W9-BEU-799

Register Your Book

at ibmpressbooks.com/ibmregister

Upon registration, we will send you electronic sample chapters from two of our popular IBM Press books. In addition, you will be automatically entered into a monthly drawing for a free IBM Press book.

Registration also entitles you to:

- Notices and reminders about author appearances, conferences, and online chats with special guests

- Access to supplemental material that may be available

- Advance notice of forthcoming editions

- Related book recommendations

- Information about special contests and promotions throughout the year

- Chapter excerpts and supplements of forthcoming books

Contact us

If you are interested in writing a book or reviewing manuscripts prior to publication, please write to us at:

Editorial Director, IBM Press
c/o Pearson Education
800 East 96th Street
Indianapolis, IN 46240

e-mail: IBMPress@pearsoned.com

Visit us on the Web: ibmpressbooks.com

Project Management with the IBM® Rational Unified Process®

RATIONAL® SOFTWARE BOOKS

Software Configuration Management Strategies and IBM Rational® ClearCase®, Second Edition
Bellagio and Milligan

Project Management with the IBM Rational Unified Process
Gibbs

IBM Rational® ClearCase®, Ant, and CruiseControl
Lee

Visual Modeling with Rational Software Architect and UML
Quatrani and Palistrant

ON DEMAND COMPUTING BOOKS

Business Intelligence for the Enterprise
Biere

On Demand Computing
Fellenstein

Grid Computing
Joseph and Fellenstein

Autonomic Computing
Murch

WEBSPHERE® BOOKS

IBM® WebSphere®
Barcia, Hines, Alcott, and Botzum

IBM® WebSphere® Application Server for Distributed Platforms and z/OS®
Black, Everett, Draeger, Miller, Iyer, McGuinnes, Patel, Herescu, Gissel, Betancourt, Casile, Tang, and Beaubien

Enterprise Java™ Programming with IBM® WebSphere®, Second Edition
Brown, Craig, Hester, Pitt, Stinehour, Weitzel, Amsden, Jakab, and Berg

IBM® WebSphere® and Lotus
Lamb, Laskey, and Indurkhya

IBM® WebSphere® System Administration
Williamson, Chan, Cundiff, Lauzon, and Mitchell

Enterprise Messaging Using JMS and IBM® WebSphere®
Yusuf

MORE BOOKS FROM IBM PRESS

Irresistible! Markets, Models, and Meta-Value in Consumer Electronics
Bailey and Wenzek

Service-Oriented Architecture Compass
Bieberstein, Bose, Fiammante, Jones, and Shah

Developing Quality Technical Information, Second Edition
Hargis, Carey, Hernandez, Hughes, Longo, Rouiller, and Wilde

Performance Tuning for Linux® Servers
Johnson, Huizenga, and Pulavarty

RFID Sourcebook
Lahiri

Building Applications with the Linux Standard Base
Linux Standard Base Team

An Introduction to IMS™
Meltz, Long, Harrington, Hain, and Nicholls

Search Engine Marketing, Inc.
Moran and Hunt

Can Two Rights Make a Wrong? Insights from IBM's Tangible Culture Approach
Moulton Reger

Inescapable Data
Stakutis and Webster

DB2® BOOKS

DB2® Universal Database V8 for Linux, UNIX, and Windows Database Administration Certification Guide, Fifth Edition
Baklarz and Wong

Understanding DB2®
Chong, Liu, Qi, and Snow

High Availability Guide for DB2®
Eaton and Cialini

DB2® Universal Database V8 Handbook for Windows, UNIX, and Linux
Gunning

DB2® SQL PL, Second Edition
Janmohamed, Liu, Bradstock, Chong, Gao, McArthur, and Yip

DB2® Universal Database for OS/390 V7.1 Application Certification Guide
Lawson

DB2® for z/OS® Version 8 DBA Certification Guide
Lawson

DB2® Universal Database V8.1 Certification Exam 700 Study Guide
Sanders

DB2® Universal Database V8.1 Certification Exam 703 Study Guide
Sanders

DB2® Universal Database V8.1 Certification Exams 701 and 706 Study Guide
Sanders

DB2® Universal Database for OS/390
Sloan and Hernandez

The Official Introduction to DB2® for z/OS®, Second Edition
Sloan

Advanced DBA Certification Guide and Reference for DB2® Universal Database v8 for Linux, UNIX, and Windows
Snow and Phan

DB2® Express
Yip, Cheung, Gartner, Liu, and O'Connell

Apache Derby—Off to the Races
Zikopoulos, Baklarz, and Scott

DB2® Version 8
Zikopoulos, Baklarz, deRoos, and Melnyk

Project Management with the IBM® Rational Unified Process®

Lessons from the Trenches

R. Dennis Gibbs

IBM Press
Pearson plc
Upper Saddle River, NJ • Boston • Indianapolis • San Francisco
New York • Toronto • Montreal • London • Munich • Paris • Madrid
Cape Town • Sydney • Tokyo • Singapore • Mexico City

Ibmpressbooks.com

IBM Press Program Managers: Tara Woodman, Ellice Uffer

Cover design: IBM Corporation

Published by Pearson plc

Publishing as IBM Press

Library of Congress Cataloging-in-Publication Data

Gibbs, R. Dennis.

  Project management with the IBM Rational Unified Process : lessons from the trenches / R. Dennis Gibbs.

    p. cm.

  ISBN 0-321-33639-9 (pbk. : alk. paper) 1. Project management. 2. Information technology—Management. 3. Computer software—Development. 4. Software engineering. I. Title.

  HD69.P75G52 2006

  658.7'23—dc22

                        2006012687

This Book Is Safari Enabled
The Safari, Enabled icon on the cover of your favorite technology book means the book is available through Safari Bookshelf. When you buy this book, you get free access to the online edition for 45 days. Safari Bookshelf is an electronic reference library that lets you easily search thousands of technical books, find code samples, download chapters, and access technical information whenever and wherever you need it.

To gain 45-day Safari Enabled access to this book:

- Go to http://www.awprofessional.com/safarienabled
- Complete the brief registration form
- Enter the coupon code EMJG-TNDK-7UJ6-LMK6-D7HN

If you have difficulty registering on Safari Bookshelf or accessing the online edition, please e-mail customer-service@safaribooksonline.com.

For Robert and Katie

Table of Contents

Acknowledgments

Many people helped with the writing of this book. I am especially thankful to those at IBM Press, who were patient and encouraging. In particular, I wish to thank Bill Zobrist, Chris Zahn, Mary Kate Murray, and Kathleen Addis. In addition, the IBM Press reviewers who gave many constructive suggestions: Brenda Cammarano, Chris Soskin, Eric Lopes Cardozo, Remco Bruns, plus some anonymous reviewers. Also, I would like to thank R. Max Wideman for permitting my use of his progressive acquisition model and for his review of that chapter. Finally, I would like to thank several people at Praxis Engineering Technologies, who provided the encouragement to write this book: Bill Dunahoo and Al Dunn. Also, thanks to Mary Bordner and Mike Short of Praxis Engineering for their perpetually positive outlook and exceptionally thorough reviews and ideas. Finally, I wish to thank my best friend and wife, Marge Gibbs, for her encouragement and an occasional "kick in the pants." Last, to my son and daughter, Robert and Katie Gibbs, the best kids a parent could ever wish for.

About the Author

R. Dennis Gibbs has been immersed in a variety of roles since beginning his career in the software industry in the early 1980s, including roles in programming, software technical support, quality assurance, systems engineering, software engineering, project and program management, and consulting and mentoring. His customers have been a mix of commercial and government clients, particularly centered on the civilian federal government and Department of Defense sectors. He currently is a software architect with Electronic Data Systems (EDS) in Herndon, Virginia.

Introduction

The idea for this book came from my experiences as a consultant and project manager. As a consultant, I was focused on mentoring, training, and providing services associated with best practices in the software industry. These services centered mostly on the Rational Unified Process (RUP)® and the associated tools from IBM Rational.

During these consulting engagements, I had the opportunity to work with many software teams in government, commercial companies, and academia. I learned much from each engagement, and they all contributed to and shaped my knowledge and thinking.

At that time, I also developed quite a collection of books that I read cover to cover. These also helped hone my knowledge. I read many excellent books that discussed the RUP. As a consultant I was always interested in hearing new perspectives on the RUP and its application.

During this period, I managed several projects that were outsourced to the companies where I worked. It occurred to me that I had never seen a book that combined the RUP with project management on outsourced projects. In addition, I felt the book should provide something useful to managers of the outsourcing organization (in other words, my customers). The idea is for each side (customer and contractor) to gain a better understanding of each other, and of the issues with software development.

This book does not cover every aspect of the RUP. Many excellent books cover the RUP in great detail. Some of them are listed in the bibliography.

This book focuses on projects that are conducted as a business arrangement between a procuring organization and a contracting organization. The book assumes that these two organizations are different companies, although this is not always true. The common term used for this situation is outsourcing.

Outsourcing Versus Offshoring

I am somewhat hesitant to use the term outsourcing because it has become synonymous with offshoring. In my view, offshoring is a subset of outsourcing. My definition of offshoring is that the procuring organization and the contractors are located in separate companies, each residing in a different country. The main point is that offshore projects have additional challenges. This book touches on some of these challenges, but the primary focus is on the more general outsourcing situation. In other words, the outsourcing organization and the contractor are separate companies but are located within the same country, perhaps even down the street from each other.

When the procuring organization is a legally separate entity from the contracting organization, factors come into play that place pressures on the software development process. These pressures are nonexistent, significantly reduced, or simply different altogether than when projects are conducted in-house.

One of two major premises in this book is that projects conducted as part of an outsourcing arrangement have special risks that must be addressed to be successful. I identify and discuss these throughout this book.

Procuring Software Services for Outsourced Projects

The advancement of best practices in the software process is well known within the software development community. But one aspect of outsourced software development has changed very little in the past 25 years—the process of procuring software development services.

As best practices for software development have been adopted, the lack of a sound, disciplined development process is no longer the root cause of failure for many projects. Instead, the cause can often be attributed to the procurement of the services needed to accomplish the project's goals. The traditional customer-contractor relationship is often dysfunctional.

Procurement processes commonly used today seem to assume (and, in many cases, actually impose) the use of traditional Waterfall-style software development lifecycle models. This is contrary to current best practices, which emphasize iterative lifecycle models. Furthermore, many outsourcing organizations remain completely detached from any involvement on the projects. They simply deliver a pile of requirements documents to the contractor and expect good results. As the contractor conducts the project, he often learns information that invalidates initial assumptions. This frequently necessitates changes to the contract, Statements of Work, or other parameters. Yet, particularly on fixed-price projects, outsourcing organizations refuse to negotiate these changes. The contractor, in an effort to avoid financial loss, cuts costs. These cost-cutting moves introduce technical risk to the project. The second major premise of this book is that these behaviors (for both the outsourcing organization and the contractor) cause many of the failures so endemic in the industry today. The way to change these behaviors is to change the procurement process. Projects should be conducted as a partnership between producer and consumer, rather than as a simple customer-supplier relationship. This book identifies and suggests practices to move in this direction.

Target Audience

The first target audience is project managers and procurement professionals in outsourcing organizations. I hope this book will give you insight into the issues surrounding outsourced projects. If the material in this book helps shape your procurement processes and how your projects are conducted, I would consider this book a major success.

The second target audience is project managers and contracting professionals for contracting organizations. Persons in this role may recognize many of the situations discussed in these chapters.

Other people who might benefit from this book are quality assurance professionals, software process professionals, consultants, and anyone interested in project management in an outsourcing/contracting context.

Finally, I hope this book will encourage outsourcing organizations and contracting organizations to work together more closely. The most successful projects are those in which both organizations work in close partnership, sharing both risks and rewards.

Chapter Summaries

The following is a brief summary of the chapters in this book.

Chapter 1, "Introduction to Outsourcing"

This chapter defines the term outsourcing as it is used in this book. Four scenarios common in outsourced projects are discussed. Some of the challenges commonly faced by software teams are covered for each scenario. The first goal of this chapter is to set the stage for this book. It also identifies high-level issues encountered by the software team in these environments. The second goal is to raise awareness of these issues in the hope that they can be addressed on current and future projects.

Chapter 2, "Overview of the Rational Unified Process"

This chapter starts with a review of traditional Waterfall-based lifecycles. It identifies characteristics of projects that are suited to Waterfall-based lifecycles (sometimes called SDLC). Next, the chapter introduces best practices, such as those introduced by the Unified Process. It introduces iterative development and compares and contrasts it with Waterfall lifecycles. The four phases of the Unified Process are identified and discussed. Some common difficulties that software teams experience implementing the RUP are covered.

Chapter 3, "Getting Started: Request for Proposals (RFPs), Proposals, and Contracts"

This chapter discusses how common procurement methods cause difficulties on projects. I show how decisions made in the proposal process for projects set the pattern for difficulties on outsourced projects. A typical procurement process is described. I also present the ideas of R. Max Wideman, who originally published a series of articles in *The Rational Edge* e-zine for a progressive procurement model. This model is better suited for the iterative processes used on projects today.

Chapter 4, "Best Practices for Staffing the Outsourcing Organization's Project Management Office (PMO)"

As stated earlier, successful projects involve close collaboration between the outsourcing organization and the contractor. This chapter describes the roles needed in the outsourcing organization to foster a close partnership between the organizations.

Chapter 5, "Best Practices for Staffing the Contractor's Software Project Team"

This chapter describes the major roles on modern, high-performance software development teams. It is not meant to proclaim that all teams must have all these roles. Instead, the purpose is to describe the roles that high-performance teams seem to have in common.

Chapter 6, "Establishing the Software Development Environment"

Establishing a software development environment using modern, state-of-the-art tools is expensive. Often the cost is shared between the outsourcing organization and the contractor. In addition, sometimes the outsourcing organization has certain standards dictating the kinds of tools that should be used. This chapter describes the kinds of tools needed to establish a modern software development environment.

Chapter 7, "Inception: Kicking Off the Project"

This chapter describes the purpose and goals of a project's Inception phase. In particular, it focuses on the "soft" skills needed for a successful project.

Chapter 8, "Identifying and Managing Risks"

This chapter explains the importance of identifying and managing risks. The different types of risks are identified, and examples are given from actual projects. The goal is to help project managers recognize and address the risks affecting their projects.

Chapter 9, "Navigating the Requirements Management Process"

The need for documented requirements is well understood. However, proper requirements collection takes on added levels of complexity in an outsourcing environment. Furthermore, it is difficult to balance added and changed requirements with the fixed-price nature of many contracts today. This chapter discusses these complexities and solutions for them.

Chapter 10, "Construction Iterations: Staying on Target"

The Construction phase is a period of time when the contractor is often "heads down" implementing the software. It is also the period within the project when the bulk of the project resources are consumed. Accordingly, it is vital to verify that the project is ready to move into the Construction phase. This chapter gives some checklists to help you determine whether the project is ready to move into the Construction phase. It also discusses the factors involved in planning and structuring iterations.

Chapter 11, "Testing"

Everyone agrees that testing developed software is important, yet testing is often poorly done or incomplete—especially when the Waterfall lifecycle is employed. This chapter discusses the different types of testing and the importance of each type. You also learn why Waterfall-based lifecycles inhibit thorough testing. Finally, you learn how to integrate testing results with iteration planning for subsequent iterations.

Chapter 12, "Transitioning a System into Service"

Transitioning a new system into service for the first time is a major event, particularly if a legacy system is being deactivated at the same time. This chapter covers the activities that take place during the Transition phase. You will learn about the following:

- Managing end user expectations at the most critical point in the project lifecycle
- How to leverage the relationships developed during requirements elicitation to ease the system into production
- The data migration challenge: preparing to migrate data from a legacy system
- The issues involved in training end users

Chapter 13, "System Operations and Maintenance Issues"

Interestingly, a project's maintenance phase is not covered by the RUP. This chapter considers some of the issues arising in a project's maintenance phase. Many software projects never make it into the maintenance phase; they fail before they reach this stage. Other projects manage to complete the development cycle, only to discover that the product is unsuitable for production work. This chapter covers the following:

- Identifying what is important for proper maintenance
- Setting up and using a change control system to best advantage
- When maintenance is not enough: how to recognize product failures that are beyond the scope of typical maintenance

Chapter 14, "Using Consultants Effectively"

Using consultants on a project can be an effective way to solve certain problems. Care should be exercised, however. Consultants cannot and should not solve every problem. In this chapter, you learn about the following:

- How to determine what is appropriate for a consultant (with examples)
- How consultants can derail your project
- Monitoring consulting work
- Effective knowledge transfer techniques when working with consultants

Chapter 15, "The Project Postmortem"

For an organization to improve its ability to develop software, it must reflect on the project's successes and failures. Even failed projects have some successes. Projects considered successful often have some failures. The purpose of the project postmortem is to collect the lessons learned and instill them in the organization's memory so that they can be applied to the next set of projects. This chapter discusses the best practices for this process.

CHAPTER 1

Introduction to Outsourcing

The topic of outsourcing has gained much attention in the press. A Gartner, Inc., report dated March 10, 2004 states, "The worldwide outsourcing market is expected to grow from $161.9 billion in 2002 to just over $235.6 billion in 2007 at a compound annual growth rate (CAGR) of 7.8 percent." The article continues, "Because of the recent global economic downturn, cost reduction has been the primary driver for outsourcing over the past several years and continues as a strong driver even as economic growth returns."[1] Outsourcing of IT services clearly will be a major venue for the fulfillment of our needs for IT systems for years to come. Figure 1-1 shows the breakdown for worldwide IT outsourcing and its respective growth rates.

[1] From a Gartner Dataquest Alert, "Forecast for IT Outsourcing Segments Shows Strong Growth," by Bruce Caldwell, Rob De Souza, Allie Young, Ron Silliman, and Eric Goodness, dated March 10, 2004. Reused with permission from Gartner, Inc.

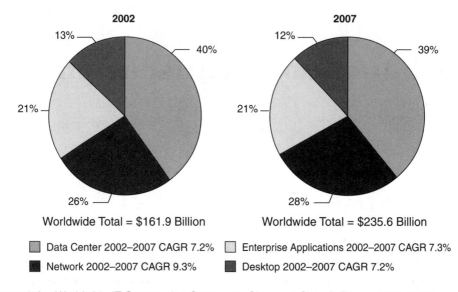

Figure 1-1   Worldwide IT Outsourcing Segments, Size, and Growth Rates, 2002–2007

From a Gartner Dataquest Alert, "Forecast for IT Outsourcing Segments Shows Strong Growth," by Bruce Caldwell, Rob De Souza, Allie Young, Ron Silliman and Eric Goodness, dated March 10, 2004. Reprinted with permission.

For a contractor, providing software development services to other companies is fascinating, challenging, and rewarding. It combines the technical challenge of applying technology to solve problems with the discipline of sound business management practices.

For a company contemplating a major software development project, outsourcing the work can be a convenient and cost-effective solution. This chapter sets the stage by describing the types of projects and environments frequently encountered in outsourcing situations.

Outsourcing Defined

Outsourcing is the practice of procuring IT services from sources external to an organization. It is important to distinguish between outsourcing and offshoring, which is a form of outsourcing. In recent years, the term "outsourcing" has become associated with organizations that employ overseas firms to perform the bulk of the work required by software development projects (offshoring), generally for cost-reduction reasons. Yet outsourcing (to domestic companies) has been used for many years, long before offshoring was commonplace.

This book defines outsourcing as "The process of retaining resources external to the procuring organization to conduct software development and related activities." The reason for this definition is as follows:

- It places no restrictions on the size or number of resources external to the procuring organization. The resources could be another company or an individual consultant.

- It places no restrictions on the location of the external resources in relation to the procuring organization; in other words, the resource can be located a long distance from the procuring organization or down the street.

- It places no restrictions on the number of organizations involved. This means that the procuring organization may hire a number of different companies or consultants, working either in a parallel or in a serial fashion. In other words, one contractor develops the system, and another contractor deploys and maintains the system after it is in production.

- It does not preclude the procuring organization from performing some of the work itself and outsourcing only a portion of a project to an external organization.

Notice that nothing in the definition specifically mentions overseas resources or offshoring. The practice of outsourcing to overseas companies for software development tasks is a fairly recent phenomenon. More traditional forms of outsourcing software development projects have been taking place for many years. In particular, the U.S. government has been outsourcing projects to domestic companies for dozens of years. That said, offshoring is increasing in popularity and also is covered in this book.

This is a broad definition of outsourcing. But it is necessary to include the multitude of scenarios that are commonly encountered today. The next section discusses the most common scenarios in outsourced projects, the variations within the scenarios, and the risks unique to each scenario.

Four Common Scenarios Encountered in Outsourced Projects

Software development projects present many challenges in an outsourced environment. In particular, these projects have the following challenges in common:

- Software developers are separated (sometimes by great distances) from the stakeholders.

- The software development team often has little knowledge of the problem domain.

- The stakeholders do not know how to express their needs in a way the development team can understand.

- The development team sometimes has difficulty articulating technical challenges to a nontechnical stakeholder group, who doesn't understand why something they are requesting may not be possible.

- Requirements frequently change.

As a result of these factors, communication between software development teams and project stakeholders is challenging at best. The result, in most cases, is wasted time and resources as development teams struggle to understand what to build and stakeholders struggle to use software that does not meet their needs.

The common thread in the challenges just listed is communication. Outsourced projects fall into four common scenarios (with some variations on each type). Each scenario presents its own advantages, disadvantages, challenges, and risks:

1. Projects in which the contractor is colocated physically with the outsourcing organization.

2. Projects that involve offshoring or employing a contractor's resources in another country, typically thousands of miles away. The work is performed at the contractor's location.

3. Variations on the first two categories, such as contractors separated a significant distance from the outsourcing organization, but still within the same country. In these situations, the work is done at the contractor's location.

4. Projects involving multiple subcontractors, typically seen in larger projects. In this scenario, the work is divided and spread across multiple contractors and the work is performed in multiple locations.

Scenario 1: Colocated Contractors

In this scenario, the contractor performs the software development activities in facilities provided by the outsourcing organization. Some companies prefer this scenario for outsourced projects, for the following reasons:

- The outsourcing organization may have security concerns over the business process or, more likely, the data involved in developing the system.

- The outsourcing organization believes that colocating the project will allow it to retain a higher level of control over the contractor and the project.

- The outsourcing organization believes that colocating project personnel makes it easier to communicate with the project stakeholders.

- The outsourcing organization can achieve some cost savings by providing facilities and IT services to the contractor.

At first glance, colocating the contractor with the outsourcing organization would seem to be a win-win situation for everyone. Yet, you must carefully consider some issues with this arrangement:

- Quality of facilities: Is enough space available? What about conference rooms and other auxiliary space?

- Will IT resources (PCs, servers, network) be provided? If so, how much control will the contracting team have over these resources?

- What are the facility's rules regarding working outside normal business hours?

- Problems could occur because of reliance on informal communication.

Let's examine each of these in detail.

CONTRACTOR WORK SPACE CONSIDERATIONS

When considering whether to have contractors colocated in your facility, keep in mind that the contractor team will spend a good portion of their lives there. Their work space needs to be at least as spacious and comfortable as what they are accustomed to. Having a personal space that each team member can adopt as his own contributes to good team morale. In addition, the space needs to be as free of distractions as possible. Software engineers work on complex problems that require intense concentration. Numerous studies have shown the negative effects of frequent interruptions and distractions on productivity. Some project cost estimation tools, such as Cost Xpert Group's Cost Xpert, even accept as input a metric on the type of office space used for project personnel. Private offices are best, whereas open areas with no isolation between desks tend to have the worst effect on productivity. Don't forget to include several small conference rooms as well. Teams frequently need quick access to conference rooms to discuss possible solutions to problems. If these necessities are not available, allow the contractor team to work in their own facilities. Look to other areas and opportunities to reduce costs.

Quality of Facilities

This seems obvious, but poor facilities and working environments are a frequent complaint I have observed from colocated contractors. I have personally experienced situations of overcrowding—as many as two or three people placed in a cubicle designed for one. I have also seen poorly environmentally controlled areas (too hot, stuffy, odors) allocated to contractors. Finally, poor access to common areas (such as conference rooms with whiteboards, telephones that can make conference calls, and informal meeting areas such as kitchenettes) is a frequent complaint of colocated teams. Poor facilities are a major contributor to poor morale. The contractor will have to deal with complaints from team members, which is a distraction that results in turnover of otherwise-qualified team members. If this is a long-term project, or just one of many colocated projects, the story of the poor working conditions will spread rapidly through the contractor's company grapevine, which will cause the contractor to have difficulty staffing the project. An outsourcing organization that spends thousands of dollars per hour for a small- to medium-sized team and then forces them to accept poor or insufficient facilities will not receive good value from the team.

IT Resources

IT resources are another area that receives little attention proactively. When I mentioned that I would cover this topic in this book, one colleague was surprised. "What's the big deal?" he said. "You don't need to waste time on this. You just have someone do it." Of course, it's often not so straightforward. These are the sorts of problems and complications that occur:

- Developers often have PCs on their desks that are "locked down," meaning that they cannot alter the operating system settings or even install software without contacting their customer's IT department. They are not given administrator privileges on their own PCs.

- The PCs are often underpowered for development tasks. Developers tend to stress PCs and therefore require lots of CPU, memory, and disk space. Providing PCs that are generally used for processing e-mail and editing documents will not suffice for most development tasks. Because they do not own the PCs, developers often are not permitted to alter the hardware configuration, such as adding memory, even if they pay for the upgrades.

- The network connecting the PCs and servers is subject to the outsourcing organization's security rules and policies. Certainly the outsourcing organization has its own proprietary information on its network that needs to be protected, even from colocated contractors. The controls needed to protect these shared resources inhibit the contractor's ability to establish control over its own IT environment, which can make using certain tools difficult.

- Access to normal IT services, such as backing up and restoring files, can be more difficult, because the outsourcing organization's IT group may not be prepared to handle the needs of a software development team. Changes that normally are done in a matter of minutes at the contractor's home location can take days or even weeks at a customer site.

- The contractor is subject to changes and upgrades made on the network and IT environment, which may be scheduled with little notice and may occur at inopportune times. This is potentially disruptive to the development team.

IT PROBLEMS IN A NEW ENVIRONMENT

I once worked as a consultant to a project for the U.S. Army. The development activities were to take place at the contractor's facilities. The contractor provided excellent hardware and infrastructure to establish a first-rate software development environment and associated tools for a multiyear project involving dozens of developers. A significant effort lasting several months was spent installing tools, configuring processes, preparing training, and customizing the tools to support and enforce the processes. Just as the software development environment was coming online, the contractor received word that the project was to be moved on-site with the customer. In addition, the contractor was not permitted to bring its PCs and servers. Everything had to be re-created on government-furnished equipment.

The transition to the new environment was difficult. The customer site IT environment had a policy against having any servers running Microsoft Windows, which prevented getting some of the development software operational. Although the desktop PCs ran Windows, the contractor had no domain administrator access. The on-site administrators gave all contractor requests very low priority, making it impossible to quickly transition to the new environment. To make matters worse, updates such as operating system patches and other upgrades were automatically pushed to all servers and desktop PCs without warning overnight. Developers would come into work some mornings and find that tools, or their application under development, would no longer work. Of course, this often happened at the worst possible times, such as right before a deadline.

Eventually, most of the issues were either solved or worked around, but in the meantime, hundreds of hours were lost. Developers could not wait for the tools to come online, so temporary methods and tools were devised to keep the team productive. This resulted in more work as the tools came online, because project data had to be migrated into the new tools.

Hours of Operation

Software development is not a 9-to-5 business. During peak project periods when the project is marching toward a deadline, overtime is common. When a bid for a project to be conducted on-site at a customer location is being considered, examine your company's history for past patterns of overtime on similar projects. Will the customer permit developers to work after hours and on weekends? If not, you need to plan for this time to be scheduled during the customer's normal business hours.

OVERTIME ISSUES

At one government site, it was known that the shop closed promptly at 7 P.M. and generally did not allow work to be conducted on weekends unless you were a government employee. Initially, this was not considered a problem. But as the project experienced some challenges (as most projects do), the overtime issue did become a problem. The customer indicated that on-site work could be conducted if a government employee accompanied the contractor. However, the request had to be made well in advance, which wasn't always possible. Furthermore, developers were reluctant to make the request because they knew it meant a government employee would have to take time out of her schedule to accompany the contractor during these overtime hours.

Communication Mechanisms

One of the advantages of being colocated on-site with the customer is quicker access to some of the stakeholders. This can also be a disadvantage. It is important to respect whatever formal processes are in place for requirements capture, as well as change requests to existing requirements. I prefer to caution stakeholders that change requests, bug reports, new requirements, and so on are to be submitted via a formal change control process, preferably whatever process the contractor defined. If they aren't submitted in this fashion, they risk being lost or forgotten. It's important to periodically remind your customer contacts of this.

Scenario 2: Offshore Projects

Projects that take place overseas face all the traditional challenges of software development projects and add many unique challenges:

- The contractor is physically located a long distance from the outsourcing organization and the project stakeholders. This raises a number of issues:
  - Real-time discussions, even via telephone, can be difficult, because the locations are a number of time zones away, and the work periods do not overlap or overlap only slightly.
  - E-mail threads discussing various topics with only a handful of replies may take a week or more to resolve. If these e-mails had stayed within the same time zone, they may have been resolved in only a few hours.

- Face-to-face meetings are rare due to the expense and time involved with travel.

- Network connectivity (particularly high-bandwidth connectivity) may be non-existent or very expensive.

- The contractor is located in a different country than the country of the outsourcing organization. Many issues are related to this issue:

  - Differences in languages spoken.

  - Cultural differences.

  - Political differences. Some projects may have representatives from around the world, creating not only cultural differences, but also mixing nationalities who have historically been in conflict with each other. These situations can result in very politically charged situations.

  - Differences in laws protecting intellectual property.

  - Understanding that certain problem domains may differ significantly between the countries involved.

  - Differences in work practices in other countries.

Let's take a closer look at these characteristics.

Dealing with Offshore Projects

Successful projects usually result from building a high-performance team. The key to building a high-performance team is to establish trust through good working relationships with other members of the team. The distance between team members is a problem that can be partially overcome through the application of technology. Another contributor to building a high-performance team is to develop an understanding of the culture, laws, and business practices that are standard in the country where the other team members are located. When trying to build your connection with the offshore members of your team, you need to understand as much as possible about the cultural, work, and legal practices of the offshore country.

Using Technology to Help Establish and Maintain Communication

Although face-to-face communication is the most desirable form of communication, it's not possible for most offshore projects. Fortunately, technology offers many solutions that help alleviate these difficulties. Organizations considering offshore projects should think about adding the following capabilities for communicating with the project team:

- Audioconferencing equipment has greatly improved in the past few years. Despite being a relatively "low-tech" solution, audioconferencing remains an excellent low-cost solution for meetings. Recent innovations have reduced the "echo" that is common on overseas long-distance connections. This solution is best applied when most or all the conference participants are acquainted and can map the voices to the people on the team.

- Videoconferencing has been around for many years, but its use is still not very common. It is much less expensive than arranging face-to-face meetings with overseas participants, but it is often too costly for small companies unless its cost can be amortized over many projects. It also requires a large amount of network bandwidth, which may be prohibitive for connections to some countries. Still, it is worth investigating as an alternative, particularly for large companies in which the cost can be shared among projects.

- Electronic whiteboards are growing in popularity. Electronic whiteboards allow the writing on a whiteboard in one location to automatically appear in another location. They can be purchased for as little as $2,000 to $3,000. Installation and setup may involve additional costs, but the total cost is generally within reach of most small companies. When used in conjunction with a high-quality audioconferencing system, many of the advantages of videoconferencing can be obtained without incurring its cost.

- Many inexpensive group collaboration tools, such as scheduling, calendar tracking utilities, and address books, exist. Although they are relatively simple, I encourage usage of these, because they help you communicate major deadlines, meetings, and milestones across multiple teams.

- Many software development tools come with Web interfaces that can effectively be used over the Internet. The following are some examples from IBM Rational's product line:

  - RequisitePro provides requirements management capabilities. It offers a Web interface that contains most of the features of the native Windows interface.

  - ClearQuest is used for change request tracking. It is commonly used for defect and enhancement tracking, but it can easily be customized to handle nearly anything that is tracked via a formal process. This tool also offers a Web interface. An optional feature called ClearQuest Multisite is useful for geographically distributed projects in which high-speed connectivity is not possible.

  - ClearCase is a popular configuration management tool that lets you check in and check out files and manage baselines. This tool provides two features for remote usage. The Web interface is best suited for small projects. Like ClearQuest, ClearCase also has an optional feature called Multisite, which is highly recommended for geographically distributed development efforts.

  - Project Console is a unique product that extracts information from many other tools (mostly other IBM Rational tools) and produces metrics illustrating project progress.

- Project Web sites, or portals, are a useful means to exchange information. In the past, I have set up project Web sites for the exchange of project information. The project Web site can also function as a conduit for access to the Web-enabled development tools just described. Chapter 7, "Inception: Kicking Off the Project," contains suggestions on setting up a complete project Web site.

Understanding Differences in Cultures, Work Practices, and Laws

Some aspects to consider include the following:

- Some countries, particularly in Europe, have strict laws controlling or limiting the use of overtime. In those countries, it is a major issue to suggest that staff work extra hours. In other countries, such as Japan, long hours are common.

- Be careful about assuming basic knowledge surrounding the understanding of the problem domain. For example, if you are outsourcing a project to build a system for processing mortgages, does the country you are outsourcing to even use mortgages to acquire property? If not, you need to educate the contractor on the topic of mortgages (which wouldn't be necessary if the project were outsourced to a domestic contractor).

- Laws concerning intellectual property vary widely between countries. If the project being considered for offshoring involves sensitive information, be sure to consult an attorney who specializes in the intellectual property laws of the countries involved.

- Find out about the contractor's practices regarding trade-offs among schedule, quality, and completeness. In some cultures, releasing a product before it is fully completed or tested is unthinkable, even if this means missing a deadline.

- Understand the culture and practice of the contractor's approach to analysis and design. Some cultures tend to focus first on lower-level details, and others tend to focus on the big picture. Still other cultures insist on a full engineering approach and process.

EXTENDED VACATIONS

I overheard one project manager discussing an interaction with his counterpart on a project that had been outsourced to a Scandinavian country. His company was unaware that it is often a custom in Scandinavian countries to take an extended vacation (often up to a month) in July, when the amount of daylight is near its peak. During that time, it was nearly impossible to get in touch with most of the key project members.

Further examples on this topic may be found in the publications listed in the bibliography. In particular, refer to Erran Carmel's excellent book, *Global Software Teams*.

Deciding Whether to Use Offshoring for a Project

By now, hopefully you understand that offshore projects can potentially incur a much higher amount of overhead, mostly due to the costs of establishing and maintaining effective communication. Although the labor costs may be much lower, you should consider this overhead and the delays inherent in an offshoring arrangement, as well as the additional risk incurred. It may be that these costs outweigh the potential savings involved. Yet, many successful offshoring projects have occurred. How do you decide whether to outsource to a domestic company or an overseas one? There is no magic answer, but you should consider the following points:

- Is the project's purpose to develop a new system? Will much requirements elicitation and business modeling occur? (See Chapter 9, "Navigating the Requirements Management Process.") For projects like these, extensive and frequent interaction with stakeholders and potential end users is necessary. Offshoring can be an excellent alternative if one or more of the following conditions are true:
  - The additional time and cost of enabling frequent contact (via travel) between the contractor and the stakeholders are not an issue.
  - The project is not on an unusually tight schedule and budget.
  - The contractor has built and successfully delivered many similar types of systems, and the teams that performed the work are available for your project.
  - Both the outsourcing organization and the contractor are well-equipped with the latest tools (such as audioconferencing and videoconferencing) to assist working in geographically dispersed environments.
- Is the project's purpose to augment or enhance an existing system? Offshoring can be a viable alternative in this situation. The added caveat (in addition to the previously mentioned criteria) is that the source code of the system being modified can be accessed, and so can the tools and documentation needed to build the system.
- Tasks involving testing and verification are excellent for offshoring. These tasks involve intensive "hands-on" work with a developed system and usually do not require much stakeholder interaction, except at the start and end of the task—ideal for an offshore environment. This is one of the few software development disciplines that can be sent entirely offshore. In most cases, with testing being one of the few exceptions, it is best to send entire subsystems or components offshore. The more robust and modularized your architecture, the greater the chances of success in offshoring certain components. The more dependencies there are between code developed in remote locations, the more difficult the task becomes.

Scenario 3: Distant Contractors, Same Country

This situation is similar to offshoring a project, except that the cultural issues are not as significant. In this case, the considerations for the type of project outsourced to a distant, same-country contractor are the same as for an offshore contractor. In addition, the same tools to enable communication between the outsourcing organization and the contractor are highly recommended.

Scenario 4: Multiple Contractors

In this scenario, the project being outsourced is large enough to divide the work among multiple contractors. The complexities in these situations can multiply quickly, depending on how the work is divided between contractors. Consider the following:

- Will the software being built by one of the contractors need to interface with the software being built by the other contractor?
- Will the contractors be working in parallel on different portions of the same system, or will they work on different tasks in a serial fashion?

If the answer to the first question is yes, or if the contractors are working in parallel, the following practices are recommended:

- During requirements elicitation meetings, all contractors should be represented. When partitioning the building of single system (or a "system of systems") is undertaken, the boundaries between the systems can be blurry. Because each contractor is focused on the performance of its individual contract, there is a natural tendency to avoid accepting responsibility for any work that is not clearly delineated as part of the contractor's Statement of Work. This can be a detriment to the system as a whole. When representatives from all contractors gather with representatives of the outsourcing organization, this is less likely to occur.
- When you form a Change Control Board, representatives from all contractors should be present. A change that seemingly affects only one part of the system could, in fact, affect the work of other contractors as well.
- It is incumbent upon the outsourcing organization to ensure that the vision for the system as a whole is consistent across all contractors. Is the system mission-critical? Is each contractor taking the necessary steps to ensure that redundancy, failover, and scalability are incorporated into the system architecture? Pay close attention to the supplementary requirements covering these areas.
- Will each contractor be developing portions of the user interface? If so, close coordination between the contractors will be necessary to ensure that the interface's look and feel is consistent. Also, each contractor should use the same technologies, languages, tools, and so on to build the system to make it easier to maintain the system after it is deployed.
- Do all portions of the system being built require persistent storage, or an application or Web server? If so, each contractor will want to build the system with its own servers, database instances, and so on. This is acceptable for the development environment, but if it is extended to the production operating environment, it will result in unnecessary duplication and increased costs. To avoid this problem, an appropriate arrangement must be made that consolidates these requirements without unnecessary duplication. At the same time, each contractor will want some control over its environment without delays. It may be appropriate for each contractor to have its own development environment, with the requirement that the production environment will run on a consolidated set of servers. Be sure that each contractor understands this.

- If one or all contractors are offshore, every contractor on the project needs to have the infrastructure to communicate effectively—not just between the outsourcing organization and each contractor, but between the subcontractors as well.

Overall, using multiple contractors increases the burden on the outsourcing organization. The outsourcing organization needs to have the staff to handle this added burden. This is discussed further in Chapter 4, "Best Practices for Staffing the Outsourcing Organization's Project Management Office (PMO)." In addition, a centralized repository for requirements, designs, documents, and so on is advisable. It should be accessible by all contractors involved in developing the system.

Where Does the Rational Unified Process Fit in All of This?

Thus far, we have discussed many of the challenges faced by outsourced projects, but we have not mentioned the Rational Unified Process (RUP). In fact, we have not discussed any aspects of software development. Why? The reason is simple. The challenges faced by outsourced projects mostly center on communication, cultural, business management, and other "soft" issues. A disciplined process (such as the RUP) does not provide all its intended benefits when the environment surrounding the project is in chaos or disorganization. Many projects that otherwise would have been successful have failed due to poor communication between the technical team and the business managers, poorly set expectations, and poor management from a business perspective. In these situations, no software process—RUP or otherwise—will result in success.

The RUP stresses close collaboration between teams and stakeholders. It is vital to break down as many communication barriers as possible before many of the RUP's benefits can be realized. The next chapter examines the RUP to help you understand what makes it different from traditional development processes, such as the Waterfall lifecycle process.

Summary

- When outsourcing to a colocated contractor, be sure to consider whether proper facilities can be provided. Consider allowing the contractor to create its own local-area network (LAN) that it can completely control.

- When working with a colocated contractor, be sure to adhere to any formal processes and mechanisms that are in place for managing requests, changes, and so on.

- During the beginning phases of a project that uses an offshore contractor, consider cultural awareness/sensitivity training to familiarize project staff with the business practices and philosophies common in the country in which the offshore contractor is located.

- If offshoring is to be used for a project that will require extensive requirements collection and analysis, be sure that the proper infrastructure is in place to provide the level of communication needed.

What's Next?

The next chapter reviews and summarizes the Rational Unified Process for software development. I will compare and contrast it with traditional Waterfall lifecycle models. If you're already familiar with the RUP, you might want to skim the next chapter or skip it and continue with Chapter 3, "Getting Started: Request for Proposals (RFPs), Proposals, and Contracts."

CHAPTER 2

Overview of the Rational Unified Process

If you are new to the Rational Unified Process (RUP), this chapter gives you an overview of the process, including how it differs from traditional processes and why it is advantageous for software projects. The RUP cannot be thoroughly covered in a single chapter. If you prefer a complete introduction to RUP fundamentals, refer to the references given in the bibliography.

When undertaking a significant project of any kind (software-related or not), it's important to approach the work in an organized fashion. This is especially important when teams are involved. Following a defined process helps coordinate the work of teams and keeps them focused on the right activities at the right time. It also reduces project risk.

The Traditional Software Development Process

For many years, and even today, many projects have used a traditional process commonly called the Waterfall lifecycle process, shown in Figure 2-1. Even if you are unfamiliar with this term, you have probably used this lifecycle before without knowing it. The basic tenets of the Waterfall lifecycle are as follows:

- You cannot effectively create or build anything until you know the requirements.
- Development should not begin until the requirements have been completely collected and frozen, because you don't want to have to redo work that has been completed.
- You cannot begin work on a subsequent phase of the project until the preceding phase is complete.

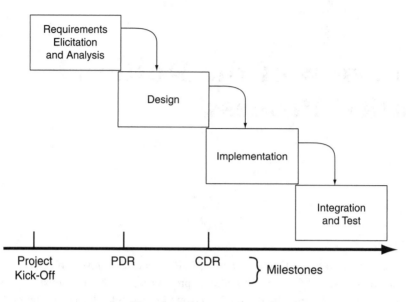

Time and Resources

Figure 2-1   Phases of the Waterfall lifecycle model

In addition to the preceding basic tenets, some practices are commonly associated with use of the Waterfall process:

- Requirements and design are extensively documented.

- Reviews of documentation are conducted at significant project milestones:

  - Preliminary Design Review (PDR)

  - Critical Design Review (CDR)

  - Test Readiness Review (TRR)

- Detailed project planning and scheduling for the entire project are performed at the beginning of the project.

- Success is measured by adherence to the milestones and dates in the original detailed project plan.

Advantages of the Waterfall Process

The Waterfall process has been around for many years. It began long before large software development projects were common. The Waterfall process originated in the manufacturing sector. It has been practiced in the manufacturing and building construction industries for many years and is well understood through years of application. Given that the main topic of this book is applying the RUP, you might expect to see the horrors of the Waterfall process revealed here. Although this process certainly has some disadvantages, it also has many advantages. It is still commonly used, and it will continue to be used. The key is applying the right process to the situation at hand. Let's start by listing the advantages of the Waterfall process:

- It's intuitively obvious what activities should be conducted at a given point in time.
- As a result, it's an easy process to learn.
- It's easy to determine staffing needs, because each phase requires a specific skill set during a specific time period.
- It's easy to schedule.
- It's easy to gauge *apparent* progress by comparing work completed with the expected completion of work according to the schedule.

Based on these advantages, the Waterfall lifecycle is well suited for projects that have the following characteristics:

1. The requirements are known completely at the beginning of the project and do not change significantly for the duration of the project.
2. The requirements are understood completely at the beginning of the project.
3. The risks are identified and understood at the beginning of the project.
4. It is known that the requirements can be implemented utilizing the technologies to be used for the project.
5. The technologies employed on the project do not change for the duration of the project.
6. The team assembled for the project is experienced and familiar with the problem domain and the technologies applied on the project.

A project exhibiting these characteristics is an excellent candidate for the Waterfall process.

Disadvantages of the Waterfall Process

The Waterfall process actually has few disadvantages per se. The problems with using the Waterfall process stem from applying it to projects with the wrong characteristics. Let's revisit the list of characteristics of projects that are well suited for the Waterfall process. This provides a convenient way to discuss the problems created by the mismatch of situation and process.

1. The requirements are known completely at the beginning of the project and do not change significantly for the duration of the project.

   This is not the situation for most software projects of significant size today. With many projects, the stakeholders must be carefully guided through a requirements elicitation process. In most cases, users are unable to articulate what they truly want or need, but they know what they like when they see it. This is related to requirements changing. As stakeholders learn, they become better able to articulate their needs. Significant changes are the bane of the Waterfall process. Why? The Waterfall process is strictly sequential.

After you have completed the Requirements and Design phases, the process dictates that you work on implementation. A contractor will strongly resist new or changed requirements at this point, because it means going backward—revisiting existing work and modifying it to accommodate the changes and additions. This results in delays and increased expenditure of resources.

2. The requirements are understood completely at the beginning of the project.

For a system to meet the needs of its stakeholders, the requirements articulated by those stakeholders must be completely understood by the system's creators and builders. This takes much more than simply reading documents provided by stakeholders at the beginning of the project. It involves working closely with the stakeholders over a period of time. Furthermore, the burden is on the contractor to convince the stakeholders that this understanding has been achieved. This can be difficult to do with a Waterfall lifecycle. Typical lifecycle milestones in the Waterfall process, such as Preliminary Design Review and Critical Design Review, assess status and understanding through documentation of design, snapshots of screen prototypes, and other "static" artifacts. Seldom are there any interactive, executable implementations, or partial implementations. Nothing is coded or implemented until the Implementation phase, which occurs after the Critical Design Review. Therefore, understanding of requirements is based on assessment of documentation. Furthermore, some of the documentation consists of design diagrams that the stakeholders might not understand. Overall, extensive documentation is not a reliable predictor of ultimate project success.

3. The risks are identified and understood at the beginning of the project.

There is no way to completely discover and eliminate all risks on a software project of significant size, regardless of the process used. The phrase "You don't know what you don't know" comes to mind. The best you can do is engage in activities that allow you to discover the risks early enough to be able to take action to mitigate them. In the Waterfall process, each phase is conducted once. Let's examine examples of risk discovery in a typical project using the Waterfall process. Figure 2-2 shows three unexpected risks that were discovered at different points in the project lifecycle.

Risk 1 was discovered during the Requirements Elicitation and Analysis phase. Because it was discovered fairly early in the lifecycle, it may be possible to take corrective action without much difficulty. Risk 2 was experienced during the Implementation phase, roughly halfway through the project schedule, after approximately one-half of the project resources had been expended. Depending on the nature of the risk, it may be possible to recover, but not without some heroic action on the part of the project staff. Risk 3, on the other hand, is discovered late in the project lifecycle, not far from project delivery, after most of the project funds are exhausted. Chances are if this risk has a serious impact, this project will not be delivered on time. Given that Risks 2 and 3 were disruptive because they were encountered near the middle and end of the project lifecycle, how can you discover them earlier so that they won't be so disruptive? The answer is that you can't if you are using a Waterfall lifecycle. The section "Practice 4: Demonstrate Value Iteratively" explains how iterative development, one of the six best practices emphasized by the RUP, helps with this situation.

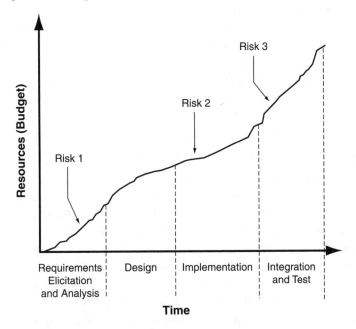

Figure 2-2   Risk discovery in the Waterfall lifecycle process

4. It is known that the requirements can be implemented utilizing the technologies to be used for the project.

   In many cases, the technologies already have been selected for implementation of the project requirements by the time Requirements Elicitation and Analysis takes place. Furthermore, requirements are elicited strictly from the user's perspective, without regard for the implementation technology (as it should be!). Occasionally, a situation occurs in which implementation of some requirements may not be possible, or perhaps it is unusually difficult, with the technologies chosen. With the Waterfall process, Implementation does not begin until the Requirements and Design phases are complete. This means that discovery of problems is likely to be delayed. In addition, when the problem is discovered, you must spend time re-eliciting the requirements and altering the design to accommodate the changed requirements, increasing the delay.

5. The technologies employed on the project do not change for the duration of the project.

   Given the rate at which new developments in hardware and software are being introduced to the marketplace, any project lasting longer than a year or so is likely to experience this situation. The question is whether the customer wants to incorporate the new technology into the product being built. In the Waterfall lifecycle process, introducing new technologies during the Implementation or Integration and Test phases is both risky and disruptive. Depending on the nature of the changes, close examination (and possibly significant rework) from the artifacts produced in the first two phases must be performed. If significant rework is required, forward progress slows or even stops as this examination takes place. In some cases, project managers, under schedule and budget pressure, try to skip this examination and incorporate the technologies by shear brute force, without determining whether the changes are compatible with the work done so far. The risks of this approach tend to surface during Integration and Test. At that point, correcting the problems guarantees that the project will be late.

6. The team assembled for the project is experienced and familiar with the problem domain and the technologies applied on the project.

This issue relates to risks and understanding requirements. Clearly, if the project team has built similar systems, they will have encountered and mitigated the risks that are likely to occur on the current project. In addition, because the team is already familiar with similar systems, they will be better able to guide the users during requirements elicitation. This also means the team can incorporate lessons learned from their earlier experiences and thus are less likely to repeat mistakes. Because the Waterfall lifecycle does not easily allow for correction of mistakes made in earlier phases, having an experienced team is a key advantage for Waterfall-based projects.

Unfortunately, turnover within the software development industry tends to be fairly high. Software developers also like new challenges and may be unlikely to sign on for a project similar to one they have done previously. Finally, even if the developers have completed similar projects, the technologies may not be the same as those employed on the earlier project, negating the applicability of some of the lessons learned on earlier projects.

The development of new software systems more closely resembles the invention of a new product. Each project typically involves new stakeholders, technologies, project personnel, tools, risks, and environments for both the creation and operation of the project. As a consequence, these projects cannot be easily planned or predicted months in advance. A more flexible approach that is resilient to change and discovery is needed. The Waterfall approach generally involves detailed planning for the entire project before the project even begins. The nature of software development makes this impractical and unreliable. It is clear that many software development situations call for approaches other than the Waterfall process. One such approach is the RUP.

Introducing the Rational Unified Process

In introducing the RUP, it is best to begin with a historical overview before getting into the specific practices that make up the process.

History

The setting for development of the RUP began in the early 1980s at Rational Software Corporation. Founded by Paul Levy and Mike Devlin, Rational was dedicated to the successful development of large, complex software systems. At the time of its founding, large, complex software projects were mostly in the domain of government systems, particularly at the Department of Defense. Rational specialized in providing proprietary hardware platforms and environments for Ada, the preferred language of the Department of Defense at that time.

In the late 1980s, several trends in the marketplace converged that led Rational to rethink its strategy. First, proprietary hardware platforms were giving way to open systems. This made Rational's premier product offering, the R1000 Ada software development platform, obsolete and too expensive in the emerging marketplace for open systems. In addition, the newer open-system platforms (such as those being offered by Sun Microsystems) were becoming increasingly powerful. Even personal computers were rapidly becoming more and more powerful. This made it practical for Rational to port its Ada Software Development System to these platforms.

The second trend was the slow death of the Ada programming language. Although intended to support modern software engineering principles, Ada was perceived as a bloated, difficult-to-use language designed by committee. This perception was especially true in the rapidly growing commercial market, which favored languages such as C++. An update to the original 1983 Ada standard was continually delayed until 1995, at which point it was viewed as too little, too late. Ada is now a very small player in the Department of Defense marketplace.

The final trend that helped shape Rational's strategy was the explosive growth of microprocessors in consumer goods, such as automobiles and appliances. This led to software projects of increasing complexity and size by commercial companies that had little experience with developing software.

The advent of the World Wide Web led thousands of companies to develop a business presence on the Internet. It also led them to develop Web-based systems that placed back-office functionality into the hands of its customers through Web applications.

These trends culminated in a tremendous opportunity for Rational Software. Rational recognized and embraced these trends. Interestingly, Rational's mission did not change. The mission was still to ensure the success of customers developing large, complex software systems, but the tactics and product offerings for supporting this mission changed entirely.

Lacking sufficient product offerings to support this emerging market, Rational went on an acquisition binge. Pure-Atria was acquired, providing the ClearCase configuration management tools, as well as the Purify line of testing tools. Requisite was acquired for its Requisite Pro requirements management tool. SQA was acquired for its suite of testing tools. Rational already had Rational Rose, its analysis and design tool; ClearQuest, a change-request tracking system; and SoDA, an automated documentation generation tool. A number of other acquisitions occurred, but those mentioned here were the most important. Together with its existing product offerings, Rational now had a complete set of products that supported the entire software development lifecycle.

Almost simultaneously, two other major efforts took place at Rational Software. The first was an effort to create a standardized methodology for modeling software systems. In the early 1990s, dozens of modeling languages were in use, including Booch, Buhr, Object Modeling Technique (OMT), and Shlaer-Mellor. The marketplace was fragmented, which made it difficult to develop a single tool to support the majority of software development efforts. Rational's answer to this problem was to use Grady Booch (who invented the Booch Methodology and who was already a Rational employee) and to hire James Rumbaugh (OMT) and Ivar Jacobson (the Objectory Process). Together, these three (known as "the Three Amigos") began work that would culminate in the development of a single modeling language (appropriately named the Unified Modeling Language [UML]) that would replace the plethora of languages currently in use. Rational also acquired Jacobson's company, Objectory. The RUP drew much from the Objectory Process, particularly the notion of use cases for describing how people interact with systems.

The second major effort Rational embarked upon was to develop a documented set of best practices for software development that could be supported by the tools in Rational's arsenal. This, of course, is what led to the creation of the RUP.

IBM acquired Rational Software in early 2003. The RUP continues to evolve and be updated as industry practices change. The RUP, therefore, will continue to be at the forefront of software development methodologies and best practices.

The Six Best Practices

When the RUP was developed, it centered on the application of six best practices. From the initial version of the RUP through most of 2005, these best practices were as follows:

1. Develop iteratively.
2. Manage requirements.
3. Use component architectures.
4. Model visually.
5. Continually verify quality.
6. Manage changes.

These six best practices were developed from Rational's experience in helping develop large, complex software systems. They were also designed to help drive the use of tools offered in Rational's product line. The designers of the RUP continue to evolve the process as methods and practices mature through their application. In October 2005, an article appeared in the IBM Rational e-zine *The Rational Edge*. In it, Per Kroll and Walker Royce updated the six best practices, as follows:

1. Adapt the process.
2. Balance competing stakeholder priorities.
3. Collaborate across teams.

4. Demonstrate value iteratively.

5. Elevate the level of abstraction.

6. Focus continually on quality.[1]

Let's take a closer look at each of these best practices.

Practice 1: Adapt the Process

Every project is different. Large projects with many people and teams who are geographically scattered require more formality and control than do small projects with few people. Furthermore, within each project, the level of control may vary depending on the amount of "invention" and novelty required. It is difficult to be creative when lots of heavy, formal controls must be followed. On the other hand, a project involving maintenance or enhancement of mission-critical software where failures can cause loss of life requires a much higher level of formality. The point is to assess the situation and adjust the process to fit it. The amount of control needed also varies throughout the project's duration. For example, during initial development, developers need the freedom to quickly try new approaches without overhead controls getting in the way. However, after the ideas solidify and releases are delivered to the user community, changes to these baselines need to be controlled. The following is a list of characteristics illustrating where more control and formality are needed. Evaluate your project against each criterion. Projects meeting all or most of the criteria require more formal control and process than projects meeting fewer (or perhaps none) of the criteria.

- The project team is geographically scattered. This includes the outsourcing organization and the team developing the product.
- The user community is large and geographically scattered.
- The project team is composed of multiple contractors, each building a different portion of the product.
- The product must meet stringent standards that must be verified.
- The product to be developed is technically complex.
- The project is in the later part of the project lifecycle. In other words, earlier lifecycle phases require less formality, and the later phases require more.

The process should also be adapted across projects. As a contracting organization becomes more experienced with the process, it should incorporate the lessons learned into its corporate memory and apply them to subsequent projects. This topic is covered in Chapter 15, "The Project Postmortem."

---

[1] From "Key Principles for Business-Driven Development," in the October 2005 issue of *The Rational Edge*, by Per Kroll and Walker Royce. *The Rational Edge* is owned and operated by IBM.

Practice 2: Balance Competing Stakeholder Priorities

For many software teams, it has become an ingrained habit: First, gather all the detailed require-ments, and then develop to those requirements. But this pattern ignores possible opportunities to satisfy stakeholder needs in simpler and safer ways. One way to reduce the inherent risk involved in all custom software development is to avoid custom development wherever possible through the use of Commercial Off-The-Shelf (COTS) or other predeveloped software. Before going this route, the project team must understand the users' business process and needs. The users must understand that they must make trade-offs between custom functionality and the ability to satisfy their mission with cheaper, faster methods such as the incorporation of COTS. One way to facili-tate consideration of these other methods is for the project team to help the stakeholders under-stand exactly what requirements are must-haves and which ones can be deferred or negotiated in favor of cheaper or faster solutions.

Note that "other predeveloped software" might include, in addition to COTS, legacy sys-tems, services such as those provided by Service-Oriented Architectures (SOAs), and reusable components.

Practice 3: Collaborate Across Teams

Collaboration is much more than just communication. It means building teams that share risk and reward, working cooperatively to further a project's mission and goals. It means teams proac-tively providing information to other teams when that information may affect or assist the other team. It also means creating a culture of integrity in which team members are empowered and are willing to take risks as well as responsibility. Because of the importance of team building, Chap-ter 4, "Best Practices for Staffing the Outsourcing Organization's Project Management Office (PMO)," is devoted to building a Project Management Office (PMO) in the outsourcing organiza-tion. Chapter 5, "Best Practices for Staffing the Contractor's Software Project Team," is devoted to creating a team in the contractor organization.

Note that collaboration across teams also means including organizations that often are ignored or are peripherally involved. This includes the people who will operate the system being built, and the associated business organizations (including, but not limited to, the contracts office).

Practice 4: Demonstrate Value Iteratively

Demonstrating value iteratively is perhaps the most significant of the six best practices. Similar to the discussion of the Waterfall lifecycle, let's discuss the major tenets of iterative development:

- You can better develop a complex software system by breaking it into a series of smaller problems to solve. This is applied common sense. When you're faced with a complex problem, it's much easier to "divide and conquer" by creating a series of less compli-cated problems. In the aggregate, you solve the entire problem by solving the individual problems first. This helps you deal with complexity by allowing you to focus on one subset of the problem at a time.

- It is impossible to fully understand a system's requirements (or complexities) by writing everything down first. Documentation is still important, but it doesn't prove that you have identified the proper requirements and have a thorough grasp of the complexities involved in building the system. Furthermore, it is easier for stakeholders to recognize that development is on the right track if they get "hands-on" time with a partial implementation of the system. Most users do not understand (nor do they care to) design and analysis artifacts written on paper or produced on slides.

- Greater risk identification and mitigation are possible if more of the activities of a software project are exercised earlier in the project lifecycle. As you will recall, in the Waterfall lifecycle model, many important activities (such as implementation and testing) are not exercised until well into the project lifecycle. This means that problems discovered through the conducting of these activities are not identified until that time. In contrast, with iterative development, these activities are exercised earlier. Earlier problem detection leads to earlier resolution. In addition, the iterations' content is ordered by risk. In other words, the earlier iterations in a project should focus on the aspects of the system that have the most risk. I will cover this more in Chapter 8, "Identifying and Managing Risks." To put it another way, if development of a system is destined to encounter serious problems, you want to force the problems to occur as early as possible. This allows you to regroup and determine how to solve the problems while meaningful amounts of time in the schedule and numbers of resources remain.

- Each iteration should result in a demonstrable, executable release of a system. Of course, only a subset of a system's functionality will be provided in each release. Each release should be demonstrated to stakeholders wherever possible.

- Creating executable, demonstrable versions of a system early in the project lifecycle provides a more meaningful and accurate way to gauge the project's true progress. Projections can then be made based on actual experience with developing parts of the application, rather than guesses based on documentation alone.

Advantages of Demonstrating Value Iteratively

Iterative development offers the following advantages over Waterfall development:

- It provides earlier discovery of serious problems and risks than traditional Waterfall-based lifecycles.

- It is more adaptable to changes in requirements than Waterfall lifecycles. The requirements are frozen only for the duration of a single iteration, and only the requirements affecting that iteration are frozen. Any changes to requirements in a current or previous iteration can be planned for a subsequent iteration. Also, for all requirements not yet implemented in an iteration, the priorities can be reassigned, and the order of requirements assigned to iterations can be reordered, or new requirements can be incorporated in the order.

• It allows stakeholders to have "hands-on" time with the application well before the project's end date. Thus, useable feedback can be obtained earlier in the process, allowing the development organization to adjust if the reaction is negative.

• If the schedule becomes a problem, it may be possible to deploy an early version of a system, minus some of its features. Because each iteration delivers an executable release, users may be content to deploy an earlier version of a system on time rather than wait for the development of every single feature. This is not possible with a Waterfall lifecycle model.

Refer to Chapter 10, "Construction Iterations: Staying on Target," for suggestions on the proper length of time for iterations.

Practice 5: Elevate the Level of Abstraction

Many software systems built today are quite complex. Even experienced software engineers cannot adequately cope with all the details at one time. The notion of abstraction helps you deal with complexity and understand a system's architecture.

You're probably familiar with object-oriented paradigms, which introduce the notion of abstraction. One important concept used in object-oriented methodologies is the idea of a class. A common use of a **class** is to encapsulate a data object and provide functions that manipulate the data object in some manner. In this fashion, the data object's important attributes and operations can be accessed in a controlled fashion, the way the author of the class intended. The implementation details are programmatically hidden from users of the class.

A component extends this concept and broadens its use to a single unit of functionality. Continuing the example of a class, a **component** could be a collection of classes that are logically grouped. Each component is a self-contained "chunk" of functionality that has a well-defined interface and that does something of value for a system. The interface represents the attributes and operations that the developer of the component believes are necessary for a client to effectively use the component.

Figure 2-3 shows an example of a three-tiered architecture. Note that all access between components occurs at the application programming interface (API) level. In other words, the components interact with each other, but all calls from one component to the other are made to the component's interface.

Figure 2-4 illustrates another example of a layered architecture, with each layer dedicated to a specific aspect of the application's functionality. Interaction between components in other layers occurs only with layers immediately adjacent to the level initiating the interaction.

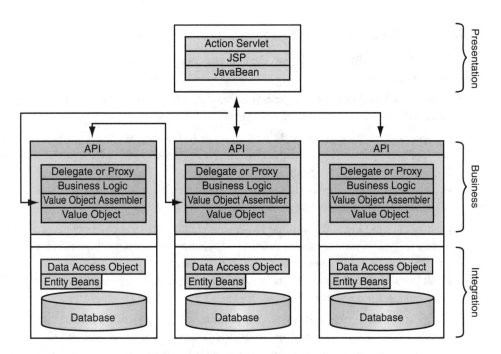

Figure 2-3 An example of a layered architecture with APIs

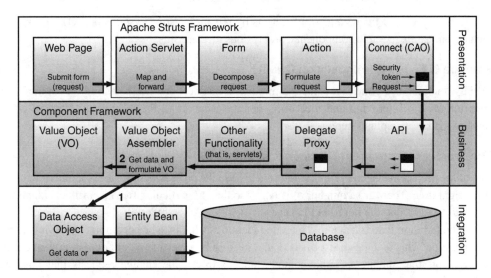

Figure 2-4 Another example of a three-tiered architecture, illustrating layers showing separation of concerns

Applications that use component-based architectures reap several benefits:

- A component's API clearly defines the boundary between the component itself and the users of the component.

- Component-based architectures help you understand how a system is designed at a high level, without getting lost in a sea of detail.

- Components are easier to reuse. In fact, entire architectures are often reused from project to project. The notion of the three-tiered architectures shown in Figures 2-3 and 2-4 is quite common. Components also aid in reuse at the individual component level. Because a component performs a specific function and has a well-defined interface, it's easier to reuse a component on other projects.

- Component-based architectures are easier to maintain. Because components programmatically "hide" implementation details, and dependencies on a component are made at only the API level, changes to a component's implementation are less likely to affect client users of that component. This means that code changes are less likely to "ripple" throughout other portions of a system.

- Component-based architectures enable portions of the system's functionality to be developed by separate teams. If the team strictly adheres to the conventions defined by the component's interface, the teams developing the code to implement the functionality can operate separately. This fact is particularly helpful for distributed teams.

Another way of managing complexity is by reusing existing systems or COTS packages, such as databases, reusable components, and various mechanisms.

Practice 6: Focus Continually on Quality

Usually, the first discipline that comes to mind with this best practice is testing. Yet in the RUP, opportunities for improving and measuring quality occur in all the disciplines. We will cover some of the key disciplines here.

The Project Management Discipline

One of the project manager's primary duties is to keep the project team focused on the right goals at the right time. There are a number of ways to do this. In particular, two key artifacts identified by the RUP stand out: the Iteration Plan and the Iteration Assessment.

The Iteration Plan is a detailed plan that identifies what is to be accomplished during a specific iteration. This includes a list of risks that need to be investigated or addressed, a subset of requirements that should be implemented, and possibly some change requests that must be addressed.

The Iteration Assessment is a balanced, intellectually honest evaluation that examines the goals set forth in the Iteration Plan. It determines whether the iteration's goals were met. This is more than simply whether the requirements allocated to the iteration were successfully implemented. More important is whether the risks investigated through the iteration's activities were successfully resolved or mitigated. Also, were new risks identified, or did new problems arise? The results of the Iteration Assessment are used to help plan the remaining iterations.

Other measures available in the Project Management discipline include some of the traditional measures, such as tracking actual resources expended versus planned resources, earned value metrics, and so on. It is important to note that the RUP stresses adaptive planning instead of predictive planning. Projects using iterative lifecycle models (such as the RUP) should not be planned in detail for the project's duration in the beginning. Instead, detailed plans are created only for the current iteration and perhaps the next one. Detailed plans for subsequent iterations are created along the way to incorporate lessons learned, new requirements, and so on. Therefore, attempting to create detailed plans for the entire project and tracking adherence to that plan is not meaningful. In other words, if you must track adherence to schedule or planned resources due to contractual requirements, deviating from the plans made at the beginning of the project does not necessarily mean that the project is in trouble. It is important to adapt plans as the project is executed.

The Requirements Discipline

The keys to verifying quality in the requirements discipline involve careful review of document requirements from three perspectives:

- Do the documented requirements truly reflect the needs of the stakeholders?
- Are the documented requirements testable or verifiable?
- Are the documented requirements of sufficient detail that they are unambiguous and can be understood by the developers? Can they be understood by other stakeholders as well?

In addition, requirements should be baselined when they reach a sufficient point of stability. Beyond that point, any changes must be carefully documented and controlled, and the results communicated throughout the team, preferably through an automated tool designed for tracking changes.

The Analysis and Design Discipline

The key ways of verifying quality here involve reviewing the artifacts created, with particular attention given to the following:

- Do the Analysis and Design artifacts trace directly back to the requirements artifacts? The goal here is *not* to trace every individual piece back to a requirement, but rather to understand its role in accomplishing the requirements.
- Are the artifacts consistent in the level of detail?
- Can they be understood by the developers who will translate the design into executable code?

The Testing Discipline

In the Waterfall lifecycle model, testing does not take place until very late in the lifecycle. It's really impossible to test any earlier, because nothing is available to test! When a project is running behind schedule, because testing is one of the final activities, it is often cut short or even eliminated. As a result, the product is often riddled with bugs. In contrast, with the iterative lifecycle model, testing takes place within each iteration, especially toward the end of the iteration. Defects found are corrected, tests are reverified, and a stable baseline is created for demonstration to stakeholders.

Figure 2-5 illustrates this process. In the iterative lifecycle model, each iteration has a specific goal, and specific requirements are allocated to it. Testing can begin, even in iterations within the Elaboration phase.

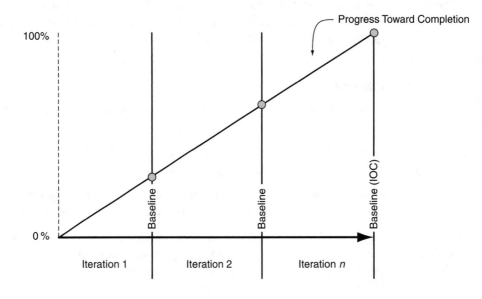

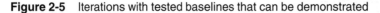

Figure 2-5   Iterations with tested baselines that can be demonstrated

RUP Lifecycle Phases

In the RUP, the project lifecycle is divided into four phases: Inception, Elaboration, Construction, and Transition. Each phase has a different emphasis that affects the content of the individual iterations within the phase. Figure 2-6 illustrates the four phases, together with the trends of levels of effort within each discipline throughout the project lifecycle.

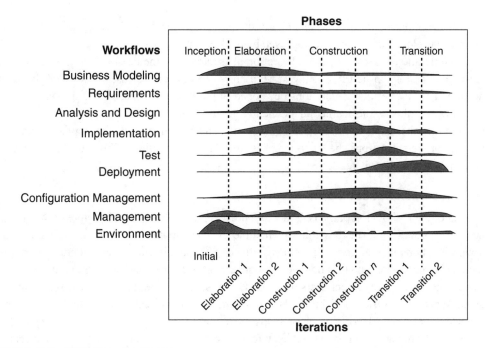

Figure 2-6   RUP lifecycle phases

Derived from *The Rational Unified Process Made Easy: A Practitioner's Guide to the RUP*, by Per Kroll and Philippe Kruchten

Goals of Each Phase in the RUP Lifecycle

Each phase in the RUP lifecycle has a specific purpose and goal. Let's examine each.

The Inception Phase

The goal of the Inception phase is to reach the lifecycle objectives milestone. At this milestone, you decide whether to continue with the project, change its scope, or cancel it. You do this by carefully examining evaluation criteria such as these:

- Do stakeholders agree on the system's key requirements? At this point in the project lifecycle, in the RUP, not all the detailed requirements are known, but the key high-level requirements are, especially those detailing the system's scope. Exactly who are the system's stakeholders? Who are the users? How many people will use the system? Which business processes will the system manage? Will the system be Web-based or some other type of system?

- Do the stakeholders agree with the cost and schedule required for producing the system?

- Have the significant risks been identified and mitigation plans developed for each risk? Do the stakeholders understand the risks and the consequences if the risks materialize?

Of particular importance in this phase, the project business case, vision, and list of risks should be developed in writing and approved by the key stakeholders.

The iterations developed in the Inception phase are often the most difficult, because they may be exploratory in nature or may serve as proof-of-concept releases. Therefore, it is not uncommon for the results of iterations developed in the Inception phase to be throwaway artifacts. However, the lessons learned in these early iterations are key.

On the other hand, if the project's goal is well understood, and the development team has built similar systems before, the Inception phase may have no iterations. This is the only lifecycle phase that might not have iterations.

The Elaboration Phase

The goal of the Elaboration phase is to identify, prove, and baseline the architecture of the system that is to be developed. This baseline is called the lifecycle architecture milestone. This is done through iterations that address requirements affecting the architecture. Key attention is paid to functional requirements and to supplemental requirements that drive the system's architecture. For example, how many concurrent users must the system support? Are there response time requirements? What about system reliability? Is the system mission-critical? The content of iterations conducted during the Elaboration phase helps prove that the system's architecture is viable. It's critical that the focus remain on the architecture. If an architecture is chosen that does not meet the supplemental requirements, the system will ultimately fail after delivery, no matter how well the subsequent phases go. Key exit criteria for the Elaboration phase include the following:

- Artifacts produced in the previous phase, such as the product vision, business case, and key requirements, are stable.

- The architecture chosen for the system is identified and proven through executable releases produced by iterations exercising key system requirements, and risks are identified and mitigated. This includes test results for each release produced during the Elaboration phase.

- Most of the system's detailed requirements are identified by the conclusion of Elaboration. Note that some detailed requirements still might be unknown, but the ones most important to the user are known. There is no exact number, but I prefer to have approximately 80% of the system requirements identified by this point.

- Trends involving expenditure of resources (time and budget) are acceptable to the project stakeholders.

- Iteration plans for the Construction phase (particularly for the early Construction iterations) should be in place by the conclusion of Elaboration. You should have a detailed plan for the earliest Construction iterations, such as the first and perhaps second iteration. After that, any plans should be high-level at the most. The reason, of course, is that discovery in the first iterations may lead you to change the subsequent iterations. There is no point in creating detailed plans for iterations that are very likely to change.

The results at the conclusion of the Elaboration phase are evaluated. If the exit criteria show that acceptable results have been achieved, the project proceeds to the Construction phase.

The Construction Phase

On RUP-based projects, the majority of the time and project resources are expended in the Construction phase. By this point, all the major risks of developing the system have been identified and mitigated, the architecture has been determined, and most of the system requirements have been identified. The goal is to produce a new, stable release at the conclusion of each iteration that contains more and more implemented functionality. Testing also occurs during each iteration, regardless of phase. This means that during an iteration, testing of new functionality begins as soon as it becomes available within the iteration. Regression testing of functionality built during previous iterations also takes place. This requires close coordination between testers and developers. Defects discovered during testing are documented and evaluated to determine their priority. The most serious defects are corrected immediately within the same iteration. Lower-priority defects may be deferred to later iterations if necessary. The goal is for each iteration to produce a release that is executable, demonstrable, and stable.

The goal of the Construction phase is to produce the initial operational capability. This is not necessarily a completely finished product, but rather one that implements all the system's key requirements. This may be called a **beta** release. Some things might be missing, such as help files and installation scripts, but the release can be used as a pilot release to gain useful feedback.

It can be helpful, when conducting high-level planning, to schedule one or two extra, "empty" iterations at the end of the Construction phase. These are iterations for which time is allocated in the schedule, but no requirements are allocated to them. This way, if additional requirements are identified, or if difficulties arise, requirements can be deferred to these empty iterations while the additional requirements or challenges are addressed. If no such circumstances arise, you can always deliver earlier than planned.

The Transition Phase

In the Transition phase, final iterations incorporate corrections for defects and other items, such as help files, installation scripts, some enhancement requests, and configuration and tuning. Other significant tasks might also be included, such as data migration if the product replaces a legacy system.

It is interesting to note that the Transition phase can be trivial or complex, depending on the nature of the product. A product that resides on a single system and involves only a handful of expert users colocated at one location is one extreme. On the other end, a very large distributed mission-critical system with thousands of users may have an extended Transition phase. This might include very close monitoring and involvement by the contractor, with a significant core group of developers and staff on alert, ready to address key problems that are discovered.

Is the RUP Agile?

In the late 1980s and 1990s, as the foundation was being laid for the RUP, a number of practitioners were experimenting with variations on iterative software development techniques. The focus was to eliminate much of the overhead and "ceremony" common with Waterfall-based lifecycles. The inspiration was the lean production techniques pioneered in the manufacturing world by companies such as Toyota. The goal was to create demonstrable releases quickly and frequently, using short (2- to 4-week) iterations. Other novel aspects involved having the software users work directly with the software team. In addition, the entire software team worked together in close collaboration. This enabled quick, efficient communication within the team as well as with the stakeholders. The process was highly adaptive and flexible. Planning for each iteration was performed based on the evaluation of the previous iteration's release. Even testing was performed during the iteration and was repeated frequently during builds, facilitated by extensive use of test automation.

These lightweight, flexible lifecycle models experienced success and attracted the attention of several prominent experts in the industry. In early 2001, a group of 17 of these practitioners met to discuss these methods. The group decided to name these methods **Agile** methods. Together, the group authored what became known as the Agile Manifesto:

> We are uncovering better ways of developing
> software by doing it and helping others do it.
> Through this work we have come to value:
>
> Individuals and interactions over processes and tools
> Working software over comprehensive documentation
> Customer collaboration over contract negotiation
> Responding to change over following a plan
>
> That is, while there is value in the items on
> the right, we value the items on the left more.[2]

Interestingly, several variations of Agile processes exist. Examples are Extreme Programming (XP), Scrum, Crystal, and others. They vary on factors such as typical iteration length, and other practices that have differing emphasis.

So, is the RUP Agile? The answer is that it *can* be. It depends on how the RUP is tailored. If the values expressed in the Agile Manifesto resonate with your team and your customer, consider the following points when tailoring the RUP:

- Choose only the most vital artifacts needed by the customer and the development team. Strive to eliminate any unnecessary processes and documents. When in doubt, eliminate it.

- Strive to keep iterations as short as possible. Remember that the goal for each iteration is to produce a demonstrable, executable release. The release should be tested during development so that the release delivered at the end of the iteration functions correctly.

---

[2] © 2001, Kent Beck, Mike Beedle, Arie van Bennekum, Alistair Cockburn, Ward Cunningham, Martin Fowler, James Grenning, Jim Highsmith, Andrew Hunt, Ron Jeffries, Jon Kern, Brian Marick, Robert C. Martin, Steve Mellor, Ken Schwaber, Jeff Sutherland, and Dave Thomas. This declaration may be freely copied in any form, but only in its entirety through this notice.

- Agile methods above all stress collaboration between all members of the development team, as well as customers or users. Whenever doubt on functionality or priorities exists, the customer is consulted and drives the decision.

- If possible, have the customer work with the testers to define acceptance tests for the various features. These tests are run at the conclusion of the iteration, and the customer signs off on that functionality at the end of the iteration. The advantage of this approach is that it eliminates the need for a massive, "all-at-once" acceptance test by the customer at the end of the project. Even if the customer still wants a complete acceptance test, the likelihood of surprises is lower.

- Agile methods stress automation of redundant tasks wherever it makes sense. In particular, testing needs to be automated. As iterations continue, the amount of functionality requiring testing increases (both regression testing of previously delivered functionality and testing of newly developed functionality).

RUP practices are completely compatible with Agile values. The key is to tailor the RUP to be as simple as possible and to focus on frequently producing releases that the customer reviews and accepts.

Summary

The key to iterative development (and, therefore, implementing the RUP) is to embrace the notion that early failure is good. An iteration that fails early in the Elaboration phase, for example, is a success, provided that the failure is for the right reasons. To illustrate, an iteration in Elaboration may have the goal of proving that a project's performance requirements can be met with a certain architecture. Yet the team is unable to achieve the required performance with the chosen architecture. At the iteration's conclusion, the team might decide to scrap the architecture or make significant changes to it. The next iteration is successful as a result of the changes made due to the lessons learned in the first failed iteration. The ultimate result is project success through lessons learned, with minimal schedule risk.

I have encountered common patterns in organizations attempting to use the RUP the wrong way. These are covered in Appendix A, "Common Mistakes Utilizing RUP."

What's Next?

Chapter 3, "Getting Started: Request for Proposals (RFPs), Proposals, and Contracts," discusses an aspect of projects many developers and other team members never see or experience—the procurement process. I invite you to examine this chapter, because it will help you understand the factors that lay the groundwork for difficulties on projects. Practitioners who have not experienced proposals and procurement efforts will gain insight into how these activities influence the eventual success or failure of an outsourced project.

CHAPTER 3

Getting Started: Request for Proposals (RFPs), Proposals, and Contracts

This chapter discusses how common procurement methods can result in project difficulties or even complete failure. It shows how inadequate Request for Proposals (RFPs) and Statements of Work (SOWs) make it difficult to employ modern iterative development methodologies such as the RUP.

I decided this chapter would be beneficial based on my experiences as a consultant and project manager on numerous projects that implemented the RUP. My experiences prior to that as a developer on various outsourced projects also contributed to the need for this chapter. I strongly encourage developers to understand the proposal process, because this is where many decisions are made that shape the experience on the project.

Having served as a consultant to various outsourced projects involving the RUP, I have spent much time listening to clients, trying to understand their difficulties with software development. As I have praised the virtues of modern development processes such as the RUP with these clients, I have often heard a response that disturbs me. A typical response is, "I hear what you're saying, but our Statement of Work/contract/agreement doesn't let us do it that way." In some cases, it is easy to work around these issues. In others, the situation becomes complex. Then, the focus turns to how to use a modern iterative development process while still conforming to the letter of the contractual agreement. This is when the problems arise. Even under the best of circumstances, software development is a difficult task. For many years, the industry has focused on methodology, techniques, languages, and process. We have come a long way. But there is room for improvement—especially in the areas of procurement and monitoring methods on large outsourced projects. To see why, let's look at how software systems are procured.

How Is Procurement Accomplished for Outsourced Systems?

At a high level, the procurement process is straightforward. Most procurements, particularly government procurements, follow these steps:

1. A Request for Proposal (RFP, sometimes also called a Request for Solution [RFS]) is released to potential bidders.

2. On occasion, proposal meetings or conferences are held, often at the client's location. Bidders attend to get an overview of the RFP, ask questions, and "scope out" the competition by observing who else is in attendance.

3. Each bidder typically forms a proposal team to examine and prepare responses to the RFP.

4. If the bidders have questions about the RFP, they submit them to the client. Whether oral or written, copies of the questions, together with the answers, are circulated to all bidders to ensure a level playing field. Depending on the complexity of the RFP, more than one iteration of questions and answers may occur.

5. For larger projects, the bidders give oral presentations to the client.

6. The written proposals are submitted.

7. The client submits questions to the bidders (if there are any). These are strictly confidential between the client and each bidder.

8. The bidders submit their answers to the questions.

9. The client requests a Best and Final Offer (BAFO), which the bidder submits.

10. The client makes a decision and notifies all the bidders.

This process has several variations. If there are many bidders, the selection process may occur in phases. This is known as a "down select" or prequalification process, in which the pool of bidders is narrowed down to a select few. There are other examples, but they do not directly affect this discussion.

The Ten Steps in the Procurement Process

Let's take a closer look at each of the ten steps just described.

Step 1: An RFP Is Released

Most contractors have marketing departments and track key developments with their customers. This means, in many cases, that contractors are aware that an RFP will be forthcoming, although they are unaware of its specific contents. When the RFP is obtained, the contractor decides whether to respond to it. (This decision often already has been made by the time the RFP becomes available.) The contractor then forms a proposal team and examines the RFP in detail. In most cases, the written response has a specific page limit, and if oral presentations occur, a time limit is given for them.

The information supplied in an RFP varies widely. Most commonly, high-level descriptions of the tasks to be performed are given. A vision statement may be included, explaining why the customer needs the system and why any current systems in place are inadequate to solve the problem at hand. An SOW may be given, which directly describes the tasks the contractor is to perform. On occasion, if any prior analysis work has been done, the high-level requirements are provided. Sometimes, a glossary is provided that explains the key terms in the problem domain.

Step 2: Proposal Meetings and Conferences

If you are considering responding to an RFP, these meetings are "must-attend" events. In addition to meeting the customer (and possibly some of the key project stakeholders), you can observe who will be competing with you on the bid. You'll also see how much interest there is in the proposal, judging from the number of attendees. The client typically gives a presentation summarizing the contents of the RFP, and perhaps some background on the client's business and organization. This is usually followed by a question-and-answer session.

Step 3: Forming a Proposal Team

The criterion for choosing the members of the proposal team varies from company to company. Large companies often have dedicated proposal teams and marketing departments. Small companies may have to pull people from billable projects to respond to an RFP. The bidder may have someone familiar with the specific problem domain or customer. Also, anyone with certain skills that are deemed critical for a given proposal will be asked to participate to some degree on the proposal team.

A quick schedule is drawn up, and tasks are assigned to each member of the proposal team. This is important, because with most proposal efforts, time is of the essence. It is common for the proposal team to work late into the night on proposals. All-nighters are not unheard of as the proposal due date approaches.

Step 4: Questions from the Bidders

The bidder, while preparing a proposal, may have questions about certain aspects of the RFP. In most cases, questions cannot be asked directly of the project stakeholders. They must be submitted in writing through the contracts office. The contracts office then obtains the answers to the questions from the project stakeholders. This controls the flow of information between the prospective bidder and the project stakeholders. If bidders were permitted to speak to stakeholders directly, one prospective bidder might obtain information the other bidders might not have. This opens the door to potential "award protest" litigation as other bidders may claim the information gave the winner an unfair advantage. The questions collected from the bidders are then consolidated, along with the answers, and are distributed to all the bidders. When these questions and answers are provided, the identity of the contractor asking the question is omitted. (But in some cases, it's possible to guess who asked the question if the pool of bidders is small.) This ensures that all bidders receive the same information from the client to prepare their bids, thus guaranteeing fairness in the process.

Step 5: Oral Presentations

Oral presentations are common, especially on medium to large procurements. Oral presentations generally occur after a down select process. The contractors remaining after the down select have their own private presentation session with the project stakeholders. Other bidders cannot be present. The contractor generally has a fixed amount of time in which to give an overview of its corporate capabilities, its assessment of the RFP, how it will respond to the RFP, and the proposed costs. An overview of the skills of key personnel is given. A question-and-answer session usually follows, and the presentation is concluded. Most oral presentations are one to two hours long.

Step 6: Written Proposal Submitted

The written proposal is submitted at the conclusion of the oral presentations or shortly thereafter. A strict page limit is usually imposed on the proposal (because on large procurements, the outsourcing organization may have many proposals to read and evaluate). At this point, the majority of the work by the bidder for the proposal is completed, and the bidder waits to hear from the outsourcing organization.

Step 7: Questions and Answers

When a bidder receives questions from the outsourcing organization, it's generally considered a good sign. If the bidder has been eliminated from consideration, there would be no questions. The contractor scrutinizes the questions to try to gain an understanding of the outsourcing organization's motivation. The contractor typically has several business days to respond.

Step 8: Answers Submitted

The contractor submits its answers to the questions. Note that the questions and answers may go through a couple of iterations.

Step 9: Best and Final Offer (BAFO)

The contractor may ask one or more of the bidders to submit a Best and Final Offer (BAFO). If a bidder is asked by the outsourcing organization to submit a BAFO, it knows it is on the short list to potentially win the bid. The contractor examines the bid's history, particularly the questions and answers, and any marketing intelligence that may have been gathered. It then uses this information to change its bid to make it more attractive. Usually, this means cutting the price through either reduced amounts of labor, a different mix of staffing levels resulting in a lower price, or possibly a change in assumptions that limits the contractor's risk so that it is more comfortable submitting a more aggressive price. All these assumptions during the bidding (and BAFO) process are documented and are submitted with the bid documents. The assumptions become part of the contract if the bid is awarded to that contractor.

Step 10: Contract Award

The contractor that produced the winning proposal is notified, and then the other bidders are notified. A debriefing is usually scheduled for those that did not win the work.

Advantages of the Procurement Process

I have described the process commonly used in government procurements. Commercial procurements are similar, but they have fewer steps. At first glance, nothing seems wrong with this procurement process. In fact, it has a number of advantages. Let's discuss these first before we identify the challenges:

- Competition ensures that the bids will focus only on what is requested, to be produced in a way that is the most cost-competitive. This ensures that the outsourcing organization is obtaining a good value.

- Great care is taken to ensure fairness in the process. All bidders obtain the same information from the outsourcing organization.

- The RFP typically requests a specific capability within a specified amount of time. This means that the outsourcing organization knows in advance what capabilities it will have in the future and how much money must be committed in its budget to obtain the capability. This helps the organization plan its future budgets.

These are key advantages for the outsourcing organization. Yet from a software development perspective, the procurement process causes a number of problems. Why? Let's take a look.

What's Wrong with This Procurement Process?

The problem with this procurement process is that it assumes that the item being procured is a simple commodity. In other words, given a general description of the system, a vendor should be able to determine the cost to make such a system, add a percentage of profit, and produce the bid. Of course, the software industry is far from the level of maturity seen in other industries. Given the same requirements, bids for an identical system from different contractors have large variations that can't be explained solely by one contractor's being more proficient than another. Specifically, consider the following issues:

- A limited number of inputs describe precisely what needs to be done. Most RFPs do not supply the detailed requirements needed to truly determine the size of a software system. Many RFPs ask for a single bid for the cost of an entire project, from requirements elicitation through delivery of the final product. How can you determine a realistic bid before you know what the project's requirements are? You can't. Worse still, the RFPs for these projects sometimes request Firm Fixed Price (FFP) proposals! This is a recipe for disaster before the project has even started. Most bidders respond to this situation in one of two ways:

1. They bid a high price to cover the worst-case situation. Most bidders don't do this because doing so wouldn't make them competitive with other bidders that are willing to accept a higher level of risk.

2. They load the proposal with so many assumptions and stipulations that the proposal becomes meaningless early in the project's lifetime. Although this protects the bidder legally, it is ultimately harmful to the relationship between the client and contractor. This is also risky, because if there are too many assumptions or the proposal is not specific enough, the bidder risks being eliminated due to being considered nonconforming or unresponsive to the client's needs.

Ways to handle this situation are covered later in this chapter.

- When the outsourcing organization attempts to produce a detailed set of requirements, they are often poorly done and incomplete. Unless the outsourcing organization has the proper expertise, the requirements do not follow the best practices for requirements that are clear, concise, unambiguous, and testable. Furthermore, many stakeholders are not even sure what they want (although they usually recognize a good solution when they see it). This makes it even more difficult to properly articulate the requirements.

- The bidders have a limited amount of time to properly analyze the inputs. Even if accurate, detailed requirements are supplied, there is insufficient time to read and thoroughly understand them. The primary goal during the proposal process is to produce a winning bid that compares favorably with the other bids. Many proposals are analyzed and produced within a few weeks. As stated before, most proposal teams work very long hours, with little time to contemplate the long-term effect of many of the decisions made in the bid.

- Questions and answers about the RFP take place in a competitively charged environment. When a bidder has a question about the RFP, it knows that any question it asks will be shown to the other bidders. Therefore, any question that hints at a bidder's approach to the problem or its difficulty in understanding the RFP is not submitted. This means that important questions go unanswered, or the bidder makes assumptions about the RFP that may be inappropriate.

- Questions that do get submitted are not allowed to go directly to the stakeholders. They first go through a contracts department. Questions and answers are in written form only. Often, the question is misunderstood or the answer is insufficient. There is no opportunity to interact with the stakeholders during the question-and-answer process.

- The BAFO phase is often counterproductive. A detrimental psychological process seems to occur during this phase with bidders. A bidder works many hours to painstakingly produce what it believes is a viable, workable plan backed up with as many facts as possible. When BAFO occurs, the bidder knows it is one step away from winning the bid. This pressure often leads a bidder to ignore the work previously produced, slashing estimates to get the cost lower to win the bid. This results in a proposal cost based on wishful thinking and luck rather than facts. An estimate that is prepared through a careful analysis of the facts is a nonnegotiable figure. The only way an estimate can be changed honestly is to change the assumptions made as a condition of the estimate—or possibly, one of the inputs to the estimate is changed. Of course, during the proposal process, the bidder does not have control over the inputs. Occasionally, errors occur when an estimate is produced. But many contractors simply look at their budget and schedule figures, slice a percentage off those figures to meet the competitive pressure, and hope for the best.

- At many companies, especially medium to large companies, the members of the team who produced the proposal are not the same as the members assigned to the team after the project is won. Often, the team running the project is shocked to learn of the assumptions, budget, and schedule set forth by their teammates in the proposal. Of course, by that time, there is no choice but to live with the situation.

Given these difficulties, it's no wonder so many projects are behind schedule and over budget. And we have not even begun to consider the usual technical challenges that come into play on projects. Clearly, a better way is needed.

How Can Procurement of Software Systems Be Improved?

The Rational Unified Process incorporates iterative development as the core of the process. Why? As discussed in Chapter 2, "Overview of the Rational Unified Process," you can best solve a large problem by breaking it into smaller, more easily understood parts. As you learn more through the execution of iterations, risks are resolved early, and the subsequent iterations can be adjusted. Why not apply these ideas to the procurement process?

A Proposed Progressive Acquisition Model for Small Projects

For small projects, the question is how to implement an iterative, progressive model without so much procurement-related overhead that the Return on Investment (ROI) becomes poor.

A two-phase acquisition process solves this problem. The first RFP, referred to as a System Specification Contract, is issued strictly for the project's Inception and Elaboration phases. The second RFP, called the System Realization Contract, covers the project's Construction and Transition phases, as shown in Figure 3-1. Note that the RFP for the System Realization Contract can be prepared before the completion of the Elaboration phase to minimize delays in the project.

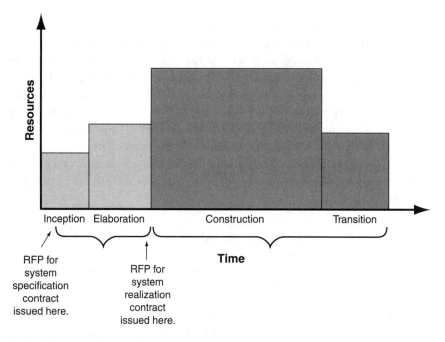

Figure 3-1   Two-phase acquisition process

The key to this model is the tremendous amount of information that is learned during a project's Inception and Elaboration phases. Yet, the bulk of the cost to implement a project occurs in Construction and Transition. Splitting the project into two separate procurements has the following advantages:

- The project team can conduct the requirements elicitation by interacting directly with the stakeholders.
- You can estimate the portions of the project that use the most time and resources from useful artifacts produced during Inception and Elaboration.
- The project estimation is performed outside of a competitively charged environment.
- The project estimation can be accomplished over a reasonable period of time, instead of during the hectic period during a proposal.
- The contractor is motivated to produce high-quality artifacts, because it can potentially win the System Realization Contract if it performs well.
- The outsourcing organization has more flexibility. It can retain the existing contractor or hire a different one for the System Realization Contract.
- If the size, schedule, and budget needed for the System Realization Contract are much larger than the outsourcing organization anticipated, the subsequent RFP for the System Realization Contract can be canceled, rescoped, or modified before the majority of the overall project schedule and funding are consumed.

Outsourcing organizations should be aware of some issues with this model:

- Careful planning is needed to avoid delays between the System Specification and System Realization portions of the contract. The deliverables produced in the System Specification portion of the project that are needed for the System Realization Contract must be completed, at least in draft form, early enough so that the RFP for System Realization can be produced.

- If the outsourcing organization decides to award the System Realization Contract to a contractor different from the one performing the System Specification portion of the contract, a significant amount of "ramp-up" time is needed. The new contractor needs time to review the deliverables and understand the project's business processes.

Several examples of projects that have used this model exist. On August 29, 2003, the Department of Commerce, National Oceanic and Atmospheric Administration (NOAA) awarded a contract for a project known as Grants Online. The purpose of the NOAA Grants Online project is to provide a fast, coherent, flexible, and robust application to support the Grants evaluation, award, and long-term management and operations process. Grants Online will deliver a standardized set of capabilities for viewing, retrieving, modifying, and deleting application- and award-related information, including (but not limited to) applications, awards, amendments, audits, proposal scoring and commentary, budget and finance information, and technical and panel reviewer information.

This award was for the equivalent of the System Specification portion of the project. The contractor for the System Specification portion of the contract produced the following deliverables:

- A complete set of business and system use cases

- An architecture road map, which provided an overview of the key architectural attributes and decisions that would be made to develop the system

- An initial draft of the project's Configuration Management Plan

- A Development Case, illustrating which artifacts should be created and developed from the Rational Unified Process

- A draft of the Requirements Management Plan

- A Reference Architecture document, containing a proposed reference architecture for the Grants Online system

- A Unified Modeling Language (UML) model

- A list of key project risks with suggested mitigation steps

- A Supplementary Requirements Specification

- A Vision document explaining why the system is needed, who the stakeholders are, the environment, and other key information

It is far easier to produce a proposal (with realistic schedule and budget estimates) with this accompanying information. Accordingly, RFPs with this accompanying information are more likely to receive accurate bids, and they have a better chance of concluding successfully.

Organizations that are considering implementing a two-stage acquisition model (with one contract for Inception/Elaboration and another for Construction/Transition) should consult Appendix B, "Implementing a Two-Stage Procurement Process." It discusses the artifacts that should be produced by the system specification contract and included in the RFP for the System Realization Contract.

A Progressive Acquisition Model for Medium to Large Projects

For larger, long-term projects, the two-phase acquisition model described in the preceding section is too simplistic. Although it's better than a single, one-shot award for an entire project, it is still insufficient. Large, long-term projects have these additional challenges:

- The project's long-term nature means that the technologies available at the beginning of the project are likely to change during the project.

- The organization's business processes may change during the project.

- The stakeholders themselves are likely to change. New stakeholders may not agree with the needs of previous stakeholders or with the project's current direction.

- Larger projects involve more people and often multiple contractors. The lines of communication, therefore, are much more complex and take considerably longer to traverse.

The end result is that multiple adjustments may need to be made throughout the project.

In a series of articles written for *The Rational Edge* e-zine, R. Max Wideman defines a progressive acquisition solution for contracting that addresses these issues. In one of these articles, he states, "a contract agreement should consist of two levels":

- A Head Contract that sets out terms and conditions for an anticipated long-term relationship.

- A system of Contract Work Orders (CWOs) that progressively enable the work.[1]

More specifically, in the article "Progressive Acquisition and the RUP, Part II: Contracts that Work," published in the January 2003 issue of *The Rational Edge*, Wideman says the following:

> The Head contract should include most of the required standard boilerplate: administrative and technical provisions such as hourly or unit rates, change management procedures, payment cycles, testing processes, and so on. If the acquiring organization has done its homework, this part can also include a target budget figure based on reasonably accurate conceptual-level estimates. This document spells out a broad framework for an ongoing relationship; it provides the acquirer with the necessary financial control and the supplier with a reasonable expectation on which to base its competitive pricing.

[1] From "Progressive Acquisition and the RUP, Part II: Contracts that Work," copyright R. Max Wideman and IBM Corporation 2002–2003. All rights reserved. Used with permission.

The second level of the contract defines specific deliverables associated with a shorter period of time, and the actual technical work is released as a sequence of CWOs. These CWOs are prepared and awarded to the supplier for each stage of work, based on the latest information and development of the solution, and as a result of technical negotiations between the parties. The initial set of deliverables will be recorded in the first CWO. The earliest CWO or CWOs will be cost reimbursable ... then, as successive elements of work are accomplished, the requirements should become sufficiently firm, at least for the next iteration that a firm price can be agreed upon for the next CWO.[2]

Figure 3-2 illustrates this process.

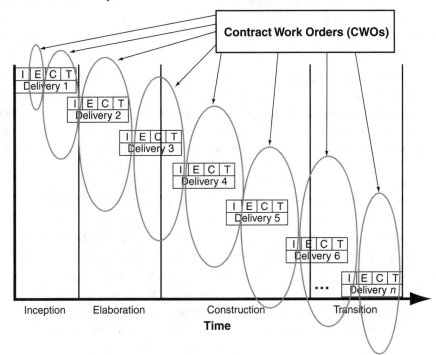

Figure 3-2 Progressive acquisition model for medium or large projects

Derived from "Progressive Acquisition and the RUP, Part II: Contracts that Work," copyright R. Max Wideman and IBM Corporation 2002–2003. All rights reserved. Used with permission.

As Wideman states:

Note that a first small contract might be issued to help define the first delivery—part of the Elaboration Phase for the first increment... The second CWO would cover completion of the Delivery 1 and include the technical discussion necessary for setting up Delivery 2—in other words, the Inception Phase of the second increment. Depending on the confidence level of the parties regarding the extent or effort required for this second CWO, the payment arrangement could be either cost reimbursable or fixed price.

[2] Ibid

By the time we get to Delivery 2 (i.e., the third CWO), both the relationship between the parties and their understanding of the work should be solid enough to let them arrive at a satisfactory fixed price for the scope of work in this CWO. Specifications should include not only the amount, but also a payment schedule and end date. The acquirer should avoid imposing unreasonable time constraints so that the work can be done properly.[3]

The pattern repeats until the final CWO is reached and the full functionality of the product becomes available. Figure 3-2 shows eight CWOs. Although there is no specific recommendation for the number of CWOs that are needed for a long-term project, Figure 3-2 represents a project that might take several years to accomplish.

This model provides many advantages over traditional procurement models. But the outsourcing organization must be closely involved when using such a model. In particular, the following are true:

- The progressive model is more than a simple series of mini-contracts. For it to work, deliverables and goals must be clearly defined in the beginning of each CWO. Government contract professionals may notice that this model appears similar to an Indefinite Delivery, Indefinite Quantity (IDIQ) model. In fact, there are some similarities, but there are important differences as well. The key difference is that the progressive model is a series of steps in the lifecycle of a single project. Each step is based on what was accomplished in the previous step, similar to the iterative development model. A careful evaluation is conducted near the end of one step before the RFP is developed for the next step.

- Near the end of a CWO, its deliverables are examined and its goals are evaluated to determine the proper goals for the next CWO. This requires periodic involvement from the contracting professionals in the outsourcing organization, as well as the project stakeholders.

- The outsourcing organization must pay especially close attention to the results of the first two or three CWOs. If the work in the first CWO is not advancing significantly toward the project's final goals, work should be stopped and the situation evaluated to determine whether the project can continue or if it needs to be rethought.

Advantages of the Progressive Acquisition Model for Larger Contracts

A progressive acquisition model solves many problems inherent in the traditional "single RFP" model. In particular, the following are true:

- The estimates for the subsequent phases of the project can be adjusted as more information is learned during the earlier phases. The estimates have the potential to be much more accurate because they are based on useful information obtained through actual hands-on experience with the project.

- As the needs (requirements) change over time, through either changes in the business process or changes in technology, the contracts for the subsequent phases can be adjusted accordingly.

[3] Ibid

- Contractors have a strong incentive to perform well and maintain good relations with the outsourcing organization. This ensures that they will be invited to bid on subsequent phases of the project.

- The next contract is not established until performance on the current phase has been determined to be successful.

- If performance at the conclusion of a phase is unsuccessful, the situation can be analyzed to determine the cause of the failure and correct it before subsequent time and resources are spent.

If these advantages sound strangely familiar, it is because many of them are very similar to those of iterative development. The underlying principle of the progressive procurement model is identical to that of iterative development: Attack risky areas first, apply lessons learned to subsequent iterations, and establish and enforce entry and exit criteria for each phase.

Potential Weaknesses of the Progressive Acquisition Model

Any process for procuring large, complex systems has risks, even the progressive acquisition model. These risks can be managed, but the results can still be disastrous through lack of attention.

- Continuity is lost if contractors are changed between phases. Presumably, this should not happen unless there is a serious issue with the contractor's performance.

- The progressive acquisition model requires strict monitoring of the project's success, particularly at the end of each phase. This cannot be a "rubber stamp" process. It requires the stakeholders to carefully examine the artifacts and released product at the end of the phase. Planning on the subsequent phases is then based on these artifacts. Without this involvement, many of the advantages of the progressive model are lost.

- The progressive acquisition model requires a significantly higher level of involvement from the outsourcing organization. This is also true of the contracts organization, which may be unaccustomed to multiple RFPs and contracts for a single project.

Issues with Managing Fixed-Price Projects

Earlier, I mentioned that entire projects are sometimes implemented with a single contract—from requirements elicitation all the way through final delivery. Although it's not possible to bid these with any certainty, the fact remains that until progressive acquisition models become more prominent in the industry, this situation will continue. Although these types of projects (one contract for the entire project lifecycle, Firm Fixed Price) are difficult, it is still possible to achieve success. The utility of iterative development is the key.

In any project, four variables must be continually managed:

- Cost: The total projected cost of the entire project, through to the end of the contract
- Schedule: The progress against the schedule of the entire project

- Quality of the system as it is being developed, verified through testing
- Functionality: The complete collection of requirements desired by the system's stakeholders

With iterative development, the project manager can measure actual values for all four of these variables with each iteration. After a few iterations have been completed, you can project the measured values for the number of requirements or features implemented, the funding expended, and the schedule. This information will determine whether the project goals can be achieved within the original cost and schedule proposed.

Iterative development has yet another benefit. If projections indicate that the project cannot be completed with the remaining amount of budget and schedule, the customer can decide whether to commit additional time and funding to the project. The customer can evaluate the executable releases produced by the project. If the customer likes what it sees produced so far, it can commit additional time and funds with the confidence that the project is on the right track. Contrast this with traditional Waterfall methods, which usually have nothing to show for resources expended except documents and PowerPoint presentations. Projects with early releases that show solid progress are more likely to receive added funding.

Monitoring Project Performance

Project performance can be monitored in a number of ways. This section briefly mentions one inherent in the RUP and then discusses another, Earned Value, in more detail.

Releases

The RUP, due to its iterative nature, provides the best opportunity to observe real project status through demonstrable, executable releases. I encourage outsourcing organizations to work with their contractors to determine the appropriate time to examine these releases. These releases amount to snapshots in time of the state of the actual product being produced. Having the people who will use the project evaluate the executable releases is the best way to measure progress.

Earned Value

Earned Value has become an increasingly popular technique for tracking true project performance. Outsourcing organizations sometimes ask, or even require, their contractors to use Earned Value techniques to help them monitor a project's progress. To understand what Earned Value is, examine Figure 3-3. Is the scenario shown in Figure 3-3 a good situation? At first glance, it would seem so. Figure 3-3 shows that the project is running under its planned budget, which would seem to be a good situation. But in reality, you cannot tell if the project described by Figure 3-3 is running well or is having problems, because you cannot tell how much work has been done. If very little work has been accomplished, the project may be in serious trouble even though it is running under budget. On the other hand, if the work to be completed by the point identified by Time (x) has been completed successfully, the project is in excellent shape. Thus, Earned Value is useful because it integrates the number of resources (time and budget) with the amount of work actually performed.

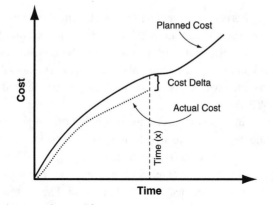

Figure 3-3   Is this project running well?

Derived from "Earned Value, Clear and Simple," used with permission from Primavera Systems, Inc.

Figure 3-4 illustrates some of the fundamental metrics that are computed as a part of Earned Value analysis.

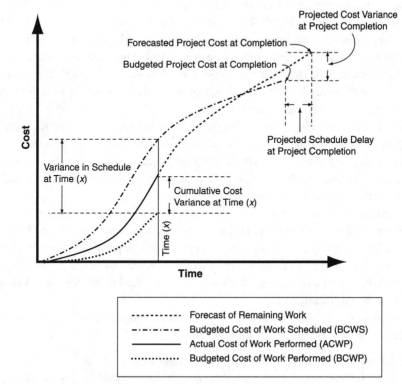

Figure 3-4   Fundamentals of Earned Value management

Ibid

Most projects using Earned Value require the metrics illustrated in Figure 3-4 to be calculated each month. To properly calculate Earned Value, the contractor must track hours spent by project staff at a higher level of granularity than they may be accustomed to. This requires the contractor to closely track not only the total number of hours each person spends on the project, but also how many hours each person spends on each major task defined in the project's Work Breakdown Structure (WBS).

Monitoring Earned Value is quite useful to ensure that the project stays on task. If projections of cost and schedule begin to move significantly beyond budgeted amounts (10% is a reasonable figure), this does not necessarily mean that the project is in trouble. It means that something is happening on the project that requires investigation. The fluctuation may be due to a change in project scope or an unscheduled event that occurred. The contractor should discuss this with the outsourcing organization and decide whether corrective measures are warranted.

Points to Consider When Using Earned Value on Software Projects

The use of Earned Value techniques is not without controversy. Earned Value is more appropriate on projects involving a predictive lifecycle model, such as Waterfall-based projects. It is also common in the manufacturing and construction industries, where it is easier to quantify certain variables, such as the cost of materials. This does not mean it cannot be used on iterative lifecycle projects. It does mean that additional aspects must be considered. For example, to track and calculate Earned Value, you must estimate the value of each task. The values of all these tasks add up to the project's total cost. As the project progresses, the percentage of completion of each task is recorded, along with the funds expended. This, together with the budgeted amount of each task, allows you to calculate the Earned Value for the task.

One challenge with using Earned Value on software projects involves the Budgeted Cost of Work Scheduled (BCWS). This figure is based on rough estimates or guesses made early in the project's lifecycle, particularly on Waterfall lifecycle projects. As noted earlier in this chapter, these figures may be completely unrealistic. As a consequence, the result of the calculation of Earned Value in this situation is questionable.

Another challenge using Earned Value with iterative projects is that the scope of the development tasks may change. As iterative projects progress, new requirements may be discovered and added during the project, or the existing requirements may change. Finally, the knowledge gained as the project progresses might lead you to conclude that the earlier BCWS figures were wrong. This changes the budgeted cost of some of the tasks. As a result, the Earned Value calculation result can be misleading.

One possible way to make Earned Value useful and to integrate it with an iterative lifecycle is to calculate it for each individual iteration:

- Calculate the budgeted cost of an iteration right before it begins. This should be easy, because iterations are time-boxed. You can calculate the cost simply by taking the number of hours of labor performed for the iteration by each person and multiplying it by the person's hourly rate.

- Determine the estimated effort for each requirement or feature that is planned for the iteration. You should already be performing this activity in some capacity to determine what is reasonable to expect to accomplish within the iteration.

- As the iteration is conducted, individual features or requirements are marked complete only after they have been successfully tested.

- If you complete exactly what was assigned to the iteration and finish at the end date of the iteration, the cost and schedule variances should both be zero.

At the end of the iteration, calculate the actual Earned Value. You can also calculate a cumulative figure using the results from the earlier iterations. These results will give you useful data for consideration. The advantages of calculating Earned Value in this way are as follows:

- The BCWS becomes more accurate with each iteration. As the project progresses, the staff becomes more familiar with the problem domain, as well as the environment. Estimates made at the beginning of each iteration improve with each iteration.

- The criterion for Earned Value is tied directly to an executable, observable, and verified unit of functionality. Thus, you calculate the percentage complete by dividing the number of verified, tested requirements or features by the number planned for the iteration. Therefore, this is not a subjective estimate.

Projections for the remainder of the project can be made from the iterations completed up to the date the projection is made. This technique also stresses the importance of prioritizing requirements.

Here are some additional points to consider using Earned Value:

- Most decisions to use Earned Value are driven by the outsourcing organization. In fact, some organizations mandate its use. However, it is less meaningful on Firm Fixed Price contracts, since the burden and risk of delivering the product within budget fall entirely on the contractor. In that case, the budget data, while interesting, does not provide significant value to the outsourcing organization. If the outsourcing organization still wants to use Earned Value on this type of project, the schedule variance information should be the prime focus.

- The most tedious part of employing Earned Value is collecting the data. Care should be taken to choose tasks at a high-enough level for collecting data so that the staff is not overwhelmed with a flood of different charge codes to use. Software developers are not likely to accurately track their time if they must use more than two or three charge codes per day.

- If the organization requires staff to fill out time sheets, it is helpful if charge codes can be set up for each specific task on the project directly in the time sheet. In other words, don't require staff to fill out one time sheet for calculating Earned Value and another for the organization to which they belong. The staff will become frustrated at having to keep track of time data in two separate places.

For more information on Earned Value, refer to the references in the bibliography, especially the book *Earned Value Project Management*, Second Edition, by Quentin W. Fleming and Joel M. Koppelman.

Project Estimation

The proper estimation of effort required on a project is a controversial topic that has received much attention in the industry. Many useful and innovative methods have been developed and described by my colleagues. Each method has unique advantages, so I find it difficult to recommend one method over another. This discussion is beyond the scope of this book. A number of useful estimation tools are available. I encourage any organization bidding on software projects to invest in acquiring one of these tools and in training on estimation methodologies as well. Despite these methods and tools, one of the major impediments to estimation is human behavior.

Only rarely does any estimate turn out to be exactly correct. The actual experience usually ends up producing higher or lower numbers than the estimated number. For many software projects, the sad fact is that actual experience ends up producing far higher numbers than estimates, for both schedule and budget. I believe that the primary causes are as follows:

- The software industry as a whole is still very immature compared to other industries. Each company typically has its own development process and personnel competency level. There are wide variations from company to company and project to project. There is no consistency of methods from one company to another. If an outsourcing organization receives many bids for the same project, this does not necessarily mean that the lowest bidder is better at building software systems and can build them successfully for a lower cost. It could mean that the low bidder does not have a complete understanding of what is involved in building the project, or perhaps it cut corners to produce a lower bid. Likewise, a company that bids high is not necessarily less competent at building software. It could mean that it has a more complete understanding of the tasks and risks and adheres to a more disciplined process that produces a more predictable result, so therefore it costs more. In other words, software is not a commodity.

- Software projects that are put out for competitive bid receive estimates that do not reflect reality. The estimates are produced in an artificial environment where the emphasis is on producing a winning bid. This means that there is significant pressure for contractors to produce estimates that are on the low side.

The procurement models described in this chapter help alleviate the problems created by estimates produced under competitive pressure. The estimates can be produced collaboratively in a better environment where the contractor knows it has the work, provided it continues to perform well.

To judge an estimate's viability, I often use the "50% rule." A proper estimate has a 50% likelihood of being too high and a 50% likelihood of being too low. If the organization can honestly make this statement about an estimate, it's probably a good estimate. For example, if someone estimates that it will take 10 months to complete a project, I often ask under what conditions they can finish in less than 10 months. If the response is "None," I know the estimate is not viable. Many estimates produced under competitive pressure suffer from this problem. No wonder software projects are so frequently late. The estimates assume a perfect world.

Selecting a Contractor Proficient in the RUP

Suppose you are a manager in an outsourcing organization, and you have read enough about the RUP to believe that it is a better process for developing software. How do you select a contractor that is fluent in the RUP? How can you be sure the contractor really follows the best practices? Consider these points when evaluating contractors:

- Look for contractors that have established a partnership with IBM Rational. One way to do this is to attend the annual IBM Rational Software Development Conferences. Many partners of IBM Rational present papers regularly at these conferences on a variety of topics. Some also have booths at the exhibit hall where you can speak to representatives of the company.

- Find out if the contractor certifies its engineers. IBM Rational partners can obtain many certifications for their engineers. Certainly, certification in the RUP is valuable, and also for the supporting tools.

In addition, ask the contractor questions about previous projects on which it has applied the RUP. Some of the suggestions in the following list do not necessarily have right or wrong answers, but they can provide insight into the contractor's philosophy regarding the RUP:

- How do you tailor the RUP for individual projects? What factors do you consider when tailoring the RUP for a given project?

- Give examples of projects in which major problems were averted as a result of uncovering risk early through iterative development.

- How long are typical iterations on a project?

- How do you identify the appropriate architecture for a project? What factors do you consider, and how do you prove that the architecture is viable?

- What process do you use to elicit and manage requirements? How are changes to the requirements managed? How do you manage changes in scope to the project requirements?

Lessons Learned for Outsourcing Organizations

Outsourcing organizations can follow a number of practices to help their projects run more smoothly:

- When reviewing proposals from bidders, examine assumptions very closely, particularly for Firm Fixed Price contracts. Evaluate the assumptions and determine how they will affect the project and how they probably will come into play. Ask the contractor what could happen if the assumptions are incorrect or fail to occur.

- Question estimates closely. Ask the contractor under what circumstances the estimate may be invalid. Ask the contractor how likely it is that it could favorably beat the estimated amounts.

- On Firm Fixed Price contracts, be flexible and willing to negotiate functionality so that the contractor can meet budget and schedule constraints.

- Stay involved with the project. If possible or practical, monitor trends in requirements, change requests, and so on.

- Be aware that traditional contracting practices may be in conflict with modern iterative development processes such as the RUP. For example, specifying that all requirements, documentation, and so on must be completed before any coding begins is contrary to iterative lifecycles. Similarly, requiring all development to be completed before testing begins suggests that a Waterfall lifecycle be employed. Consider having an RFP reviewed by someone fluent in the RUP before releasing it.

- Encourage the contractor to demonstrate releases made at selected iterations during the project lifecycle. This is an opportunity to observe progress on the actual product instead of through status reports and Earned Value charts.

- Consider applying one of the two progressive procurement models described in this chapter.

Lessons Learned for Contractors

Here, I discuss lessons learned relating to contracts and contracting:

- When bidding on projects, try to involve selected individual developers and other technical personnel deployed on other project teams. They can supply useful lessons learned based on other relevant projects from your organization. In addition, they may be in a better position to determine whether the proposed cost and schedule are reasonable for the functionality requested in the RFP.

- When producing estimates for the project, have at least two people estimate the time and resources for the project independently. If the estimates vary widely, determine why.

- Consider providing a probability figure with the estimate. Applying the "50% rule" described earlier produces a valid estimate. But what if you want to bid a more aggressive estimate to win the business? In other words, some contractors bid low knowing that they will take a loss on one project so that they can win business with a new customer. In that case, it may be worthwhile to produce two estimates. The first estimate follows the "50% rule," and the contractor gives the customer the second estimate to win the bid. The difference between these two estimates is the estimated exposure the contractor will have to absorb if the more aggressive estimate doesn't work out. The contractor's business organization needs to know this information to prepare for a possible overrun.

- Consider computing and tracking Earned Value to help determine if the project continues to focus on the right activities as defined by the contract. Be aware that this requires tracking staff hours at a lower level of granularity than the level to which you may be accustomed.

Summary

The past several years have seen great progress in software development methodologies and processes. The next wave of progress will come from contractual mechanisms that set the right environment in which to practice these modern processes.

What's Next?

The next chapter provides guidance to those who manage an outsourcing organization. If you are such a manager and you are managing your first outsourced project, the next chapter helps you define important roles for people in your organization. The people in these roles work with the contractor to help the project be successful.

Best Practices for Staffing the Outsourcing Organization's Project Management Office (PMO)

Given the complexity of today's projects, the days of delivering a pile of requirement documents to your contractor and then hoping for the best are over. A common characteristic of successful outsourced projects is the close collaboration or partnership formed between the outsourcing organization and the contractor. This collaboration occurs on many levels and does not happen by accident. The RUP and other modern iterative development methodologies have gone a long way toward helping software developers build software better and faster. Yet not much attention has been given to the relationships formed between the outsourcing organization and the contractors. Most literature I have encountered discussing the RUP seems to assume that the entire software development team (and, in most cases, the customer) belongs to the same company or organization. This is not the case in an outsourcing situation. Large projects may involve a number of contractors in addition to the outsourcing organization itself. Even when an organization outsources a project, it still has significant involvement. The purpose of this chapter is to assist those in the outsourcing organization who may be embarking upon their first outsourced project. This chapter defines the key roles in the outsourcing organization's staff and how they can interface with the contractor to increase the chances of success on projects. It also explores the key activities of each role. This helps the project manager in the outsourcing organization plan the staffing of his organization. Finally, some practices should be established as part of forming a Project Management Office (PMO) in an outsourcing organization.

Key Roles Defined

This section describes the key roles in an outsourcing organization. Depending on the project's size, some of these roles may be shared by the same person. Also, some roles may be needed in only certain circumstances. These roles are the project manager, lead user representative, PMO project architect, internal project champion, contracting officer, and IT manager. Figure 4-1 identifies these roles in relation to the project manager. Let's examine each of these roles and how they interact with the contracting organization.

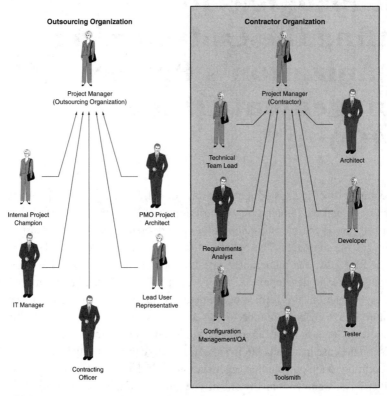

Figure 4-1   Roles in the outsourcing organization

The Project Manager

Certainly one of the most common and familiar roles is that of the project manager. This role is required for all projects. The project manager in the PMO has different responsibilities than one who manages software development directly (such as for the contractor). However, the position is similar in that most of the activities involve making sure all members of the extended team are engaged in the proper activities at the right time. In essence, the project manager serves as a "traffic cop." The next section lists and discusses the responsibilities of the project manager for an outsourcing organization.

Responsibilities of the Project Manager for an Outsourcing Organization

The responsibilities of the project manager of an outsourcing organization include the following:

- Ensure that all contractual mechanisms are established and in place to permit all contractors, subcontractors, and consultants to perform their work. The project manager should examine each Statement of Work (SOW) to ensure that it clearly specifies the responsibilities and tasks of the applicable organization. This is not a one-time task. It's not uncommon for the nature of a contractor's tasks to change during a project, particularly on long-term projects. The project manager should take the initiative to review these SOWs periodically and, if necessary, involve the contracts personnel to modify the SOW as needed. This is of great importance to contractors. At the conclusion of the contract, some organizations (particularly in government projects) rate the contractor's performance against the tasks listed in the SOW. The tasks listed must be an accurate reflection of the actual work performed, or the contractor risks getting a poor performance rating.

- The project manager must arrange for the user community to work with the contractors so that they are available to help determine the project's requirements. This generally involves a representative (or group of representatives) meeting with the contractor analysts to discuss the business process and the specific problem that needs to be solved. The project manager should ensure that these user requests are properly documented and recorded. (This artifact should be listed in the contractor's SOW.) A good project manager ensures that users are available whenever needed so that the contractor doesn't have to chase them down. The more efficiently this process is, the more likely it is that the requirements artifacts will adequately capture the users' needs.

- The project manager monitors contractor performance, typically through a number of different methods:

  - Regular written status reports

  - Periodic status meetings

  - Monitoring of Earned Value calculations, perhaps once a month

  - Monitoring of other trends, such as defects, requirements, and enhancements

- On most contracts, especially fixed-price contracts, users have a tendency to request everything and anything they anticipate needing to perform their work with the software to be built. In fact, they probably have been encouraged to do so. Despite this fact, a finite amount of time and resources is available to the contractor, and the contractor may not be able to accommodate every request. The project manager in the outsourcing organization should serve as the mediator to help the users narrow down their "wish list" to an amount that the contractor can accommodate. In other words, the project manager should prevent the contractor from having to negotiate directly with the users in this regard.

- The project manager needs to inform the contractor exactly what its responsibilities are when development is complete and the software is ready for production. The following are some typical issues that must be dealt with:

  - Will a formal User Acceptance Test occur? If so, when will it be conducted, how long will it take, and who will have the authority to sign off on the results? What will the contractor's responsibilities be during this test?

  - Will there be a "pilot" period or a "beta" release where users can try out the system before depending on it for production work?

  - Must the product meet any security standards? Who will conduct the evaluation? What are the criteria for passing any applicable tests?

  - Who will conduct any applicable training? Who will produce the training materials?

  - If the system under development is replacing another system, is any data migration necessary?

  - Will a Help Desk be set up by the organization operating the software, or does one already exist? Who will train the Help Desk staff? Is any special documentation required for Help Desk personnel?

  - Who will maintain and troubleshoot the software if this is not already accommodated for in the existing contract?

- Project managers also need to help manage change. For software projects of significant size, project managers should set up and chair a Change Control Board (CCB). The participants on the CCB should include the contractors (project manager, analyst, and technical lead) and lead user representatives. The purpose of the CCB is to analyze change requests, prioritize them, and agree on what is within the project's scope. The CCB should also agree on what constitutes an enhancement not covered in the work's original scope. Although this is an important function, it becomes even more vital when multiple contractors are involved. Multiple subcontractors could all be affected by a proposed change. Depending on the nature of the contract, subcontractors have a tendency to focus only on what is in their own SOW. In other words, there may be little communication between subcontractors. The CCB is an opportunity to discuss and resolve how the change may affect each contractor's work.

- Finally, project managers are responsible for the project's financial performance as well. Is the project on schedule and within budget? Is the outsourcing organization receiving a good value for the money spent? In this capacity, the project manager works closely with the contracts officer to be sure proper accounting practices are being followed and that the financial milestones are met.

Attributes of a Good Project Manager for an Outsourcing Organization

Good project managers need the following qualities to be able to function well:

- Knowledge of software engineering standards that are applicable to the organization, such as the RUP, CMMI, and PMI.

- Ideally, experience as a software developer, IT manager, and end user. You may not find someone who has been all of these, but experience in as many areas as possible is helpful.

- Experience managing enterprise software development projects. If an experienced individual is not available, a strong support system, including a senior project manager that can act as a mentor, must be available.

- If development will take place overseas (offshore), experience with the culture, business customs, and language of the country involved is very helpful.

- The ability to manage and negotiate with stakeholders who have opposite goals (such as users who want the maximum functionality possible and contractors who want to be able to deliver on time and make a reasonable profit).

- An understanding of and experience with supporting organizations, such as IT, Training, and the Help Desk.

- A demonstrated ability to motivate people is a requirement. Any software project has many stakeholders, and there are times when the project will run well and other times when problems occur. The ability to motivate when the situation is difficult is one of the most important attributes of a project manager.

- A demonstrated understanding of managing a business. Understanding profit and loss, hiring the right people, and so on are important skills.

The Lead User Representative

The lead user representative in an outsourcing organization acts as a liaison between the organization's user community and the analysts who work for the contractor. This person's purpose is to communicate the needs of the user community to the contractor analysts.

Responsibilities of the Lead User Representative

The responsibilities of the lead user representative include the following:

- The person in this role participates in the outsourcing organization's CCB. In that capacity, this person's purpose is to communicate the importance of requested changes and enhancements and rank their priority.

- The lead user representative should also be involved in reviewing significant artifacts produced by the contractor, such as prototypes or executable releases produced by iterations.

- The lead user representative also advises the contractor and the outsourcing organization's project manager on transition issues, requirement issues, and anything else that reflects the end users' desires, concerns, and issues.

Attributes of a Good Lead User Representative

The attributes of a good lead user representative include the following:

- A typical lead user representative has been with the outsourcing organization for many years. She must be familiar with all aspects of the organization's business processes.

- For those areas of the business in which she might not have the latest information, the lead user representative should know exactly who to contact. In fact, the person in this role is generally very well known and respected throughout the organization and is recognized as an authority figure.

- The lead user representative should be able to carefully and fully articulate the organization's needs. This person needs excellent oral and written communication skills.

- The lead user representative should be able to take the time to answer ad hoc questions from both the contractor and the outsourcing organization's project manager.

Typical lead user representatives are very busy people who have other jobs they must perform and are not dedicated to a specific project. However, it is vital that they have the time to adequately support the project and to answer questions. The attitudes of other users in the outsourcing organization often depend on their perception of the lead user representative's attitude.

The PMO Project Architect

This role is optional, because it may not be needed on smaller projects. It is generally required when a project is large enough to need multiple contractors, and each contractor is developing a portion of the system.

Why Is This Role Needed?

I have been involved in several large projects that had multiple contractors. As with any project, SOWs are written and given to each contractor. At that point, most contractors adhere to working on the tasks specified in their SOW. This makes sense, because by definition, if the contractor successfully completes all the tasks in his SOW on schedule and within budget, he has done his job. Accordingly, the following are actions I have seen on projects in this scenario:

- Each contractor performs development on his own servers. If the application has a Web interface, the contractor acquires his own Web server, application server, and application server software. If persistent storage is required, each contractor has his own database server, database software, and database instances. This decision is good for the contractor, because he maintains control over the environments in which he develops. This minimizes interruptions from other contractors, the customer, and so on, thus ensuring maximum availability of the environment required by the contractor to meet his deadlines. The problem happens during integration, when the use of different servers by different contractors results in difficulties. In some cases, the system gets delivered with multiple database servers, multiple application servers, and so on, which is unwieldy and more expensive to maintain.

- The contractor tends to make decisions about the environment that are not specified in the SOW. In some cases, the information may be conveyed to the outsourcing organization, but it seldom gets communicated to the other contractors.

- Although each contractor presumably has been given a different portion of the system to develop, some data elements are common to all portions of the system. This makes sense, because the project as a whole is for the same customer, and the same business process drives the system design for all portions of the system. Unless specific measures are taken, each contractor develops her own code to describe and manipulate these data items. This code should be written only once. Developing her own code is a duplication of effort and can result in problems during integration because the common data items might be treated or defined differently by each contractor.

- "Glue" code is developed. When integrating portions of large, complex systems, some code might be needed to interface the components. An example is a component's application programming interface (API) and the associated code for integration. These items may not be anticipated and spelled out in the contractor's SOW. If they are not, the contractors will not pay much attention to them, to the detriment of the system as a whole. The PMO project architect recognizes these situations and takes steps to ensure that this aspect of the project receives the proper attention.

It is not possible to anticipate all these situations when a SOW is written. Without someone to champion the cause of the tasks in the SOW, these and similar issues can undermine the architecture and the integrity of the system as a whole. This is the purpose of the PMO project architect. The PMO project architect reports directly to the project manager of the outsourcing organization. As an important member of the PMO, this role is empowered by the project manager to work closely with the individual architects and technical leads at each contractor.

Responsibilities of the PMO Project Architect

The PMO project architect provides many benefits to a project. This person works to establish architectural standards and ensures that all contractors consistently follow these standards on the project. The responsibilities of the PMO project architect include the following:

- The PMO project architect identifies and establishes standards for the environment in which the software to be produced will operate. For example, does the outsourcing organization operate only Windows-based servers in its data center? If so, a solution involving UNIX may be unacceptable. If these sorts of decisions are known before the project starts, the architect's job in this regard is to publish the standards and then make sure all contractors abide by them. Otherwise, the PMO project architect works with the architects on each contractor team to develop standards that satisfy the needs of all the stakeholders involved.

- When the system has been partitioned in such a way as to allow the work to be delegated to two or more contractors, there may be interfaces between the portions of the system. The PMO project architect works with each contractor to make sure that the interface is accommodated in the design and that any appropriate APIs are built.

- If the organization has established an Enterprise Architecture, the PMO project architect should ensure that the solution proposed by the contractor is compliant with it.

- The PMO project architect either develops or provides a set of user interface design standards to each contractor. If each contractor's portion of the system has a user interface, these standards enable consistency between the user interfaces built by each contractor. The PMO project architect verifies enforcement of these standards.

- The PMO project architect should establish or provide standards for other software needed by the systems as well. Some examples are database, application server, report generation, and other Commercial Off-The-Shelf (COTS) code. Many outsourcing organizations with large IT needs may already have site licenses for some applications, thus making certain choices cost-neutral.

- Every IT application has certain abstractions and core functionality that are part of the environment and that are needed by applications operating in that environment. When multiple contractors are involved, each contractor focuses on developing their portion of the system. This means that without careful coordination, each contractor develops his own code to manage and represent the abstractions and functionality that are part of the environment. This means that each contractor is creating duplicate code. In addition to wasting resources, this can result in integration problems, because the representation of the data defined by this code may vary between the implementations. The PMO project architect should identify potential areas of duplication and prevent it from occurring. Refer to the "Other Role Issues" section near the end of this chapter for a suggestion on managing this situation.

- The PMO project architect should work closely with the architects of each contractor. In particular, the PMO project architect should be satisfied that the architecture proposed by the contractor architects will meet supplementary requirements, such as performance, response time, scalability, failover, reliability, and redundancy.

Attributes of a Good PMO Project Architect

The PMO project architect is technically proficient but is more interested in seeing the big picture. Most likely, the PMO project architect was once a very experienced developer and technologist. Instead of progressing to a project management role, his desire to "stay technical" and his disinterest in the more mundane activities of project management led him to this role. The PMO project architect is fascinated by technology and is knowledgeable about the latest technologies. He is also a trusted advisor to the project manager of the outsourcing organization. The PMO project architect has technical depth, plus the time to investigate technical issues at length, and he advises the project manager on these issues. The PMO project architect is also very familiar with the needs, plans, and goals of the IT organization for which he works.

The Internal Project Champion

The internal project champion is vital to a project, especially during the initial stages of the product's being rolled out to the user community. Ideally, the internal project champion is a respected member of the user community. Occasionally, on smaller projects, this person may also perform the roles of lead user representative, project manager, or PMO project architect.

Why Is This Role Needed?

The internal project champion can have a significant impact on a project's success during two periods in the project lifecycle. As explained in Chapter 9, "Navigating the Requirements Management Process," user involvement during requirements elicitation activities is vital to ensure that the developed product meets user needs. Users generally are very reluctant to get involved with these activities. The internal project champion role generates enthusiasm in the user community to encourage active participation in the requirements elicitation activities.

The second period when the internal project champion is important is during the project rollout. The acceptance of a new product and the incorporation of it into the users' work generally follow a standard bell curve. The acceptance and attitudes developed toward the product are heavily influenced by perception. The internal project champion, forever the optimist, encourages users to try the product, to overlook its immediate shortcomings, and to see value in adopting its use. If the internal project champion is a respected member of the user community, her message will be heeded and will positively influence acceptance of the product by the user community, making the project a success.

The Contracting Officer

The contracting officer is an often-neglected role on projects. This person manages all contracts relating to contractors and vendors for a project. His expertise is strictly related to managing a project from a business perspective. This person's work helps ensure that all contracts adhere to the laws, rules, and regulations affecting the project. If the project involves offshoring and use of vendors from other countries, this person needs to be familiar with the differences in contracting law between the countries involved.

I frequently hear contracting officers complain that they never hear from members of a project (even the project manager) unless the project is in trouble. Although the contracting officer may not have expertise in software, his opinions can offer a unique perspective on the project's performance from a financial viewpoint. Furthermore, during any contract negotiations, if the contracting officer understands the project manager's position, he can negotiate more effectively.

The IT Manager

In most organizations, the IT manager is responsible for operating and maintaining the product developed by your project. The IT manager is not hired for the project's purposes. You will work closely with the IT manager in your organization. The IT manager's typical concerns and responsibilities are as follows:

- When will the application be installed in the environment?
- What additional hardware will be required to run the new application? Does the hardware conform to the specifications required by the IT manager's organization?
- When will the IT manager assume responsibility for the new application?
- Have all the outsourcing organization's applicable standards been taken into account? These include the following:
  - Does the application conform to the organization's security needs?
  - Does the application work with the current configuration of the systems used by the end users? In other words, is any special software required to be installed on end-user systems? Can the new application work with the versions of browsers, operating systems, and so on currently running in the organization?
  - Does the application have any special consideration for backup and restoration? Can the current backup/restoration solution in use by the organization work correctly with the new application?
  - What COTS software does the new application use? What software licenses need to be maintained, and how much will this cost annually? When are the licenses due to be renewed?
- What does the Help Desk need to know to successfully field calls about the new application? What is the expected level of usage? How many calls will the new application likely generate for the Help Desk?
- If your IT organization also handles the training for your users, who will train the trainers? What training materials will be produced, and by whom?
- Who will be responsible for maintenance and upgrades of the new application?
- Will any legacy applications need to be deactivated when the new application goes online? If so, which applications? Who uses those applications?

These are some of the questions the IT manager is likely to face. The project manager of the outsourcing organization should have the answers. The most common complaint heard from IT managers is that they are not involved in the advanced planning for new applications. They often find out shortly before the application is delivered that they will be receiving a new application and a new set of servers to maintain. Involving the IT manager well in advance helps the new application's transition to production go much more smoothly.

Other Role Issues

I have identified the key roles to be enacted by the outsourcing organization's PMO, but we should discuss some additional role issues in the outsourcing situation.

Developing a Data Model

On large projects involving complex business domain processes, developing a single data model can help the contractor analysts understand the business. Figure 4-2 shows the logical placement of an individual in this role as analyst/data modeler.

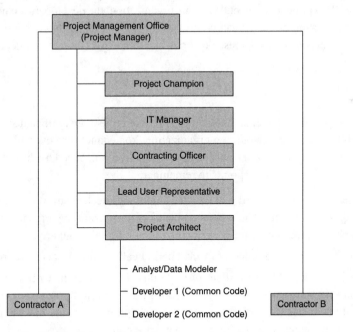

Figure 4-2   Organization for data model and common code development

Developing Common Code

The earlier section on the PMO project architect mentioned contractors duplicating effort by developing common code. On large projects, where multiple contractors need code to manage the same abstractions in the problem domain, the question is, who should develop this common code?

Having the contractors direct the development of the common code creates as many problems as it solves. Here are a couple examples:

- The developers are controlled by the contractor for which they work. There is a strong tendency for the contractor to have that developer first focus on common code needed only by the contractor, possibly contrary to the project's needs as a whole.

- If the contractor gets behind schedule, it might pull that developer off the common code tasks to focus on the contractor's scheduled items. This helps the contractor but may be detrimental to the project as a whole.

Consider the organization shown in Figure 4-2 as a possible solution. In this organization, the developers shown may, in fact, work for the contractor, but in this capacity, they report directly to the PMO project architect. With this organization, the developers are not subject to the pressures on the portion of the project controlled by that contractor. Note that depending on the amount of common code needed, these positions under the PMO project architect may need to be only part-time.

Summary

You should now understand that an outsourced software project of significant size carries important responsibilities for the outsourcing organization. You cannot turn over all responsibility for project success to the contractor. The project must be actively managed by the outsourcing organization to succeed. Here are other points to remember:

- A Change Control Board (CCB) is an important mechanism to manage and prioritize changes on a project. The project manager of the outsourcing organization should form this group and chair the meetings, which should be held regularly.

- Keep the contracting officer informed periodically of the project's progress.

- The IT manager can help identify important deliverables that need to be produced to ensure the developed product's successful transition into production. The IT manager should be consulted during the contract's inception to be sure that the deliverables are identified and incorporated into the contract for the contractors.

- The PMO project architect should take the initiative to provide and define all standards pertaining to software development for the contractors.

- Multiple contractors on a project increase the burden on the outsourcing organization, because the need for oversight and coordination increases.

What's Next?

The next chapter discusses the key roles on a contractor team that interface with the outsourcing organization. The managers of both the outsourcing organization and the contractor are invited to review these roles to gain an understanding of how the two groups can collaborate. In addition, for managers of a contractor, the next chapter covers important attributes of each role. This can help you identify good candidates to staff these roles.

CHAPTER 5

Best Practices for Staffing the Contractor's Software Project Team

Software development has been and will continue to be very dependent on the caliber of the individuals involved. The reason, of course, is that software development is an intellectual exercise. More importantly, teams produce successful software development projects. The trends of outsourcing and offshoring extend this concept further by introducing groups of teams that must work well together (hence, the reason for a separate chapter covering the outsourcing organization's team). In his book *Object Solutions: Managing the Object-Oriented Project*, Grady Booch, one of the creators of the RUP, states, "It is time that I come clean and unveil one of the dirty little secrets of software engineering: People are more important than any process."[1]

Successful teams are fascinating to analyze. After observing hundreds of teams over the years, I believe that good teams transcend process and technology. A successful software development team has much in common with a successful sports team. In particular, the following are characteristics of a good team:

- Each person on the team respects his company, customer, and, especially, fellow team members.

- Each person on the team trusts the other members of the team completely.

- Although individuals take pride in their accomplishments, they recognize that their accomplishments are diminished unless the team succeeds.

- Although individuals have specific expertise and roles on the team, they are quick to assist others on the team if help is needed.

- The team has a certain "chemistry" that customers, management team members, and others recognize.

[1] From *Object Solutions: Managing the Object-Oriented Project* by Grady Booch. Quoted with permission.

- Major decisions affecting the project's or team's direction are not made without consulting the team.

This chapter describes the major roles on a modern, high-performance software development team. It discusses the best practices for creating a team that will eventually exhibit the characteristics just listed (but this does not occur overnight!). This chapter also discusses how these teams are best managed.

Governing Principles for Staffing the Team

The first step toward building a cohesive team is to recognize that you must evaluate a prospective team member in two areas. The first is to understand the candidate's attitude and disposition toward working on a team. The second is to evaluate the person's technical abilities for the role in question. This section considers the former.

When evaluating a candidate to join your team, focus first on attributes that give insight into the person's attitude and propensity for working on a team. Here are some suggestions and ideas for when you interview candidates:

- When discussing the candidate's accomplishments, pay attention to whether the candidate mentions other teams of which he was a part. For example, suppose the candidate says, "In my last position, I worked closely with two other developers on a project that was behind schedule. We worked many extra hours, and as a result, we caught up and delivered on time." Statements like this are a good sign. Notice the reference to other team members and the use of the word "we." This suggests that the candidate is team-oriented.

- Try to assess the candidate's ability to learn. Rarely can you find someone who has all the technical skills your team needs. In general, you are better off with someone who works well in a team culture and who can learn quickly than with someone who has technical skills but who doesn't work well on a team.

- Have several team members interview prospective candidates. This has four advantages:

  - It provides multiple perspectives on a candidate's suitability for the position. After several team members have interviewed the candidate, schedule a briefing to discuss each interviewer's impression. Try to achieve a team consensus. If the consensus is negative or an agreement cannot be reached, keep looking at other candidates.

  - When decisions are made as a team, the team feels ownership of the decisions. If the team decides to hire the person, they will work collectively to integrate that person into the team, making it more likely that the person will succeed as a team member.

  - It gives the candidate a better picture of the position and the other team members. This enables the candidate to make a more informed decision.

  - Having several team members interview the candidate separately shows that you value each team member's opinion.

- Try to assess how the candidate would respond to a recent challenge on your project. Describe a recent scenario, explain the problem, and ask how the candidate would respond to it. This gives you insight into the candidate's problem-solving ability. It also acquaints the candidate with actual issues that have affected the project recently.

The exact answers to these questions are not as important as how the candidate answers the questions.

Roles on the Contractor's Software Development Team

This section describes the major roles on software development teams, their responsibilities, and the attributes of strong performers in each role. Figure 5-1 illustrates these roles. The roles described here are for software development teams ranging in size from 6 to 30 people. On the lower end of this range, the same person may perform more than one role. I do not pretend to believe that this is the only organization that works, or that these are the only roles needed. Your specific situation and organizational norms will dictate the exact staffing profile. That said, I have organized several teams around these roles and found them to be successful. In the absence of any guidelines from your organization, the roles described here are a good starting point upon which to build a successful software development team.

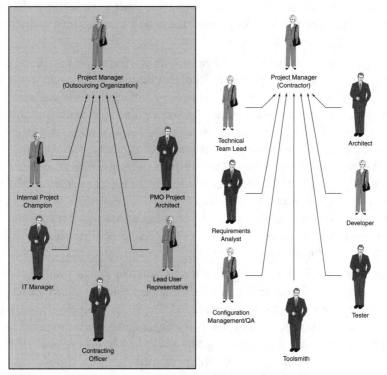

Figure 5-1   Roles on the contractor's software development team

The Project Manager Role

Certainly a common and well-recognized role, the project manager role has evolved in recent years. The project manager was once a role of authority. The project manager would identify the tasks, delegate the tasks to the staff, and apply pressure as needed to push the staff to work until the tasks were done on time. The project manager would seldom share much information with subordinates, other than what was necessary for them to get the job done. This type of project manager is rapidly becoming a relic.

Project Managers and Team Interaction

Today's project manager is more of an "enabler" of teams. The project manager still identifies and delegates many of the tasks, but equally important, this person shares the vision with the team. He collaborates more closely with the team. Here are some additional characteristics:

- The project manager is focused on making sure that each team member has the resources needed for him to be successful in his role.

- The project manager protects the team from distractions. Sometimes, these distractions come from within the company. For example, other projects, proposals, and working groups can siphon valuable time needed to meet the project's schedule. In these situations, the project manager negotiates with these other groups. Rather than making the project team member fend for himself, the project manager tries to determine how to best satisfy the needs of everyone involved.

- Today's project manager shares a great amount of information with the team. The entire project schedule and the progress against that schedule are communicated to the team. In addition, many metrics can be produced by software tools (some examples are discussed in the next chapter). Teams like to know that their work is contributing to the accomplishment of a goal; sharing metrics is one way of communicating the progress. Finally, at many companies, project managers regularly participate in management activities outside their project. These activities give the project manager visibility to other projects and new business opportunities at the company. When conducting project team meetings, project managers should share this information with the team. When a project team is focused on a project, it is comforting to know that their project manager is keeping them informed. This increases their confidence, because they know someone is looking out for them.

- Project managers should avoid dictating a solution to the team and shouldn't get involved in lower-level details. Instead, the project manager allows the team to explore their own solutions to the problems at hand. The project manager should, however, recognize when the team is stuck and is no longer making forward progress. When this happens, the project manager can act as a sounding board and gently guide the team toward alternative approaches to solving a problem.

- Project managers should avoid putting excessive pressure on the team. Most software developers are proud of their work and want to produce quality work on time. (If you have team members who do not have this attitude, why are they on your team?) Excessive pressuring of the team seldom results in higher productivity.

PROTECTING A TEAM FROM DISTRACTIONS

On one project, I remember a technical lead approached me regarding a company-level activity she was being asked to perform. The activity had nothing to do with the project, but the fact that she was invited to participate was indicative of her good reputation within the company. "Get me out of this!" she said. At first, I was a bit shocked that someone would turn down such an opportunity. But I quickly realized that her dedication to the project was taking precedence over everything else. I told the other group that she could not be spared from the project. After that, I realized that one of my functions as a project manager was to protect the team from distractions.

Qualifications Needed for the Project Manager Role

The project manager is perhaps the most complex role on a software development team. The reason is because of the diverse skill set required. To be successful, a project manager must be proficient in the following areas:

- Software development technologies (such as languages, tools, and platforms). Detailed low-level knowledge is not necessary, but the project manager must have basic familiarity with the technologies involved.

- Software development methodologies (RUP, Agile, and Waterfall). Familiarity and experience with the methodology used on your project is essential.

- Financial skills. Your company is in business to make a profit. To effectively manage the company, your management will want forecasts and projections of the project's financial performance. Forecasts and projections are also important so that you know you will not exceed the amount specified in the contract for the project. If this situation does occur, the sooner you can identify this trend, the better. No customer wants to hear that it will have to spend additional funds beyond what was planned. But if you can provide several months' notice, it may be possible for the customer to find additional funds or change the project's scope to fit within the originally budgeted amount.

- Negotiation skills. All projects involve some form of negotiating. Whether it's during the proposal phase, achieving a final price, or internal negotiations regarding company resources, good negotiation skills are essential.

- General people management skills. Project management involves constant interaction with people who have a wide range of interests, motivations, and skill levels. The success of your project depends on your ability to effectively work with others.

Interfacing with Other Organizations

No project manager can work in a vacuum. You need to interface with a number of other departments within your company to be successful. Here are some examples of other groups within your company, along with the nature of the interaction you will have with them:

- Human Resources (HR). As a project manager, depending on your company's policies, you may be required to conduct performance reviews on members of your staff. Your HR department can supply guidance, form templates, and so on for these reviews. In most companies, HR also performs many recruiting functions. You need to accurately describe your needs so that HR can recruit viable candidates. In addition, as members of your team complete their assignments, you need to inform HR in advance so that they can find other assignments for these people. Finally, HR can give you guidance in special situations, such as policies for handling troublesome employees.

- Accounting. Most projects bill their clients monthly. You need to communicate the proper information to Accounting so that they can produce whatever invoices are needed. You also need to review these invoices for accuracy. I have seen otherwise flawless project performances marred by a failure to invoice the client accurately and in a timely manner. Don't let this happen to your project.

- Contracts. If your company provides outsourcing services often, it probably has a dedicated person or group devoted to managing the contractual elements of projects. You will be working with this person closely during the proposal process. She is familiar with the legal aspects of outsourcing arrangements, types of contracts, and so on. It is a good idea to periodically touch base with this person to let her know how the project is going. That way, if you run into difficulty, she will be familiar with the project's progress to that point.

- IT/Facilities. As a project starts, your company's IT department furnishes the necessary equipment, such as PCs, servers, software, and networking services. Nearly every IT organization I have worked with (regardless of the company) is typically overworked, understaffed, and underappreciated. They often do not hear from anyone unless there is a problem, and "everything" is an emergency. Being one of the easier clients to deal with may make the difference when you have a difficult problem to solve. I always make a point of notifying the IT department of any needs I anticipate as soon in advance as possible. That way, when you really do have an emergency, they will respond appropriately. When IT helps you by solving your problem quickly, make sure you mention this to the organization's manager. If you follow these practices, your IT department will be grateful, which will pay dividends later.

- Upper management. Your company's upper management wants to be kept informed of client satisfaction issues, as well as opportunities for additional business with that client. If the project is going well and the client is satisfied, you may have nothing more than a

30-second summary explaining this. If there are issues requiring your management's attention, keep it short and to the point. If there are action items requiring management involvement, make these clear, with a specific time line.

Aspiring to the Project Manager Role

Most project managers come from either the development ranks or nontechnical ranks. Each has strengths and weaknesses.

A project manager coming from a development role already is acquainted with technologies and software development processes. You will be strongly tempted to get closely involved with coding, design, and other detailed activities. You need to resist this temptation. Remember the importance of other aspects of the project manager position, especially financial tracking and forecasting. Your ability to foster the relationship with your customer, and to work closely with the other departments in your company, is of paramount importance. Finally, team building, particularly for developers, is especially emphasized. For you to successfully resist the temptation to get involved with technical details, you need to have complete trust in the people who make the technical decisions on your team.

A project manager who comes from a nontechnical background might find managing a software development project to be a bit of a culture shock. For project managers in this situation, your selection of the technical lead role on your project is especially important. In fact, you may want to choose a technical lead who has experience managing projects. The technical lead will become a trusted advisor.

The most frequent frustration I hear from project managers in this situation is that software development in general seems very unpredictable. Seemingly small changes can have significant effects on cost and schedule. My advice to these project managers is not to commit to any changes without first consulting the project team. You need advisers you can trust, because you will encounter situations requiring judgment tempered by experiences you might not have. Another frustrating aspect is that measurable progress seems intangible. An iterative lifecycle process can help mitigate this. As executable releases are produced, some "hands-on" time with the releases can alleviate this frustration.

The Developer Role

Most projects have many developers. In contrast with the project manager role, the developer's role appears straightforward and simple: Apply technical skills toward implementing the project requirements, and solve related problems. However, it is not always that simple. The developer role is an interesting balancing act of creative problem solving versus conformity to requirements. It also involves adapting to changing situations while working to control change. Finally, it involves quickly cranking out code versus building in quality along the way through unit-level and some integration-level testing. The best developers balance these factors well.

Aside from the governing principles for team building in general, the specific skills needed for developers depend on the technologies used by your project, so we will not cover them here.

Another consideration is the type of process used on the project. A large project with lots of formality and ceremony may not be a good fit for developers who have experienced only small, unstructured projects with no formal process in place.

There is one caveat to observe with hiring developers. In addition to the usual skills with the languages and platforms used for software development, make sure that the developer is willing to use the tools provided as part of your software development infrastructure. In other words, tools such as configuration management, change management, visual modeling, and testing are important to the success of the team as a whole. I have seen a few otherwise excellent developers who are either reluctant to use these tools or who outright refuse to use them. If adherence to software process is important, make sure that the developer is on board with consistent use of these tools and adherence to the practices used by your team.

The Architect Role

Architects usually rise from the developer ranks. The typical architect is a senior developer rising in her career who eschews management roles in favor of "staying technical." This is an important role, because the architect identifies and develops the foundation or framework of the system being developed. Poor choices and decisions made in designing the architecture can lead to disaster later in the project. One of the underlying principles of the RUP and iterative development is that the architecture is the first priority in development and receives attention in the project's initial iterations. This makes sense, because the architecture is a major risk area, and the consequences of failure are high.

Qualifications Needed for the Architect Role

Qualifications for the architect role are similar to those of the developer role, but with some important additions:

- The architect is one of the first people to join the team, along with the technical lead.

- The role of architect involves an aspect of salesmanship. When a candidate architecture is identified, the architect must "sell" the idea to the rest of the development team. Accordingly, the architect must be someone who commands respect from the other developers on the team. The elements that the individual developers will use must be very clearly documented and communicated to the developers. The architect should also monitor the developers' work to ensure that the architectural decisions are being adhered to. In addition, the architect needs to be available to solve problems when issues arise.

- Because of the importance of the system architecture, I recommend that the architect have prior experience with the same technologies on at least one other project. Ideally, the candidate architect has experience both as a developer using the technologies on the prior project and as an architect on a prior project with the same or similar technologies. This provides the best of all worlds. The architect will have an understanding of the developer concerns as a result of her experience, and your project will benefit from lessons learned on the architect's previous projects.

The Technical Lead Role

The technical lead is typically the most senior developer on the team. This person directs the day-to-day activities of the developers, testers, and analysts. He also mentors the more junior developers. He may also have some development tasks of his own.

The technical lead is often a senior developer who aspires to be a project manager. In fact, the technical lead performs many of the tasks normally associated with the project manager. However, being a developer, the technical lead works every day with the other developers on the team and can delegate tasks according to the developers' specific skills and talents. Put another way, the technical lead is more of a tactical leader, and the project manager role is a strategic one.

Qualifications Needed for the Technical Lead Role

The technical lead role qualifications are similar to those for the architect. The technical lead must be respected both as a competent developer and as a leader. In addition, the technical lead is the project manager's right-hand person. In other words, there should be complete trust between the project manager and the technical lead. They should have similar philosophies regarding managing and motivating people.

The Toolsmith Role

The toolsmith role is one I seldom see mentioned, but it is still important. On all software development projects, the software development team uses numerous tools, technologies, and processes. Most projects need to customize or tailor some of these tools to the project's specific needs. The toolsmith installs and configures the software development environment toolset and readies it for use. In addition, the complexity of the tools used means that, at some point, problems will be experienced, often at the worst possible time. Someone who is familiar with the tools needs to solve these problems fast to minimize the impact on the project schedule.

The qualifications to be a toolsmith are simple: knowledge of the tools, and the ability to customize them according to the organization's needs.

Who Pays for the Toolsmith?

Because this role is somewhat of a novelty, many customers do not understand this role and will question a bid that includes one. The customer clearly understands why a project manager, testers, and developers are needed, but a toolsmith sounds like a questionable item. Here are guidelines to follow:

- If the customer dictates usage of specific tools your organization has not used extensively, bidding a toolsmith makes sense and can be justified.

- Another scenario that occurs occasionally is that the customer pays to acquire the tools, which means that they must be installed and set up first. Bidding a toolsmith in this scenario is warranted as well.

- If the customer wants the contractor to work on-site, be sure to ask who will customize and maintain the tools used for software development. If the customer has its own group to manage the environment, you will not be able to bid a toolsmith. However, to avoid the potential for misunderstanding later, ask what level of support you can expect later. You don't want to find out about this right before a deliverable is due when your configuration management system crashes.

- Another possibility is to pay for the toolsmith through company overhead. The disadvantage of this is that the toolsmith may not be available immediately when you need him.

The Requirements Analyst Role

The requirements analyst role is unique in that the person in this role probably has the most contact with the customer—possibly even more than the project manager. The requirements analyst is responsible for translating the customer needs into specific requirements that are implementable, testable, and documented. This person also is consulted by the technical lead, developers, project manager, and testers whenever there is a question about the project requirements.

Qualifications Needed for the Requirements Analyst Role

The following are guidelines for the skills necessary in a requirements analyst:

- Experience in the problem domain. For example, if the client is a bank and the application automates the processing of loans, some financial tracking experience is essential. The analyst's prior experience may not be with the exact same type of loan system. But in this example, the requirements analyst would need basic familiarity with terms such as simple interest, compound interest, amortization, and other terms commonly found in the problem domain. The reason is simple. In requirements elicitation meetings, the customer expects to come prepared to explain its functional requirements needs for the system. They do not expect to spend a significant amount of their time educating the analyst on basic terms of the problem domain.

- The requirements analyst needs to be skilled in managing meetings. Requirements elicitation meetings can be challenging, because with some of the topics discussed, the participants in the meeting may not agree with each other. The requirements analyst needs to detect situations in which forward progress is no longer being made in the meeting and take steps to get it back on track again.

- Because the requirements analyst works with people of widely varying backgrounds and personalities, he should nurture an open, friendly relationship with the customer representatives so that they will want to open up to him. The analyst also needs to be able to detect when stakeholders are uncomfortable with the proceedings and to take steps to meet with the stakeholder privately to determine the cause.

- Finally, the requirements analyst needs to be very detail-oriented. He needs to create a complete audit trail linking each initial customer request with the final requirement that is delivered to the development team. He also needs to work closely with the tester (and possibly quality assurance) to ensure that each requirement is testable, succinct, and within the scope of the system to be built.

The Tester Role

The tester represents the last chance to catch problems before the system reaches the customer. Interestingly, the tester role has much in common with the requirements analyst role. Specifically, the tester needs detailed knowledge of the requirements.

As with the developer role, the tester role is not really simple and straightforward. With the increased complexity of software systems today, software testers must be increasingly technical themselves. Testers need knowledge of testing techniques, methods, and associated tools. They must be able to hold meaningful conversations with developers and be able to glean useful information from them. They must be meticulous and organized (much like the requirements analyst) to be able to thoroughly validate a system's requirements.

In the RUP, or any process involving iterative development, the tester needs to join the team much earlier than with projects that follow conventional Waterfall-based processes. The reason is that the development team will produce executable releases early in the project lifecycle, possibly as early as the Inception phase. Testing is covered in Chapter 11, "Testing."

The Configuration Management/QA Role

On small to medium-sized projects, the same person performs the configuration management (CM) role and the quality assurance role. As a team grows beyond 20 people or so, there is enough work for two people to perform these roles.

The Configuration Management Role

For the configuration management role, the primary responsibility is to be able to perform independent builds of the system without assistance from development. This person also works with the developers to document the build process. Another important responsibility is to know exactly which versions of files are needed to successfully perform the build. The CM engineer also needs to produce the exact versions of all the files that went into creating a release. The purpose is to make maintenance easier. When a problem with a software release is reported, the developers will have a much easier time reproducing the problem if they have the exact same version the problem was reported against. Finally, if an emergency bug fix is needed, the CM engineer must be able to re-create the exact source files used for a specific release so that she can correct the reported problem and deliver a patched release that has the exact same functionality as before but with the problem corrected. Finally, for each release produced by the development team, the CM engineer needs to be able to produce a report showing exactly what issues and problems were corrected with a given release, as well as which requirements were implemented.

To be effective, the person performing the CM role needs a configuration management tool and should be competent in its usage.

The Quality Assurance Role

Many organizations have a dedicated quality assurance engineer. Ideally, the person in the quality assurance role does not report to the project manager to ensure objectivity. The quality assurance engineer should not feel pressured to permit items affecting quality to pass.

Quality assurance personnel should be familiar with applicable standards, such as CMMI, various development processes (such as the RUP), and many other standards. This includes coding standards, user interface standards, configuration management, requirements management, and, in general, the entire software development process.

Quality assurance personnel have a tricky job. They must be able to focus attention on deviations from agreed-upon standards without invoking feelings of resentment among the project staff. Diplomacy is the key skill needed for these situations.

Best Practices for Managing Teams

Managing a team can be a source of great satisfaction—or great misery. The following are suggestions and comments on managing teams that I have put into practice over the years. You can use these and adjust them to fit your particular style.

- Remember that team productivity is as important as individual productivity. I've seen some teams where one developer produces a tremendous amount of output that the other team members can't easily use or understand. This is counterproductive in the long run. These situations are difficult to manage, because the developer in question usually can't understand why others are displeased with his work. As a result, I discuss this during interviews for prospective team members. I give examples of this scenario and explain that an important attribute of high-quality work is that it is easily used and understood by others.

- Be a proponent of your individual team members and their accomplishments. When meeting with other company employees outside the project, I always make a point of announcing major milestones reached and the people who made meeting those milestones possible.

- Have a predetermined strategy for handling poor performers on your team. If a member of the team is determined to be a nonperformer, follow your strategy closely and consistently. In general, I strive to understand the cause of poor performance. If it is due to external factors that the team member cannot control, I try to support that person as much as possible. In other words, think of this as a problem-solving issue. On the other hand, if the cause is a poor attitude or personality conflict, get that person off the team as soon as possible.

- If overtime becomes necessary on a project, instead of simply asking everyone to put in as many hours as they can, try to identify a day or two when the majority of the team can commit to working an extra-long day. Although overtime is seldom an enjoyable experience, it's a bit easier to handle when the entire team works the extra time together. The project manager should also be present during these times, if for nothing else but as an expression of solidarity and moral support.

- One consequence of hiring good performers is that new opportunities frequently find their way to these people. Your initial instinct will be to prevent the person from leaving. Certainly, you should try to identify any issues that are easily solved that would make this person want to remain on your team. Beyond that, it is best to thank the person for all her work on your project and wish her well. Attempts to force the person to stay will ultimately unmotivate her. Your positive embracing of a person's decision to leave also sets an example for those remaining on the project. It tells other team members that if and when a similar opportunity becomes available to them, their decision will be respected.

Summary

The key lessons learned in this chapter include the following:

- Successful software teams depend on people more than technology.

- The project manager's primary responsibility is to make the project successful. Do this by forming a team-based culture, and making sure that the team has all the resources they need.

- Make sure your team has the services of a toolsmith/tool administrator available, whether this is a dedicated member of the team, a member of the company staff, or provided by the customer.

- Involve selected members of the team in the interview process for new team candidates.

- Be supportive of team members if their productivity suffers due to problems beyond their control.

- If attitude or personality conflicts from a specific team member become a problem, remove that person from the team as soon as possible.

- Involve testers early in the project lifecycle. They can help define project requirements that can be tested.

- The architect role is one of the first technical roles on the project. The architect's focus is to identify a viable candidate architecture to serve as the project's foundation, reducing risk on the project.

- Project managers should keep their team informed of events in the company outside the immediate project.

What's Next?

The next chapter covers the kinds of tools needed to support the software development infrastructure. Project managers of organizations that will be procuring software tools will be particularly interested in this chapter.

CHAPTER 6

Establishing the Software Development Environment

Organizations implementing the Rational Unified Process (RUP) and other best practices appreciate the value of the discipline it brings to the software development process. Incorporating modern tools that automate and enforce the process adds even more value by increasing productivity and enabling team communication. This chapter discusses the issues involved in setting up a software development environment. The primary focus is on tools covering infrastructure for disciplines such as requirements management, change request management, and configuration management. Checklists of important features needed for the tools covering each discipline are introduced. Finally, a list of best practices for an organization adopting new tools is given.

Automated software development tools can be a tremendous boost to productivity. Unfortunately, they have an equal propensity to be a source of great frustration and can even drag down productivity.

Build, Buy, or Borrow

A team that wants to create an arsenal of tools to support software development infrastructure faces an important decision. Should the team purchase off-the-shelf tools from a commercial vendor, should they use shareware tools, or should they build their own custom tools? This is a complex decision that involves more than it would seem. Each of these three choices can be very expensive. The differences between the choices involve the timing of funds and resources expended. The following sections examine these choices.

Shareware Tools

A number of shareware tools can be procured with minimal up-front investment. They may make sense for your project, given the proper set of circumstances.

Shareware Advantages

The advantages of shareware tools are the following:

- Shareware generally requires little or no up-front investment.

- Much information on shareware tools often is available in the public domain. By conducting simple Internet searches, you can find documentation, usage tips, question-and-answer forums, and other information for free.

- Source code for shareware is often available. This allows knowledgeable users to modify the tool's functionality or tailor it to better fit their needs.

Shareware Disadvantages

Shareware also has significant disadvantages, including the following:

- In most cases, no support is available.

- Little or no training may be available.

- Updates are unpredictable. If your organization updates the version of the operating system on its client PCs, for example, and this means that the software no longer functions, there is no way to know in advance when a new version will be available to support the OS upgrade.

- There may be no third-party consulting or services available to assist with customization and mentoring.

- Integration with other tools may not be possible, or you may need to build the integrations yourself.

In spite of the long list of disadvantages, shareware may be the best option for projects short on funds. Just be sure you have extra development resources available to address the disadvantages without shortchanging the project for developers.

Commercially Available Tools

Perhaps, the option most projects choose is the many commercially available tools in the marketplace. This is a major industry, with companies large and small competing for billions of dollars of product sales.

Commercial Tool Advantages

The competitive landscape in today's marketplace has yielded many innovative tools worthy of attention. Yet, as with any alternative, there are advantages and disadvantages. Here are some advantages:

- Software support, including phone support, periodic bug fixes and patches, and regular updates, is readily available—for a fee.

- Training and consulting services are generally available from the vendor. Often, for the more popular tools, third-party services are available as well.
- User groups and information on the Internet are often readily available.
- Integration with other tools is often offered. Some vendors offer complete suites of tools that support the entire process and that are completely integrated.

Commercial Tool Disadvantages

Despite their advantages, commercial tools are not without risks:

- Commercial tools have a high initial cost, and then they incur periodic maintenance costs if you choose to purchase maintenance and support. This may be partially overcome by the leasing agreements that some vendors offer.
- It is possible to mitigate a tool's high initial purchase cost by reusing it on subsequent projects, spreading the cost over multiple efforts. This exposes you to another risk. If the vendor goes out of business, you may be suddenly left with no support or upgrades for the tool you purchased.
- Even companies that are financially secure can be acquired, which creates questions regarding the future of the specific tools you have purchased.

Overall, purchase of commercially available tools (not surprisingly) requires significant funds up-front, but you'll have fewer headaches over the lifetime of your projects.

Custom "In-House" Tools

Once a popular alternative, the use of custom "in-house" tools is dwindling, particularly given the rise of the availability of shareware solutions.

Custom Tool Advantages

Custom tools still have some advantages:

- Custom tools can be tailored to an organization's specific needs.
- Custom tools may become a competitive advantage for the company that owns them, particularly if the tools have features that other available tools do not.

Custom Tool Disadvantages

The many disadvantages of custom tools illustrate why their popularity is declining:

- Custom tools require a significant investment of labor to create. The availability of tools is significantly delayed if the tools must be created first.
- Company resources are required to maintain and support the software.

- In an outsourcing scenario, the company that maintains the developed code for the project may not be the same company that developed the code. In this scenario, the company developing the code may not be willing to supply or deliver its custom tools to another company. This may complicate maintenance, if different tools must be used for maintenance than the ones used for development.

- Integration with other commercial or shareware tools may not be available or must be built when needed.

- No information is publicly available in user groups or on the Internet.

The creation of a software development environment populated with well-chosen tools and supported with a strong and responsive IT group can be a real competitive advantage for a company.

Requirements Management

Prior to the advent of modern requirements management tools, project organizations would often receive the requirements documents from the customer and manually enter the requirements into a database to track them. This lets you sort, search, and uniquely identify each requirement. However, this approach has several problems:

- The text in the database can become out of synchronization with the text in the written requirements document. This is especially true for requirements documents that are not completely finished. As the documents are updated and changed, the entries in the database must be manually edited to reflect changes, additions, and deletions to the document. This is tedious, time-consuming, and error-prone.

- Requirements documents and the corresponding database information are not easily shared over an intranet or the Internet.

- Sometimes, a requirement cannot be easily interpreted without the context of the information surrounding it. Therefore, when viewing certain requirements in the database, the user must manually find where the requirement is located in the written documents.

- The history of how requirements have changed over time, as well as auditing information regarding the change, must be kept manually.

- It is difficult to easily trace information concerning the requirements, such as defects and change requests, directly to the requirement.

- Relationships between differing levels of requirements cannot be easily tracked. It is difficult to quickly determine the effect that changing a high-level requirement will have on lower-level requirements traced to it.

These issues illustrate how using a simple database to track requirements creates as many problems as it solves. Project success is completely dependent on collecting and organizing a large amount of information. This information comes from people in a variety of roles, with each role potentially having different interests and goals. Your success depends on how well you collect, process, and organize this information. The next section lists the features needed in a good requirements management tool.

Important Features to Look for in a Requirements Management Tool

Requirements encompass the heart and soul of any software project. The requirements drive all activities on a project. In some cases, requirements change frequently. It is, therefore, important that the requirements management tool is helpful in managing and tracking these changes.

Core Capabilities

The following features are considered essential for proper requirements management:

- The tool must be able to create and manage requirement documentation. Most customers will want to be able to receive and circulate printed copies of the various requirements documents created.

- The tool must be able to distinguish individual requirements within the requirements document. A single document could contain hundreds of requirements. The tool needs to be able to recognize and track each requirement independently.

- In addition to tracking the text of the requirement, a requirements management tool should be able to track other information about the requirement. This information is not contained within the text of the requirement. Examples include the date the requirement was created, its priority, its scheduled release date, and its status. The user should be able to define unique attributes for the requirement.

- The tool should have a searching and sorting capability. This capability should search the requirements text and all the information associated with the requirements. It should be possible to sort and filter the list of requirements according to the information tracked along with the requirement. This makes it possible to show only requirements assigned to a certain release, to sort requirements by a rated level of importance, and so on.

- Requirements can sometimes be decomposed into closely related but separate requirements. For example, a requirement could have this form: "The system shall provide the ability to send data in the form of text messages, audio data, and audiovisual data." Although the requirement is contained in a single sentence, it has multiple parts. This is known as a parent/child relationship. The parent requirement is the portion that reads, "The system shall provide the ability to send data in the form of." The child requirements are "text messages, audio data, and audiovisual data." By tracking these portions of the requirement separately, you can manage them more effectively. For example, suppose the ability to implement the sending of text messages was needed in an earlier release of the product. If this requirement were tracked as a single requirement, it would be difficult to indicate that a portion of the requirement must be implemented earlier than other portions. Tracking them separately allows this, but the nature of the parent/child relationship still documents the fact that the requirements are closely related.

- There are different levels of requirements. Each level may be contained in its own document. Figure 6-1 shows an example of the different levels of requirements that may exist on a project.

  Furthermore, the requirements within a given level drive the requirements in the next level below. Thus, a change to a requirement could potentially affect the requirements in the level below. To make managing and controlling this process easier, the requirements tool needs the following capabilities:

  - Individual requirements defined at one level need to be traceable to one or more requirements defined in the level above. The tool must document these traceability relationships and baseline the relationships along with the requirements themselves.

  - The tool should allow the user to perform impact analysis by illustrating the effect of a change to a specific requirement. In other words, if one requirement is changed, the tool should report the entire list of requirements traced directly and indirectly to it. This helps you understand how extensively the change will affect other requirements.

- The tool should be able to create a baseline of all the requirements documents, traceability relationships, and information associated with the requirements. It should be possible to examine the artifacts in the state they were in at the time of the baseline. This makes it possible to baseline the requirements along with developed code releases and other related artifacts.

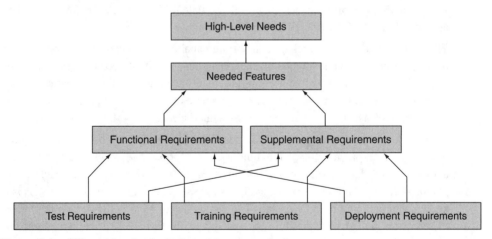

Figure 6-1   Different levels of requirements on a project

Tracking Changes to the Requirements

Requirements changes can come from many sources at any time. It is imperative that the project team be able to distinguish the exact set of requirements it is obligated to fulfill from the plethora of changes being considered. Some requirements management tools may be able to track changes as a built-in capability. Other vendors take a different approach and accomplish this effect through integration with other tools. Either way, the following list identifies the capabilities needed to manage these changes:

- If a change affects an existing requirement, the tool should indicate to the viewer of the requirement that change requests have been submitted against the requirement.

- If a change request is a submission of an entirely new (unapproved) requirement, it should be clearly separated from the list of official requirements. In other words, users who are concerned only with the set of requirements they are obligated to fulfill should not have to sift through unofficial, unapproved requirements. Why not place enhancement requests directly in the requirements repository? There are several reasons why this should be avoided:

  - Enhancement requests usually originate from the customer and end users. On most projects, a specified process should be followed to determine whether a request should be translated directly into a requirement the team is contractually bound to deliver. Once the end of this process is reached, a decision is made whether to accept the request as a requirement, defer it, or reject it. Therefore, it is not appropriate to enter a new request as an official requirement until this process is followed through to completion.

  - End users may not be able to express a new requirement in such a way as to contain all the attributes of a properly written requirement. In other words, all requirements should be clear, concise, testable, and verifiable. The initial request needs to be reviewed, and possibly modified, before it can become an official requirement.

  - End users requesting new functionality are often unaware of contractual issues, budget constraints, and so on that may prevent a new request from being implemented immediately.

  - End users and customers may not know whether a suggested new feature was previously requested or whether it might be out of scope of the system under development.

- Regardless of whether a change request is to change an existing requirement or to request a new one, the tool should create a complete audit trail of all changes to a requirement. This includes the identity of the person making the change, as well as the identity of the person requesting the change.

- E-mail notification can be a useful capability. For example, a capability that automatically generates and sends an e-mail if certain requirements are changed can alert the right people, who can react to the change.

Other Important Capabilities

The following features may not be needed, depending on the exact scenario for your project. Consider each of these features and determine whether they may be useful:

- The tool should have a Web-based interface that could be deployed over the Internet if needed. This is particularly useful in an outsourcing scenario in which the customer (or potentially other contractors) can access the requirements if needed and if appropriate.

- In some situations, there may not be network connectivity (even over the Internet) to the requirements management repository. In this scenario, the customer may communicate new or changed requirements by modifying the original requirements document and issuing a new version of the document. The requirements management tool should have a comparison tool that can compare an existing requirements document with a newer version of the document and integrate the changes.

- Security is a very important consideration, especially if many people are allowed access to the requirements repository. The tool should allow creation of groups of users with different security levels. For example, a project might want to provide read-only access to users outside the immediate project team, while requirements analysts directly on the team would have read/write privileges.

Change Request Management

All software projects need a tool for tracking change requests, defects, enhancement requests, and any information that follows a specific process. Because change requests may be submitted for potentially any artifact created on a software project, it is helpful if the tool can integrate with as many of the tools maintaining these artifacts as possible.

Features Needed in Change Request Management Tools

The following sections describe at a high level the functionality needed in a change request management tool.

Customizable Data Fields

Every software project differs in its need for the information to be tracked in a change request. Therefore, it is important that a change request tool let you create customized user interface screens containing user-specified fields for collecting information for each change request. This allows the organization to tailor to its own needs the data collected for each project.

Customizable Change Request Lifecycle Process

One characteristic of a change request process is that it typically has a series of states the request moves through as it is processed. By examining the state of the change request, you instantly know where the change request is in the process. To move from one state to another, a user performs an action that causes the change request to move to the next state defined in the process. A change request tool should allow the designer to define his own states and the actions that cause the request to move from one state to another. Just as with data fields, the change request lifecycle process is different for each organization, and even within the organization, it differs from project to project. Figure 6-2 shows a simple change request process.

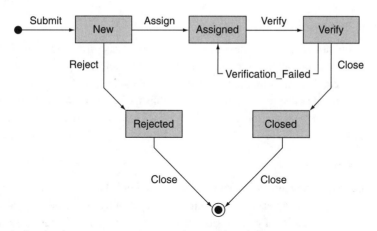

Figure 6-2   A simple change request process for tracking defects

With time, an organization becomes more comfortable with its chosen change request management tool, and its change request process becomes more sophisticated. Consequently, the change request management tool needs to be able to modify the change request process to grow with the organization. Figure 6-3 shows an example of a complex change request process that was modified over time to fit an organization's growing needs.

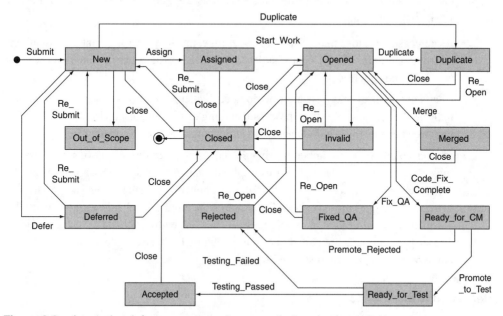

Figure 6-3   A complex defect management process that evolved over time

Customizable Behavior

Because infinite unknowns and countless possibilities exist for customizing the change request process, there is no way a tool vendor can anticipate every conceivable way a company might want to customize a tool. Therefore, the tool should be able to be modified or altered through the writing of scripts or code. The tool should have a published application programming interface (API) that can be used in conjunction with scripts to facilitate manipulation of the artifacts controlled by the tool.

Querying and Reporting

Since the change request management tool will be used to field change requests on nearly all artifacts produced by a project, querying and searching capabilities are needed to allow users to locate and find change requests of interest. It is also quite common for change requests to be discussed openly in meetings, so the tool should provide summary reports and printable reports of each change request in the system.

Metrics Collection

The change request management process is a key indicator of a project's status and health. Accordingly, the change request management tool should either provide or integrate with tools that provide metrics data on collections of change requests. As examples of the kinds of metrics needed, consider the following:

- As defect submissions trend downward over time, this may be a sign that code quality is improving. Consequently, charts and metrics that illustrate trends can be useful for assessing code quality.

- Charts and metrics that measure how long each change request stays in each state can indicate the project's ability to process incoming change requests. Used in conjunction with trend charts, this can indicate if the project organization is understaffed.

- Simple counts of the number of change requests in various categories can provide important information as well. For example, if change requests are assigned to specific individuals on a project team, it is useful to see how many change requests are assigned to a single person. This may show that although the number of change requests overall is reasonable, certain individuals might be overloaded with processing change requests. These types of charts are called distribution charts. In this example, distribution charts could be used to perform resource leveling.

Integration with Other Tools

Because change requests can affect most artifacts on a project, a useful capability is to be able to identify which change requests (if any) affect a given artifact. For example, for the requirements management tool, given a requirement, what change requests have been submitted against that requirement? For a file under control of a configuration management tool, what change requests have been submitted that affect that file? An even better capability would be that the artifact to which a change request is attached cannot be modified unless the associated change request is approved.

Another integration that is useful is with testing tools. The testing process creates many artifacts, such as test plans, test scripts, and test results. The testing process itself can generate new change requests in the form of defects that are submitted when tested behavior does not meet the expected result. In addition, changes to requirements may necessitate changes to test scripts. Integration between the testing tool and the change request management tool can help you understand and track these changes.

Other Important Features

Other important aspects of change request management tools include the following:

- Customizable e-mail notification is useful if specific conditions can be defined where the tool automatically sends e-mail to notify a predefined list of people when a certain condition occurs. For example, when a developer has fixed a defect and the code is ready for independent testing, the tool could be customized to automatically send e-mail to the testing group when the developer marks the change request as completed.

- Of all the tools used on a project, the change request management tool is one tool that may need to be accessible to both end users and customers. Accordingly, it is imperative that the tool is as easy to use as possible.

- In an outsourcing situation, the change request management tool needs a Web-based interface that could be deployed over the Internet if needed.

Configuration Management Tools

Controlling change is one of the best practices identified in the RUP. Configuration management tools provide developers with check-in and checkout capabilities for the files under development.

Features Needed in Configuration Management Tools

The most difficult aspect of employing configuration management tools is that it is difficult to achieve a balance between complete control over all changes and ease of performing changes. There is a direct trade-off between these two qualities. It is important that the tool chosen for configuration management provide the flexibility to enable both qualities to be achieved. Without this balance, developers may be impacted and become frustrated, because it is difficult to make routine changes. The following sections discuss important capabilities needed in a configuration management tool.

Workspace Management

Configuration management tools on the market today usually use one of two methods for managing the environment workspace. The first is a copy-based model, and the second is a real-time, repository-based model. Each has its advantages and disadvantages.

Copy-Based Models

In copy-based models, a physical copy of a selected set of files is placed on a local disk on the client's PC. Therefore, all the files needed by each developer are placed locally on their respective PCs. The work performed in a copy-based model is made in isolation from that of other developers, until the developer owning the files on the local disk explicitly indicates that she wants to synchronize her files with the latest contents of the changes made by other developers. This model is very similar to the model used by commonly available configuration management (CM) tools, such as CVS. Copy-based models are preferred in the following situations:

- Developers need absolute top-speed access to files. Because the files in a copy-based model are located directly on the client PC, there is no network overhead for file access.
- Developers need to disconnect from the network, such as when using a laptop. Because a physical copy of the files can be made directly on the PC, developers can disconnect from the network and work on files remotely.
- Network access to the files is either slow or unreliable. In this situation, having a local copy of the files needed is more practical than attempting to access them over an unreliable or slow network.

Repository-Based Models

Repository-based models differ from copy-based models in that usually the files in a repository-based model physically reside in a centralized repository, not on the developer's PC. This is similar to how someone would view files on a file server. Repository-based models are generally preferred over copy-based models because they have the following advantages:

- Developers can have real-time access to updates in the repository. The moment the update is checked in by one developer, it is available to other developers.
- New workspaces that re-create older baselines can be created nearly instantly, because there is no physical copying of files.
- Repository-based workspaces require very little disk space on client PCs, because most of the files accessed reside in the repository on the server.

Ideally, tools that provide both models are best, because both models may be useful on the same project.

Managing Parallel Development

On many projects, many activities happen simultaneously. For example, some developers may be performing maintenance on a previous release, and other developers may be working on creating a new release at the same time. In addition, developers performing these different tasks may need to make changes to the same file or set of files. This process is known as parallel development. It is important that the chosen configuration management tool provides comprehensive capabilities and rich functionality for managing branches and using branches for parallel development.

A series of successive versions of a file is called a branch. When changes must be made in parallel to the same file, the tool should make it possible to isolate the changes on separate branches.

Figure 6-4 shows a single branch with no parallel development involved.

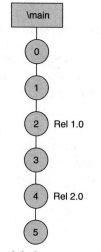

Figure 6-4   A single branch with release labels

All files belong to a main branch, whose version number starts with 0. To facilitate parallel development, a separate branch is created for each developer. This allows each developer to have his own branch on which to perform work. Because each developer has his own branch, they are free to check out and check in files independently (in parallel) from the work being performed on other branches. The labels "Rel 1.0" and "Rel 2.0" are examples of labels documenting the baseline in which those particular versions participate.

Figure 6-5 shows an example of a main branch with parallel branches created for two developers, Bill and Jane. Whenever a branch is created, it starts with an exact copy of the version from the source branch on the source tree. In other words, in Figure 6-5, version 0 on both the Bill and Jane branches is exactly the same as version 0 on the main branch. After that point, subsequent versions on each branch (versions 1 and forward) are modified independently and in parallel. Thus, Bill and Jane can check out and check in on their own branches completely independently without interfering with each other's changes.

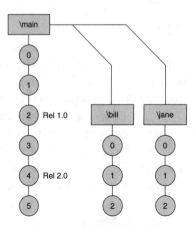

Figure 6-5   A main branch with parallel branches for developers

When development reaches a point where the developers have completed making their changes, the changes must be integrated. A special branch called the integration branch is created for this purpose. Files are not checked out and checked in individually on the integration branch. Instead, as each developer is ready, a CM administrator (or someone with that role) merges changes from the source branch (owned by the developer) to the destination branch (called the integration branch). Merges are performed from each individual developer's branch when he indicates he is ready. After merges from all developers are completed, integration testing can begin.

Figure 6-6 illustrates this process. The chosen tool should provide a utility for managing the merging process.

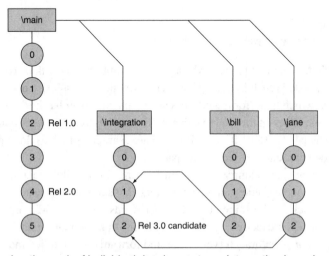

Figure 6-6   Merging the work of individual developers to an integration branch

After all developers have merged their changes to the integration branch, a label can be applied to create a baseline of that release. After testing on this candidate release has successfully completed, it can be merged back to the main branch. Figure 6-7 illustrates this process.

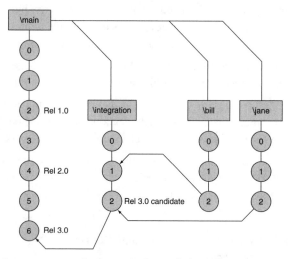

Figure 6-7 Delivering an approved release to the main branch

It's not uncommon that specific fixes or corrections to prior releases need to be made to a baseline without including any other changes other than what is required to correct the problem. The chosen configuration management tool must accommodate this scenario as well. Figure 6-8 shows a branch that was created specifically for making corrections to the Release 1.0 baseline. By using branching in this manner, the original 1.0 baseline is preserved, yet a copy of the 1.0 baseline can be modified and corrections made. At the conclusion of this activity, a label is added to reflect the bug fix (release 1.0a, and subsequently, 1.1).

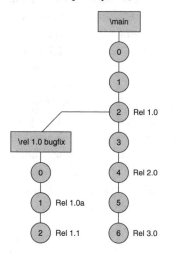

Figure 6-8 A bug fix branch showing corrections to the previous release

Other Features and Capabilities Needed

- If possible, the chosen configuration management tool should be integrated tightly with the other development environment tools used frequently by the developers. This improves productivity because the developers do not have to move to another interface to perform common commands, such as checking in or checking out files.

- Another useful feature is creating a bill of materials for a release. This is the ability to determine exactly which versions of files were used in a given release.

- The configuration management tool should maintain a complete audit trail of all versions created through checking in of new versions. Versions should be able to be compared to each other to discover the exact changes between one version and another.

- Similar to change request management tools, the behavior of the configuration management tool used should be customizable. This makes it possible to cause the tool to conform to and enforce the configuration management process used by the organization.

Considerations for Servers for the Software Development Environment

A side effect of an automated software development environment is that you become completely dependent on the reliability of the computing environment. If a server containing all your requirements, change requests, or configuration managed files fails, you lose access to all the artifacts stored there. This means an entire team becomes less productive, or possibly completely unproductive.

Requirements for Servers

Many tools supporting the software development process use databases. For most installations, database performance is not a bottleneck, because the demands placed on the database server tend to be intermittent. The key feature for the database server is to use disks in a Redundant Array of Inexpensive Disks (RAID) configuration. If a disk drive crashes, you want to avoid any downtime if possible. The ideal configuration is a RAID configuration in which online spares are maintained. With this technique, if a disk drive fails, the server storage controller detects it and automatically begins using the online spare disk. An alert or alarm is set so that system administrators can replace the faulty disk. On most servers with this configuration, the users never even know a disk failure occurred. In general, memory and I/O performance are more important than raw CPU speed, so if funds are scarce, focus on memory and fast disks. If possible, redundant power supplies are recommended. If possible, an uninterruptible power supply (battery backup) is useful to allow a graceful shutdown of the servers in the event of an extended power failure. They can also prevent shutdowns in the event of a short power spike or brownout. Even a very short power glitch (enough to cause the servers to reboot) can result in an hour of lost time across the entire team.

Other Considerations

Don't forget to include the cost of backup software and media when setting up a server. This is more critical than it may seem at first. For example, many databases must be locked, or quiesced, before a backup can be made. The files may be open for writing while being quiesced, so the backup tool must be able to copy files open for writing. Don't forget to store a copy of the media off-site so that it will be available in the event of a major mishap, such as a fire. The backup strategy should be tested to ensure that the development environment servers could be successfully restored when needed. Don't wait until a disaster occurs to find out your backup strategy has problems!

Another important consideration is security. If you create a project Web site or deploy software development tools that can be accessed over the Internet, be sure to use best practices for security. It would be a serious embarrassment if the project Web site became the victim of a hacker. In addition to embarrassment, important information could be corrupted or destroyed. Not only is this a setback for the project, but it could compromise your customer's business secrets, as well as those of your company.

Considerations for Client PCs

PCs used by the development team should also receive attention. In particular, developers and testers both use tools that stress PCs in the areas of disk space, memory, and CPU speed. A small investment can pay dividends in the form of improved productivity and increased morale among staff.

Also, don't forget to determine the client computer resources needed to run the new application once it is delivered. Will the end-user PCs have sufficient power to run both the newly delivered application and other applications the user may use concurrently? Will the network be able to handle enough traffic and still meet system response time? These questions must be answered as early in the project lifecycle as possible.

Best Practices for Deploying New Tools

Deploying any tool in the software development environment takes advanced planning. Carefully consider the following points before deploying new tools to your user community:

- It is important to distinguish between the tools and the process automated by the tools. In other words, a poor process carefully implemented by good tools is still a poor process! Exercise caution when introducing change request and configuration management tools in an organization that previously had no formal process. Introduce the process to the organization and obtain its concurrence before rolling out these tools to the end users. UML state diagrams are useful to illustrate the states and actions and to obtain feedback from the organization. Failure to obtain buy-in from the organization can result in the organization's rejecting the tools, when the real problem was not the tool, but a poorly designed process.

- Keep initial processes simple. You can always modify and change the processes as your organization becomes more comfortable with both the tools and the processes. Figure 6-3 showed an example of a defect management process that evolved over many months of experience with the tool. Attempting to implement a complex process before the organization is ready will result in the tool's being poorly utilized or rejected.

- Take small steps one at a time. Organizations need time to adjust and become comfortable with new tools and processes.

- Determine which lifecycle processes will be automated, and automate only one process at a time. Some tools are so easily customized that it is tempting to automate all your processes at once. Avoid this temptation. Take one step at a time, and leave the organization wanting more.

- Few organizations get it right the first time. Assume you will have to adjust the process and tools as you gain experience with them.

- A common complaint of users is that the tools slow them down. Explain that the tool's purpose is not necessarily to make an individual's work faster, but rather, the productivity of the team as a whole better. This is accomplished through the control and management of information, which always slows down individuals to a degree, but makes it much easier because the process is managed.

- Set expectations carefully.

- Use e-mail notification selectively. If users receive too many e-mail notifications, they become an annoyance and will be ignored.

Summary

Industry developments for the functionality and capabilities of software development tools for project infrastructure over the past several years are truly amazing. Consider the following best practices when deploying these tools:

- Although the tools described here can significantly improve productivity and efficiency on software teams, the improvement does come at a cost. The best way to accelerate the learning curve is to employ someone on your project team who has deployed and used the tools extensively in the past.

- Don't forget that there is no substitute for formal training. You probably have a group of talented individuals who can learn and solve problems on their own. If that's the case, make an investment in the team and obtain training in the tools they will be using.

- The Return on Investment for these automated tools increases greatly if the same tools can be reused on subsequent projects. Always assume that the first project in which these tools are deployed will actually experience a negative impact as the team learns to use the tools.

- Don't skimp on hardware for the servers running these tools. As the team grows more proficient with the tools, they will also be more dependent on them. This means that server downtime seriously impacts team productivity. A few extra dollars spent on redundant disks, and a strong backup and recovery plan, can make the difference between making a deadline and missing one in the event of a server crash.

What's Next?

The next chapter covers the start-up activities undertaken during a project's Inception phase. It lays the groundwork for conducting the entire project. It also covers selected artifacts suggested by the RUP.

CHAPTER 7

Inception: Kicking Off the Project

All projects start with excitement and high expectations. Successful projects harness this excitement and maintain it consistently throughout the project. How is this accomplished? Certainly a large part of this is communication among all members of the project team. Another factor is establishing a sense of mission and using it to instill a sense of urgency in the project team. This chapter covers the following:

- The purpose and goals of the Inception phase
- Artifacts to be produced in the Inception phase
- The "soft" skills needed on a successful project, such as
    - The importance of setting the project vision
    - Best practices for maintaining communication throughout all organizations involved in the project
- Establishing a project Web site with suggestions on content
- What can go wrong in the Inception phase
- Establishing a sense of ownership for the project

Purpose and Goals of the Inception Phase

Simply stated, the goal of the Inception phase on a project is to achieve the first major milestone on the project, referred to in the RUP as the Lifecycle Objectives Milestone. What does this mean? The following must be true at the conclusion of the Inception phase:

- The system's key requirements have been identified. Not all the system requirements might be completely defined, but the most important functionality has been specified formally. Furthermore, the customer, end users, and contractors have demonstrated to each other that the understanding of these requirements across the three parties is congruent.

- A candidate architecture for the system has been identified.

- All significant risks have been identified, and plans for managing and dealing with the risks have been prepared.

- All parties agree on the estimates for cost and schedule, along with the project's overall scope.

As part of accomplishing the purpose and goals of this phase of the project, the team produces a number of important artifacts.

Artifacts Produced in the Inception Phase

The RUP defines several artifacts that are produced during the achievement of the Lifecycle Objectives Milestone. I will define each artifact and add perspective from the point of view of an outsourced project.

The Project Business Case

The Business Case defines the economic advantages obtained from successful project execution. What overall problem would be solved by the project's results? What would happen if a decision not to pursue the project were made? Are there other alternatives to spending funds on this project? Could the same solution be obtained from a Commercial Off-The-Shelf (COTS) product? If so, how do the costs of the COTS solution compare to a custom solution, and what are the advantages and disadvantages of each? These are the sorts of questions that the Business Case is designed to answer.

On most outsourced projects, these questions have already been answered. If your role on the project is that of a contractor, it is worthwhile to thoroughly understand the Business Case, because it will influence your judgment for the many decisions yet to come. Certainly, it is helpful to read any Vision documents produced by the customer. See the later section "Seeing the World Through the Customer's Eyes" for other ideas.

The Project Vision Statement

The Vision Statement is written from the perspective of the customer and end users. Its purpose is to define what project success looks like. In other words, if the project were successful, what would the product look like? What are its key characteristics and features, and how will this help its users perform their functions better? One key difference between the Business Case and the Vision Statement is that the Business Case considers all options for solving the problem, without delving too deeply into the specifics of any single solution, except for the costs, advantages, and disadvantages. The Vision Statement assumes that you have decided to conduct the project. It defines, at a management level, how management will be able to tell if the mission has been accomplished.

Although most outsourcing organizations may have elements of a Vision Statement identified, it may not be formally stated in a document. If this is the case, the contractor's role is twofold:

- Help the customer define and envision what the product will do and how it will help the customer.
- Work closely with your project team to communicate this vision, and promote the vision to everyone on the project. The goal is for the project team to understand the problem from the customer's perspective and to buy in to the ideas the customer has for solving the problem.

The Project Risk List and Risk Management Plan

Every project has risks. Successful projects recognize the risks and tackle them head-on. In fact, the RUP was designed to help uncover risks as early as possible in the project lifecycle.

Many projects not only maintain a list of risks to the project but also define a Risk Management Plan describing how the project risks will be identified, communicated, and managed. The concepts of risk and risk management are so important that Chapter 8, "Identifying and Managing Risks," is devoted to them.

The Project Software Development Environment

In the Inception phase, the team's software development environment is established. These tools support the disciplines, such as visual modeling, requirements management, change request management, configuration management, and testing. Some examples of these tools were shown in Chapter 6, "Establishing the Software Development Environment."

The Project Software Development Plan (SDP)

Most contractors have company procedures that dictate the contents of an SDP. The SDP defines the methodologies, tools, and processes used to conduct the project. The SDP should also define the estimated resources and roles needed for the project. It may also be possible at this point to estimate how many iterations the project will require and their expected duration. But it is not possible to plan in detail the contents of each iteration.

It should be noted that the resource estimates, schedules, and so on produced in the SDP are estimates only. As the project progresses, you must adjust these estimates. Therefore, the SDP is an example of a "living and breathing" document that gets updated periodically during the project.

The RUP also suggests the optional creation of a product acceptance plan, which may be contained within the SDP. In an outsourced project, a product acceptance plan is vital. It states what the customer will consider proof that the project has been successfully accomplished. The details of such a plan may not be completely known during Inception. But a draft of the document should be produced and shared with the customer. Even if the detailed contents of the document are not completely known, the existence of the document signals to the customer that you expect the customer to consider specific criteria that will enable it to sign off on the project. Obviously, this document can and should be updated over time, and the document should be shared with the contracting organization. I have seen several projects that have had difficulty coming to a conclusion because there was no agreed upon criteria to indicate when the project was done. This is a source of angst for both the customer and the contractor.

The Iteration Plan

The Iteration Plan is a detailed, fine-grained plan showing a list of activities and tasks that are to be accomplished in a specific period of time. These tasks and activities are driven by specific risks and requirements assigned to that iteration.

The focus of the Iteration Plan changes from phase to phase. In the Inception phase, examples of iterations might be to clarify the project's scope and vision, possibly through the creation of prototypes. In general, an iteration should always produce something executable; however, the Inception phase is the one exception to this rule.

Iteration Plans cannot be produced reliably far in advance. The nature of iterative development is such that an iteration's success (or failure) dictates the contents or order of subsequent iterations. Consequently, detailed planning too far in advance will cause those plans to be rewritten as the project progresses.

The Development Process

The RUP is a customizable process framework. For each project, a document should be prepared explaining the development process to be used on the project and which artifacts will be produced. This document is called a Development Case. It is important to confer with the customer on the Development Case. On some projects, your Statement of Work may already specify what artifacts are official deliverables to the customer. These may or may not map well to the suggested artifacts defined by the RUP. Your Development Case should take this into account.

The Project Glossary

Many are tempted to skip creating a glossary, because it seems like a trivial exercise. But the glossary serves two purposes not immediately apparent:

- It helps those new to the project to get up to speed more quickly with the key terms, abbreviations, and acronyms commonly in use on the project.
- Without a glossary, project personnel will learn the meaning of the terms through osmosis. This is not a reliable or consistent way to learn the language of the customer's environment. The glossary establishes a common repository for the proper definitions of the terms used.

The Use Case Model

A Use Case Model should be created during the Inception phase that captures the following:

- The system's key actors. This includes all the system's important users, as well as other external entities, such as other systems, that must interface with the system being built.

- The system's key use cases. You should identify the most important functionality areas of the system to be built. Each area is a use case, and for each use case, the threads of functionality (flows) should be explained step by step.

Optional Artifacts

The RUP also suggests some optional artifacts that may or may not be necessary during the Inception phase:

- Business Analysis Model. If the system to be built involves a significant or complex business process, or workflow, a Business Analysis Model should be built. This model describes the business rules of the organization that will use the system to be built. This model is created without regard for how the system will be implemented. This serves as a reference when formulating the system's functional requirements.

- Functional prototypes. If there is significant uncertainty over the conceptual ideas presented in the Vision Statement, a small prototype can be built. The purpose of the prototype can be one or more of the following:

  - Gain consensus on what the product's form or look and feel should be.

  - Demonstrate viability of a new technology or to prove that the use of a new technology is technically feasible.

  - Explore certain aspects of a system's requirements that are particularly risky, such as performance and throughput concerns.

  - Gain the confidence of potential supporters of a system by producing a proof-of-concept.

Soft Skills

In addition to concrete artifacts that need to be produced in this phase, important "soft" project elements must be attended to as carefully as artifacts such as documents and prototypes. You need to set a clear vision for the project and establish clear and continuous lines of communication.

Setting the Project Vision

What exactly does "setting the project vision" mean? It is far more than simply reading a mission statement to the project team. It is a *process*. It is the process of helping the project team understand the reasons and motivations for the team to exist. It is the process of coming to understand why the customer wants to spend money to develop the project in the first place.

Tales from the Trenches

Years ago, I spoke to a colleague in the organization we worked for. He was working on a project in another division of the company. We had previously worked together on a project that had reached a successful conclusion, and we had moved on to other projects within the company. I asked him about his new project. He told me he was working on software related to control systems aboard a nuclear submarine. "Wow!" I said with a bit of envy. "That must be quite exciting!" "Not really," he replied. "I was excited when I was first told about the project. But if they hadn't told me what this project was about, I wouldn't have a clue it had anything to do with submarines. For all I know, we could be working on software for a new model of a washing machine."

I never forgot that conversation. Without vision, and the resulting sense of urgency, the project quickly becomes just another job to team members. As a result, the normal trials and tribulations that are a part of all projects become insurmountable obstacles and the focus of team members. Throughout my experiences, I have seen similar examples of failure to instill the vision, and a sense of urgency, in project team members. Team members become disillusioned, and morale suffers. How can this be prevented? How do you instill excitement in the team? The following sections provide some ideas.

Seeing the World Through the Customer's Eyes

On most projects, some project personnel, especially the programmers and developers, seldom if ever meet directly with the customer. Consequently, they get to know the customer only through requirements documents, Vision Statements, and perhaps feedback at major milestones that occur throughout the project lifecycle. This is a missed opportunity. The person best equipped to help you meet this challenge is the person (or persons) responsible for the team's existence— your customer! Furthermore, developers are generally very creative individuals. A better understanding of the environment in which the users of the software operate on a day-to-day basis can lead to ideas for more innovative features and solutions. This is not the same as simply knowing the requirements.

Step 1: Meeting with the Customer

The first step toward the solution is to meet with your customer. If you are part of an offshore team, this meeting (and subsequent meetings) may need to take place electronically. (See Chapter 9, "Navigating the Requirements Management Process," for more discussion on this.) If possible, this initial meeting and subsequent meetings with the project team should take place at the customer's site. Explain to the customer that you want them to brief your team on the following topics:

- What problems and challenges led to the decision to create this project?
- What alternatives to the establishment of this project were explored, and why were these alternatives dismissed in favor of establishing the project instead?
- What problems relating to the project keep them up at night?

- How is this project critical to their business?
- How will a successful conclusion to this project help them?

Step 2: Meeting with the End Users

On smaller projects, the customer and end users are one and the same. If your customer and the end users of the project you are about to build are different groups of people, ask if the project team can have an on-site visit with the end users in their work environment. Obviously, this is not always possible. If the end users are onboard a submarine, as just discussed, you may not be able to visit them in their environment! The same holds true if the project team is offshore. In either case, the next-best solution is to meet with one or more of the key end users, preferably in person, or electronically if necessary. It is important to note that these are *not* requirements-gathering sessions. The purpose is to orient the project team to the customer's environment. This gives context to the requirements-gathering sessions that will ultimately follow. Be sure these users understand the meeting's purpose ahead of time. Without this explanation, most end users will assume that the group wants to hear about their wish list for the software's functional requirements. You do not want to discuss specific requirements in this meeting. Here are some suggestions to explain to the end users what needs to be covered in the meetings:

- Tell the users you want to hear about their jobs as they relate to the project.
- How do the users envision the product helping them do their jobs?
- How do the users currently do their jobs given that the product to be produced by the project is not yet available?
- Will the system to be developed replace an existing system? If so, what do people like and dislike about this legacy system?
- Does the system to be developed automate a certain task or set of tasks for the users? If so, what are some examples of other tasks related to the new system that the new system will not provide? Why weren't these tasks included in the project's scope?
- Is the product to be produced considered mission-critical by the end users? How would the loss of the product affect their jobs?
- Are end users generally in agreement on the need for this project?
- Are there some examples of related systems that users particularly like to use or that were particularly successful in fulfilling their needs? If so, what are the characteristics of these systems the users found useful?

The discussion generated by these questions will help you understand the customer, their attitudes, and their likes and dislikes. This context will help you and the teams make better decisions during the course of the project.

Step 3: Getting to Know the Customer and End Users

Many projects often start with some sort of semisocial gathering, such as a luncheon. Often, the people who hold these gatherings assume they are for executive management only. I disagree with this position. The better the members of the teams know each other, the less likely they are to engage in political battles during the project. In addition, familiarity can open informal communications channels that can make the difference in project success.

The trend toward offshoring has made frequent in-person meetings between the customer, end users, and contractor team impractical. It will be interesting to observe the long-term effects of this situation. The concern is that the ability to communicate closely will need to be replaced by technological solutions to enable the communication. Without it, projects will suffer.

Maintaining Communication on the Project

Most projects are large producers of information—in the form of meeting minutes, status reports, trip reports, and so on. Like requirements, these are important project documents that need to be produced on a regular basis and retained.

Status Reports

Most customers require their contractors to supply written status reports periodically, often once a week. Most project status reports contain the typical summary of current activities, a section for planned activities, and a section for outstanding issues and risks. These reports, while important, need to be considered from the proper perspective.

Sometimes, the intended recipients do not read the status reports, except in certain circumstances. Some customers simply do not have time to keep up with the plethora of documents that cross their desks. I have learned the hard way that status reports should never contain new information that has not been previously communicated to the intended recipients. The status report is really more of a historical record; it should not be used to raise new issues with the customer. If you believe you must use a status report to raise a new issue, be sure to call attention to the issue by telling the customer separately (perhaps through an e-mail or a verbal comment) to be sure to look at that week's status report. Otherwise, you waste valuable time by waiting for a response that may never come.

Even though status reports are sometimes neglected, you should ensure that they are complete and accurate. When projects get in trouble, status reports and e-mails are often the only written records available. If the difficulties continue to the point where the contracts office and attorneys get involved, verbal comments and statements are insignificant. Status reports and e-mails become key because they are a record that is written by one party and reviewed by the other. Don't let poorly written reports become your undoing. Take them seriously, and be sure they are complete and accurate. At the same time, don't depend on status reports as the primary method of communication.

Status Meeting Minutes

Meeting minutes are useful as well. Depending on how frequently meetings are held on your project, formally prepared meeting minutes can help prevent misunderstandings. It is difficult to make a blanket recommendation for meeting minutes. If you have many informal and impromptu meetings, it may not be practical to create minutes for every meeting. The best possible solution for the least effort would be to record all meetings between the customer and contractors. If you meet electronically, recording the meetings may be a trivial matter. The advantages of recording meetings are several:

- You are guaranteed an accurate record of all conversations that take place.
- If you are unclear about what is discussed, you have an accurate record to return to.
- Very little overhead is involved in recording meeting minutes.
- If key people are unable to make it to a meeting, they can replay the meeting at a later date to catch up.

If keeping minutes is not possible or practical, at least create a written record of all key decisions that were made, as well as a list of all action items and who they were assigned to. Then, after the meeting, send the minutes to all meeting participants to ensure that no disagreements occur over what was decided and what the action items are.

Technical Interchange Meetings

On larger projects with multiple contractors, contractors might need to meet directly with each other, with or without the customer present. I have seen many large projects experience difficulty because of dysfunctional relationships between key contractors. Similar to building a relationship with customers, familiarity with your other contractors lessens the likelihood of political battles. Open lines of communication between the organizations at all levels—executive, contractual, technical—not only lessens project risk but also makes for a more enjoyable experience, which contributes to good morale.

Establishing a Project Web Site

I am a big fan of project Web sites. Especially for larger projects, project Web sites can be very useful.

Advantages of Project Web Sites

Advantages of project Web sites include the following:

- Stakeholders can view and access project information at any time, from any location. This is particularly important if the contractor is offshore or a significant distance from the stakeholders.
- The project team can use the Web site to stay informed of project status while away from the office.

- The Web site can be used as an easy mechanism for the exchange of files, particularly large files that may not be able to be sent through e-mail.
- Some artifacts, such as user interface prototypes (if the project is Web-based), can be accessed through the client's Web browser. This allows the user to examine the user interface at his own pace, enabling him to provide better-quality feedback.

Suggestions for Content of Project Web Sites

All standard document deliverables should be included on the project Web site, such as the following:

- Status reports
- Document deliverables:
  - Project plan
  - Project schedule
  - Requirements management plan
  - Risk management plan
  - Configuration management plan
  - Project standards
  - Use cases
  - Other documents
- Meeting minutes
- Organization charts
- Contact information for project team members

With the advent of Web-based project tools, such as those from IBM Rational, the project Web site can actually be much more than a simple repository of static files and information. Users can actually access project repositories directly over the Internet. Here are some examples:

- Access to change requests. Set up the Web interface to IBM Rational ClearQuest, and make the databases accessible to the users of the Web site. This enables stakeholders to view enhancement requests, defects, risks, and anything being tracked in ClearQuest.
- Access to requirements. IBM Rational's RequisitePro product has a Web interface. This would let users view all the requirements, attributes, and traceability matrices.
- IBM Rational's ProjectConsole tool can be configured to automatically create charts, graphs, and trends and to update them automatically every night. This opens a world of possibilities for useful information to provide to the customer. I have developers update an attribute for each requirement successfully implemented and tested in RequisitePro. ProjectConsole can then be configured to show the trend of requirements as they are

completed. This gives the stakeholders a visual indication that progress is being achieved on the project.

- If the project is using a design tool such as Rose or XDE, the models can be "published" to a Web-compatible file that can placed on the Web site. This enables the users to view the actual UML diagrams for the project.

Other Best Practices for Project Web Sites

Other best practices for project Web sites include the following:

- Depending on the nature of the project, it may be desirable to require a user ID and password for the Web site. The Web site may have information that may be of value to competitors, or it may contain business-sensitive information that is valuable to your client. Requiring a user ID and password shows that you value and respect the client's sensitive information.

- For similar reasons, it may be desirable to establish secure connections using Secure Socket Layer (HTTPS) communications. This encrypts the information sent between the Web client and the Web server, keeping it from being intercepted by third parties.

- Keep the Web site up to date. If the Web site is seldom updated and contains stale content, users will quickly lose interest.

- Keep an automated log indicating who is logging into the Web site. This will provide you with an indication of the Web site's usefulness to your client.

- Despite the value of a project Web site, it is not a substitute for the more conventional means of project communication. Think of it as a supplement, not a replacement, for meetings and conversations.

What Can Go Wrong During the Inception Phase

It is my contention that most projects fail during the Inception phase, but the participants fail to recognize it. The project plods along until the risks that were not addressed during Inception come back to haunt everyone. Here are some examples of Inception phase problems:

- One common failure is establishing a formal contract for the complete design, development, and delivery of the system before the goals of the Inception phase have been achieved. As noted in Chapter 3, "Getting Started: Request for Proposals (RFPs), Proposals, and Contracts," how can you determine a reasonable bid before you know the project's important requirements and risks? Unfortunately, in an outsourcing situation, the decision to release a Request for Proposal (RFP) for a project from start to finish has already been made, and you are expected to submit a bid. These projects can (and do!) still succeed, but a constant focus on scope is mandatory.

- Failure to set expectations. Most sources of difficulty in client relationships are due to poorly set expectations. This is a manifestation of poor communication between client and contractor. Always keep your client informed of project status, risks, concerns, and goals. If you have to deliver bad news to your customer, deliver it as soon as possible. Try to supply the customer with alternatives for solving the problem as well.

- Failure to obtain stakeholder concurrence on requirements. The project's goal is to satisfy the client's needs. This cannot be accomplished without the client's concurrence that the proper set of requirements have been identified and established. Without obtaining this concurrence, progress proceeds rapidly but unravels as the client recognizes that the desired functionality has not been implemented. By that time, it is much more difficult to recover. Take the time to work with the customer. See Chapter 9 for suggestions in this area.

- Failure to identify and manage project risks. Chapter 8 covers some methods of identifying and tracking risks.

Establishing a Sense of Ownership of the Project Plan

At the beginning of this chapter, I stated that most projects start with a sense of excitement. Another factor involved in maintaining this excitement and sense of urgency is establishing a sense of ownership of and control over portions of the project with members of the project team. Depending on the project manager's management style, this may be challenging. Here are some suggestions:

- Before asking team members to produce schedule estimates, advise the team on the importance of adhering as closely as possible to schedule estimates. Indicate that they as team members are responsible for producing estimates they have a good chance of achieving.

- Ask the team members responsible for the work to produce the project estimates. This gives them a sense of ownership of and responsibility for meeting the deadlines.

- As much as possible, resist the urge to overrule the estimates of the team members. This is important for two reasons. First, the team members are the ones performing the work and, therefore, are in the best position to know how long a task will take. Second, overruling their estimate eliminates their sense of control and is detrimental to morale. If you disagree with the team members' estimate, instead of asking them to change the estimate, discuss it with them. Ask them to explain the factors and information they considered in producing the estimate. You will either become convinced of the estimate's validity, or you may be able to correct some information that will lead the team members to update the estimate to a more agreeable number. This allows the team members to retain their sense of control over and ownership of the estimate.

- Take your commitments to the team seriously. If you schedule a meeting or event, recognize that this is a commitment to the team. The team members will see your behavior as setting an example for the team to follow.

- Involve the team in monitoring the project's progress. In-group settings focus on the team's performance as a whole. If you are using a tool such as IBM Rational's Project-Console, you can create color graphs to show trend charts illustrating the progress. Post these in common areas where team members congregate.

Summary

- Remember to stay focused on the goals of the Inception phase. If a vision has already been established, try to determine if it can be achieved with the time and resources provided. If a Vision Statement has not been developed, help your customer create one.

- Try to avoid fixing price, duration, and functionality for the entire project during the Inception phase.

- Communicate the vision to your team, and obtain their commitment toward achieving the vision.

- Familiarize the team with the customer's business—not just in terms of requirements, but in their day-to-day professional lives as they relate to the project.

- For medium to larger projects, establish a project Web site. The more dispersed the stakeholders (including the project team) are, the more they will benefit from a project Web site.

- Decide how to customize the RUP process for your project. Identify the artifacts from the RUP your organization will use. It is not necessary to adopt every artifact suggested by the RUP. In addition, your organization may have other ideas for artifacts that should be adopted on the project.

What's Next?

Chapter 8 discusses the types of risks encountered on software projects. The sources of risks are identified and explained. The RUP places great emphasis on identifying and managing risks. If you're concerned about risks (particularly if you're a project manager), I invite you to peruse the next chapter.

Identifying and Managing Risks

Some projects never reach a successful conclusion because of failure to identify or mitigate specific risks. As software projects grow in size and complexity, project managers must be aggressive in identifying and dealing with these risks. This suggests that a comprehensive approach must be taken for each project.

To meet this challenge, I recommend taking a proactive approach to identifying the risks. On small to medium-sized projects, the project manager usually leads this effort. Large projects may have a dedicated risk manager role for this purpose.

Complicating any risk management strategy is the fact that risks can come from nearly any source. The following are some examples of sources of risk on an outsourced project:

- Technical risks. These risks are usually the easiest to identify and mitigate.

- Unknown risks. "You don't know what you don't know" is a common phrase that applies here.

- Political risks. These are perhaps the most difficult to identify and manage.

- Funding risks. Unexpected or unplanned changes in funding can easily derail a project.

- Business risks. If the project's success results in lost business, or the product reaches the marketplace too late, the project's success may result in a contractor's going out of business.

- Schedule and cost risks. I have placed these in the preceding category because they are very common risks and are closely related.

- Dependencies on external sources. This could be another contractor, a vendor, or any other external source providing a critical resource to the project.

This chapter discusses ways of identifying and managing these risks.

Technical Risks

Technical risks are among the easier risks to identify and mitigate. The reason for this easier management is that most of the elements relating to the risk are under the team's control. The first step toward identifying technical risks is a close examination of the supplemental requirements. Here are some questions to ask to help you identify specific risks:

- Does the system have particularly demanding response time requirements?
- Does the system have to process an exceptionally large amount of data in a specific time period?
- Do you have hardware considerations to contend with? For example, does the system have restrictive requirements for memory, disk space, or network bandwidth?
- Does the system need to interface with hardware devices or external interfaces?
- Does the system need to interface with other legacy systems?
- Is a particular technology required with which the team has little experience?
- Is a particular product or technology required on the project unproven or known to be unreliable?

These questions will help you discover and identify the technical risks existing in your system.

Managing Technical Risks

After you identify technical risks, the next step is to take positive action against them. The only way I have found to do this is to attack them directly.

More Tales from the Trenches

On one project I managed, the architect on the project determined that to meet the system's requirements, a technique known as phased transactions would need to be used. A **phased transaction** (sometimes referred to as a distributed transaction) is a set of two or more related transactions usually in separate databases that must be completed together. A common example is a balance transfer from a banking account. To be valid, a transfer involves a withdrawal transaction from an account maintained in one database and a deposit transaction in another database. You must have assurance that both transactions can be successfully completed, before committing them. There were two challenges, however. First, none of the developers on the team had any experience using this technique. Second, at the time, we had decided to use shareware application server software. We were not sure whether phased transactions could work with this application software.

It was clear in this particular situation that these two risks were directly related to the use of phased transactions. It was also clear after reviewing the requirements that phased transactions were needed. To mitigate these risks, we decided for the first iteration in the Elaboration phase to implement a complete thread of execution by implementing certain use case requirements that would require the use of this technique. This initial iteration was scheduled to be approximately 3 weeks long. After struggling with this for 2 weeks without success, the developers began to search for others who had implemented phased transactions with this application server software.

The developers discovered that this had never been accomplished with this particular application server software. They also found that implementation of this functionality in the application server software was poorly done and that portions of the functionality in the application server were either not implemented or extremely buggy.

As a consequence of these discoveries, this iteration was a failure. The goal of the iteration was to implement a thread of execution using phased transactions, but the team was unsuccessful. After meeting as a team to discuss what we learned, we decided that the best course of action was to drop the shareware application server software and instead use a Commercial Off-The-Shelf (COTS) solution. After some investigation, we found application server software that met all our requirements. As a bonus, the developers found lots of examples on the Internet of how to use this particular application server software with phased transactions. From that point on, the project never experienced any difficulties relating to the application server software.

What lessons can be drawn from this experience? In this case, a number of key lessons were learned:

- What you think may be a risk may not turn out to be significant. In this example, we identified two risks related to the same technical problem. To mitigate the risks, we chose to implement a portion of the system's functionality. It turned out that one of the risks (the developers not having experience with implementing phased transactions) was trivial and not really a significant problem. The real problem was finding out that the chosen application server software could not handle phased transactions.

- Identify and attack risks early. Because these two risks were attacked early in the Elaboration phase, it was possible to make a choice that otherwise may not have been possible had this discovery been made later in the project's lifecycle. It may not have been possible to simply change the choice of application server software late in the project's lifecycle. Changing the application server software late, after much code had been written, could have had serious repercussions. In this example, it was an easier decision to make because little code had been written that had dependencies on the application server software.

- Early failure is good, if the failure occurs as a result of a deliberate effort of risk discovery and risk resolution.

- Sometimes, unexpected benefits are uncovered through attacking risks. In this example, in the process of researching the problem, the developers found some useful assistance in the form of examples on the Internet.

Discovering Unknown Technical Risks

In the preceding example, the risk was clear and identifiable. What about unknown risks? How do you discover what you do not know? The answer is to use the principles of iterative development to your advantage.

Some best practices when employing iterative development are particularly applicable to risk management:

- For risks that are known, or suspected, schedule the implementation of requirements involving those risks in your earliest iterations. This is what was done in the preceding example.

- Have a "main purpose" for each iteration.

- Make sure that each iteration exercises as many of the disciplines employed on the project as possible. It is through exercising these disciplines—configuration and change management, testing, requirements management, project management, environment, and so on—that you discover unknown risks.

- Keep iterations short. A common mistake made by those unfamiliar with the RUP is to make iterations months long. This delays risk discovery, because it delays the exercising of each of the disciplines. In some ways, you can think of a traditional Waterfall lifecycle as the worst case of this situation—a single iteration whose length is the project's entire duration! Chapter 2, "Overview of the Rational Unified Process," covered why Waterfall lifecycles delay risk reduction.

- Be sure to schedule some time at the end of each iteration to assess what happened during the iteration. Did you achieve the iteration's main purpose? What went well, and what went wrong? Did you discover anything that bears closer attention? If so, how will you use this information? You may need to change the contents of subsequent iterations to explore any new concerns.

Political Risks

Few projects fail strictly for technical reasons. When I speak to colleagues about problems on a project, political problems always seem high on the list. This is a difficult subject to discuss, in part because every project and every customer is different. As a project manager, you must become politically savvy and aware, or you risk being broadsided by situations you did not anticipate. As with many risks, you may not be able to avoid being adversely affected by political risks, but you can at least identify the ones that may affect your project. This information may influence your decision-making such that you can avoid making a fatal political mistake. As the saying goes, forewarned is forearmed.

I believe that many political situations result in projects being set up for difficulties from the very beginning. Some of these situations were discussed in Chapter 3, "Getting Started: Request for Proposals (RFPs), Proposals, and Contracts." Many project managers find themselves joining a project too late to be able to influence some of the factors discussed in Chapter 3. Yet, there are other political risks that you can do something about. I will discuss these here.

An Example of Discovering a Political Risk

At a kickoff meeting for one project, I was discussing the history of how the project was identified and bid with my customer. On this particular project, a different contractor had already performed the requirements elicitation. My team's task was to take these requirements as input and implement the system. (This was more of a Waterfall-style project.) During the course of this discussion, my customer contact stated that an individual on his organization's upper management team had mistakenly thought the requirements elicitation effort performed by the first contractor involved delivering the completed system, not just performing the requirements elicitation. This individual had promised another member of the upper management team that the system would be completed, delivered, and in production at the conclusion of what was actually only the requirements elicitation! This caused severe embarrassment within this organization's upper management ranks. For this reason, there was great pressure to deliver the system as soon as possible. Every project has deadline pressure, but in this case, careers were clearly on the line. On this project, we therefore based our decisions on getting the project done on time, and we always chose the simplest and quickest solutions when multiple alternatives were identified.

Identifying Political Risks

To identify political risks, you need to think like a detective and ask a lot of questions of the stakeholders. Quite frankly, you can learn much by simply asking each stakeholder separately, "What do you see as the riskiest part of this project?" The stakeholders, particularly nontechnical people, will often launch into a discussion that frequently touches on political risks. This is good information, especially for an outsourced project. It is important to ask each stakeholder privately. In some organizations, political issues may not be discussed openly. Stakeholders may be more forthcoming with information if you speak to them privately. Since by definition an outsourced project involves separate organizations, you will be unaware of political situations that are common knowledge but that are seldom discussed in the open. Here are some other examples of questions to ask in these discussions:

- Were other potential solutions identified as alternatives to conducting this project? If so, what were the alternative solutions, and who was in favor of them?

- What experiences has the organization had in the past couple of years with other software projects? What projects have gone well, and which ones have gone poorly, and why?

- Was this project attempted previously? If so, what happened?

- Is anyone in the organization not in favor of the solution currently proposed? If so, why not?

Funding Risks

You probably have been on a project when funding was suddenly cut, sending management into a panic to reduce staff or cut scope to accommodate the new funding realities. Much as with political risks, you need to apply some detective work to uncover funding risks.

The first step is to identify the type of organization your customer works for. In my experience, I've conducted projects for public companies, private companies, and government organizations. Of the three, you have the most difficulty identifying and obtaining early warning of potential funding changes with private companies. There simply isn't as much information available in the public domain.

If your customer (the outsourcing organization) is a public company, take a close look at the company's financial health. Is the company profitable? Is it meeting analysts' quarterly expectations? Here are some other questions to ask:

- Is the product you are building mission-critical to the company's line of business?
- Does the company have other alternatives to the product you are building for it?
- Is the company undertaking new business initiatives that compete with the product you are building?
- Is the company undergoing a reduction in force or other cost-cutting measures?
- Examine the competitive landscape. Is the company facing new competition in the marketplace?
- How is your project going? Is it on time and within budget?

The answers to these questions will help you determine the likelihood of budget cuts happening to your project.

Funding on Government Projects

Understanding the source of your project's funding within the government, as well as who controls those funds, is key to understanding the funding's stability. Have funds been set aside for your project? Does your customer directly control how those funds are allocated and how they get spent?

Sources of Funding Often Are Not Straightforward

One project I ran for the Department of Commerce was actually funded by the Department of Defense (DoD). This led to some strange circumstances. Multiple contractors were involved on this project. The DoD actually used only a portion of the system. For the portion of the project I ran, the Department of Commerce was the customer. Difficulties arose when another contractor delivered its system. It was deemed unusable by the Department of Commerce, and it could not pass the User Acceptance Test despite multiple attempts. Unfortunately, the Department of Commerce had no contractual authority over that contractor, even though it was the system's principal user, because that contractor was hired and compensated by the Department of Defense. Sadly, this was rendered a moot point after September 11, 2001. The Department of Defense reallocated its funds for the war effort. That system never saw the light of day, despite millions of dollars spent.

Business Risks

Sometimes in the heat of battle, we become so focused on the project that we fail to see the forest for the trees. We become so busy solving day-to-day problems that we do not recognize risks at higher levels. Business risks affect your customer, your organization, and any other organizations that are stakeholders (other contractors, subcontractors, vendors, and so on). For some examples, consider the following:

- Does the product you are building provide some kind of competitive advantage for your customer? If so, what will your customer's competition do to counter this advantage? Projects in this situation place a premium on getting the product done on time. This suggests that if difficulties are encountered, scope reduction or added staff may be better-received solutions rather than extending the period of performance.

- Is the project truly the best solution for the client? Is it possible that the project, even if executed to perfection, is not the optimal solution to the client's needs? If this is the case, should you address it, and if so, how?

- Is the project staffed properly? If the project team must frequently work overtime, or if the team members are working with technologies outside their interest area, turnover could result. Your risk mitigation plan needs to address how to prevent turnover, and also what to do if turnover does occur.

- Are other projects within the company being raided to effectively staff this one? Are these other projects suffering as a result? If so, how can you address this situation?

- What are the chances that your bid for the project is significantly too low? Even if your contract is not fixed-price, your company may feel obligated to absorb additional costs.

These sorts of risks are the types of risks your company's executive management is likely to be concerned about. Keep the lines of communication with executive management open for developments related to these kinds of risks.

Risks Resulting from Dependencies on External Sources

This category of risks is quite large; it covers any requirements your project has for outside resources that the team cannot control directly. This could include other contractors, vendors, and so on. Here are some questions to ask to identify risks in this area:

- Does your project use certain products or technologies that are unavailable from other sources? If so, investigate the stability of the vendors supplying that product. What if that product were discontinued? What if the vendor stopped supporting it?

- Will another contractor on the project be making a delivery containing functionality your project requires? If so, who is tracking that contractor's progress toward meeting that deliverable?

- Will you be interfacing or integrating your product with a legacy system? If so, who controls this legacy system, and who maintains it? Can you obtain early access to it?

An Example of Managing Dependency on a Vendor

On a project at a contractor facility a few years ago, my team identified a solution offered by a vendor that seemed to be exactly what we needed to solve our problem. Two significant risks were associated with the use of this product. First, it was a niche product for which no competing solution was available. If it turned out to be unsuitable for our purposes, it would result in a serious setback for the project. Second, the product was available in only a beta release.

To mitigate the risk, we chose to implement a small portion of the project requirements that exercised the interfaces to this product's functionality. This would tell us whether the project would fit our needs.

As often happens, the result was a mix of good news and bad news. The good news was that the product was indeed a perfect fit for our needs. The bad news was that the software was riddled with bugs. Several key aspects of its functionality did not work well. The bugs could sometimes be worked around, but this impacted our team's productivity as developers spent much time developing these workarounds.

We started to work through the standard support channels with the vendor to pursue solutions to the bugs we found. After a time, it was clear that although the product was a good fit for our needs, we were continuing to lose too much time chasing bug solutions, despite the fact that the vendor's support line was helpful.

We called the product manager at the vendor, who promised to look into the problems we were experiencing. He returned our call the next day. He agreed that our problems were indeed valid issues, but he added that our use of the product was stressing it in ways they had not anticipated.

Ultimately, we worked out a solution that ended up as a win-win solution for both the vendor and our project. Because the product was a beta release, the vendor needed useful feedback and bug reports that would help it improve the product. The vendor stated that our bug reports were indeed valid issues that we had uncovered, and its developers found our bug reports easy to understand, which helped them correct the problems. In exchange for continuing to provide frequent reports on specific documented problems (usually several times a week), the vendor gave us a direct line to the lead developer responsible for maintaining the product. This allowed us to bypass the normal support channels, reducing the time spent on the phone.

This solution was not perfect, because it still required a significant investment of our time to properly identify and distill the problems into reproducible bug reports. But in return for these efforts, we received software patches to correct the reported problems, sometimes within hours of the vendor's receiving our report. We also stayed in touch with the product manager and formed an excellent business relationship with the vendor. This kept us informed of the vendor's plans for the product. It increased our confidence that the product would be viable in the marketplace, thus reducing the risk that it would "disappear" and no longer be available. The project completed its development on time as a result.

Consider the following lessons learned from this example:

- For any product required on a project, if you have no prior experience with the product, verify its viability and suitability for your project before depending on it to complete your project.

- Be willing to invest some time to help your vendor, and search for a win-win solution.

Risks from Other Contractors

It's common for large projects (especially government projects) to have several contractors. If this is the situation on your project, take the time to understand any dependencies you have on the other contractors meeting their delivery schedule. Even if you have no dependencies, if one contractor runs into trouble, it's possible that the outsourcing organization may have to divert funding and resources to the vendor experiencing the problems. Therefore, periodic monitoring of other contractors is prudent.

On the same Department of Commerce project discussed earlier, the two main contractors both reported to the same contact at the Department of Commerce. I led one of the contractors. My project required the successful delivery of the other contractor's work. Our project was required to interface directly with the other contractor's code. This meant that the other contractor was supposed to develop an application programming interface (API) to their code. Although I monitored their success, I did not dig into the details enough. They were running behind schedule but were still on target to deliver in time for our project. I did not know at the time that the other contractor's project manager had negotiated a reduction in scope to reduce the delays. It turned out that the "reduction in scope" happened to be the elimination of the API my organization required to get its work done. The contact at the Department of Commerce did not realize that the API was required. In addition, the nature of an API is such that detailed knowledge of the underlying code is needed to develop it. This meant it would take too long for my team to get up to speed on the other contractor's code and develop a viable API in time.

In the end, we received extra money from the customer, and we borrowed two developers from the other contractor to get the API completed in time. But it was a close call. I learned the hard way to strive to identify all such dependencies and to make all the stakeholders involved aware of these dependencies.

Creating a Risk Tracking System

You have seen in this chapter that risks can come from many sources. You have also seen that periodic monitoring of risks and developing mitigation plans are critical to preventing risks from derailing a project. On some projects, a risk mitigation plan document is carefully developed and then forgotten. To be successful at managing risks, you must prevent this from happening.

On several projects, I've implemented a risk tracking system for monitoring and tracking project risks. I have used IBM Rational's ClearQuest change tracking system for this purpose, but this type of system can be implemented in any similar type of tool.

Characteristics of a Risk Tracking System

A good risk tracking system should, at a minimum, track the following information:

- When the risk was identified.
- When the risk could start impacting the project.
- The person who identified the risk.

- How likely it is that the risk will impact the project. A simple five-point scale should be fine.

- An estimate of the impact's severity if the identified risk materializes.

- A complete description of the risk and how it will impact the project.

- An assigned "owner" of the risk. This is a person on the project (probably assigned by the project manager) who takes responsibility for monitoring the risk and developing the mitigation plans. A risk is less likely to be ignored if someone is assigned specific responsibility for it. Without this feature, everyone assumes someone else will take responsibility.

- The type of mitigation plan adopted (for example, risk avoidance, risk transfer, or risk acceptance).

- The date a risk is closed. A risk can be closed when it can no longer affect the project.

- The reason for closing a risk.

Figures 8-1 and 8-2 show examples of risk tracking screens developed for the IBM Rational ClearQuest tool.

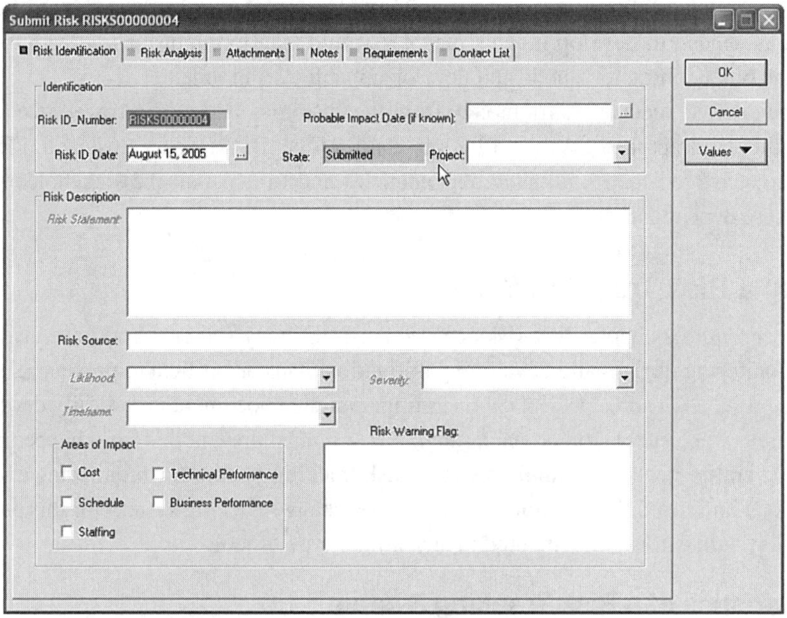

Figure 8-1   A ClearQuest form for a risk management system

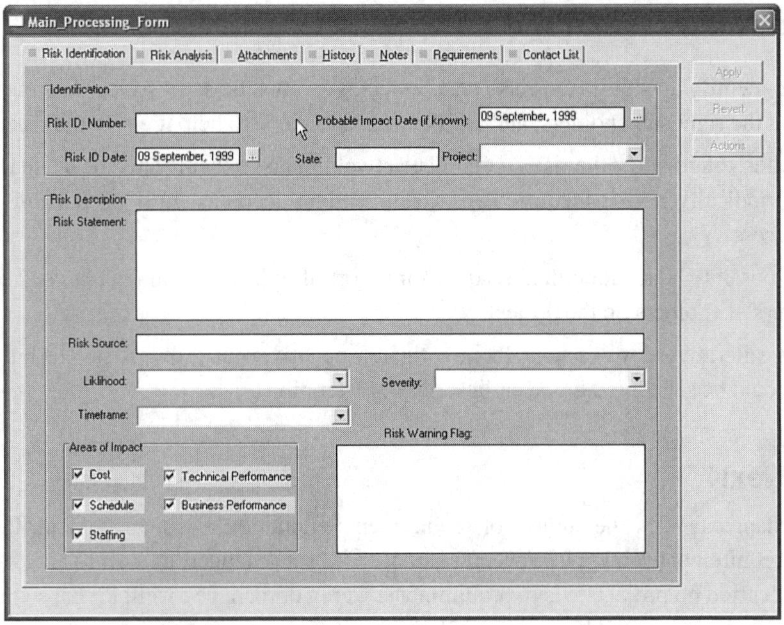

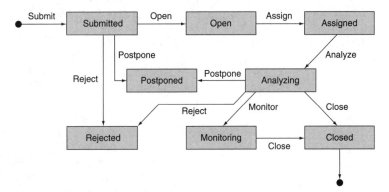

Figure 8-2 Another page of the ClearQuest form for managing risks

In addition to tracking specific items of information, the system should support the notion of a risk lifecycle. Figure 8-3 shows an example of a state diagram with a suggested risk lifecycle. Note that one of the states is called monitoring. The risk management system should be configured to proactively notify someone at a predetermined interval to remind the risk's owner. This reduces the chance that the risk will be forgotten.

If possible, your risk management system should be accessible to all stakeholders via a Web interface. This allows risks to be conveyed to the stakeholders, and also provides a mechanism for them to contribute. Information useful for confirming or mitigating a risk often comes from sources you might not expect. Also, stakeholders may identify new risks. Make sure contributions to the risk management system are acknowledged. Otherwise, stakeholders will cease contributing.

Figure 8-3 The lifecycle of a risk in the risk management system

Summary

- To identify all significant risks on a project, you must be aggressive and proactive. Seek out the right stakeholders, and ask the right questions to help identify the risks.

- After you identify the risks, you must actively manage them. This means that you must periodically revisit identified risks, and mitigation plans must be put into action as necessary.

- If possible, place identified risks in some sort of online system that can be accessed by the stakeholders on the project.

- Use iterative development to investigate and drive out risks. Risky technical issues should be scheduled in the earliest possible iterations.

What's Next?

The next chapter tackles the subject of requirements elicitation and management. It discusses sources of requirements and gives several examples of best practices, as well as actual situations that have occurred on projects where requirements were not managed well. Perhaps you will recognize similar situations that have happened on your project.

CHAPTER 9

Navigating the Requirements Management Process

The importance of proper requirements management has been discussed repeatedly for years. Traditional engineering disciplines, such as civil engineering, learned the importance of requirements management very early. Failure to properly define and analyze the requirements for a building can result in having to tear down and rebuild walls or, worse yet, risk the collapse of a building, resulting in lost time and materials, and even loss of life. It is obvious that if the requirements for a building's foundation are not adequately determined, the cost of rework is extremely high. For various reasons, this has only recently been recognized in the software industry. Because software can easily be changed, it is often assumed that requirements can easily be changed and are not as important as in the more traditional engineering disciplines. Fortunately, this perception is changing.

The conventional Waterfall lifecycle model of software development places great emphasis on creating requirements documents that *must* be frozen prior to design and implementation. Modern lifecycle processes such as the RUP recognize that requirements cannot be completely frozen and emphasize the importance of working directly with stakeholders to uncover a system's true requirements.

In the book *Managing Software Requirements*, authors Leffingwell and Widrig quote a Standish Group survey listing the three most commonly cited factors that cause projects to be challenged:

- Lack of user input: 13% of all projects
- Incomplete requirements and specifications: 12% of all projects
- Changing requirements and specifications: 12% of all projects

In addition, Leffingwell and Widrig state, "Requirements errors are likely to be the most expensive errors to fix."[1] Robert L. Glass, author of *Facts and Fallacies of Software Engineering*, confirms that "Requirements errors are the most expensive to fix during production" and "Missing requirements are the hardest requirements errors to correct." Finally, Glass states, "One of the two most common causes of runaway projects is unstable requirements."[2]

It is important to properly elicit, manage, and track requirements. But it is less obvious how to understand the circumstances that can ultimately lead to these failures and how to avoid them. This can be difficult when the stakeholders belong to an entirely different organization than the group performing the software development. This is the situation you are in when managing an outsourced project.

This chapter discusses how to identify stakeholders. It also identifies and discusses the attributes common to a successful requirements management effort. It explains the added challenges offshore projects face. Finally, it covers the consequences of failure in the requirements management process.

Identifying Stakeholders

The RUP encourages eliciting requirements directly from the stakeholders on a project. What exactly is a **stakeholder**? A simple definition is any person who is affected by the product being developed. The end user of the product to be developed is one of the most important stakeholders, but others must be identified and kept in mind as well. Consider the following:

- Who will manage the operation of the software to be produced?
- Who will maintain the software to be produced?
- Is the system role-based? If so, what are the roles, and who do the roles map to in the user organization?
- Does the system produce reports of any kind? If so, who is interested in these reports?
- Will the system interface to other systems (either newly developed or legacy applications)? If so, who develops and maintains those systems?
- Who is financially supporting the software development and is ultimately responsible for its success or failure?

An organization chart for every organization identified in these questions will be useful in identifying potential stakeholders.

Enabling Success in Requirements Management

Successful requirements management efforts on outsourced projects consistently have three main attributes:

---

[1] From *Managing Software Requirements: A Unified Approach* by Dean Leffingwell and Don Widrig. Reused with permission.

[2] From *Facts and Fallacies of Software Engineering* by Robert L. Glass. Reused with permission.

- The contractor has easy access to the proper set of stakeholders in the outsourcing organization
- A strong working relationship with the stakeholders
- Proper collection, dissemination, and leveraging of information obtained from the stakeholders

Let's take a look at each of these attributes to determine who influences them and how they are established.

Attribute 1: The Contractor Has Easy Access to the Proper Set of Stakeholders in the Outsourcing Organization

A common complaint from contractor teams is that it's difficult to obtain answers about the problem domain, the business process, and user needs in general. Often, the obstacles leading to this difficulty are in place and can't be changed by the time the contractor analysts start their work. Therefore, the first step toward a successful requirements management effort begins during the contractual process, and during the writing of the Statement of Work and other contractual documents. The key influencer of this process is the procurement specialist or contracts specialist in the outsourcing organization.

TASKS FOR PROCUREMENT AND CONTRACTING PROFESSIONALS FOR THE OUTSOURCING ORGANIZATION

The contractor needs to meet frequently with a core group of the end users of the system to be developed. The contract and Statement of Work should include statements to this effect. These meetings require a significant investment of time on behalf of the end users. In addition, the contracting team needs the end users to participate in meetings and reviews of artifacts produced by the contractor. If travel is involved, cost is an issue that must be addressed in the contract. The number and length of meetings required can only be a guess before the work begins. How quickly the contractor can gain an understanding of the system requirements is, in large part, determined by how quickly he can communicate with the stakeholders and users in your organization. Therefore, effort should be made to reduce or prevent any barriers or contractual issues that would slow down access to these stakeholders.

In addition to meetings with stakeholders, the contractor needs access to (preferably, physical possession of) documents that detail the organization's business process, business mission, organization charts, phone lists, requirements documents, and potentially other artifacts that describe how the organization conducts business and who its key contacts are. Therefore, any contractual documents such as nondisclosure agreements and security clearances need to be in place before the contractor begins work.

Finally, if the system to be developed will replace a legacy system, it is also important for the contractor to view how the users utilize the current system.

Attribute 2: Establishing a Strong Working Relationship with Stakeholders

After any contractual issues have been resolved to enable contact with the end users, the management of both the outsourcing organization and the contractor should encourage and promote activities to strengthen the working relationship between the system's stakeholders and the contractor's analysts. The key influencers of this process are the project managers—for both the outsourcing organization and the contractor. In some cases, additional management in the outsourcing organization is involved.

MANAGING STAKEHOLDERS IN THE OUTSOURCING ORGANIZATION

If you are a project manager in the outsourcing organization, this note is for you. The most important aspect of the relationship you have with the development organization is between the user community and the analysts of the development organization. You should encourage contact between the two organizations. The stakeholders identified for this project need to invest significant time on this project. This involvement consists of attending and participating in meetings concerning requirements, requirements workshops, milestone reviews, and so on. They will also need time to review and comment on artifacts such as use cases and activity diagrams. This requires some relief from or relaxation of their current job responsibilities, creating some temporary hardship in your organization. The return on investment of their time is the ability to influence the product's development. The better the development organization understands the user community and the business processes, the more likely the elicited requirements will capture your organization's true needs.

Depending on the relationship between the project management office in the outsourcing organization and the user community, this goal may be difficult to attain. For example, in many large organizations, you may have no direct managerial control over the end users. If this is the situation, you will have greater difficulty establishing those communications. It is not enough to simply ask the appropriate manager to make certain users available for a few hours. This sort of attempt will be less than successful. This kind of request is likely to result in the users being given this assignment in addition to their normal workload. This means that the users may be less than motivated to attend these important meetings and go the extra mile. Or participation will always be preempted by some "urgent" situation that arises.

To solve this problem, set up a meeting for all the managers involved. Explain that the user's time is needed, and also make them aware that the amount of effort may necessitate reduction in the participant's normal duties. To determine the amount of time these people will be needed, consult with the project manager of the contracting organization.

It's easier if the end users report to the outsourcing organization's project management office. Not only can you select the best people to represent the user community, but you also can have them participate fully by rearranging their normal duties if necessary.

Extensive involvement of stakeholders in the requirements elicitation process yields many benefits. If there is any disadvantage to involving stakeholders, it is the fact that their investment of time is long-term. The benefits are not realized until near the end of product development, or perhaps when the product is released. These benefits are as follows:

- Involving stakeholders means that the end product is more likely to meet their needs and make their jobs easier.

- Involving stakeholders gives the contractor greater confidence that the product being built is what the customer actually needs. This reduces uncertainty and makes planning (and, therefore, predictability) better.
- When stakeholders are actively involved in shaping the product, they are more likely to accept it when it is ready for use; they take ownership of the product.
- The stakeholders feeling ownership can make training the users easier. They have seen "early releases" of the system and already have some familiarity with it when it is released. These selected stakeholders can potentially become the "experts" in their respective departments on how the new product works. This elevates their status among their peers.
- Users can help identify risks that would not be discovered from any other source.

Attribute 3: Collecting and Disseminating Information Obtained from Stakeholders

One side effect of establishing a strong working relationship with stakeholders is obtaining a flood of information about requested features, functional requirements, needs, wants, and so on. Successful teams leverage this information to their advantage. Storing this information in a tool for tracking purposes is important. Chapter 6, "Establishing the Software Development Environment," covers the best practices for establishing the software development environment. IBM Rational offers Requisite Pro and ClearQuest to manage requirements. This section makes no assumptions about which tools are being used, so it covers the capabilities needed to manage information rather than tool-specific features.

Essential Needs

Information that would be considered essential includes the following:

- A list of the stakeholders in the outsourcing organization. Include all contact information, such as name, address, phone number, and e-mail. Also indicate who the person reports to in the organization and who reports to her. Finally, indicate her job title and role in the organization.
- For each feature or requirement request, indicate which stakeholders from the list of stakeholders made the request. Include the date and time the request was made and the circumstances under which it was collected. In other words, was the request made in an e-mail, phone call, or meeting? If it was a meeting, when was the meeting, where did it occur, and who else was there?
- Rate each feature or requirement request with a simple priority of importance from the stakeholders' perspective. It is important to do this when the request is made. I prefer a simple High, Medium, and Low scale. Anything more complicated results in too much time wasted trying to determine which rating fits best. Remember that this priority may change over time. At this point, you simply want a general priority rating.

- For every meeting that occurs with stakeholders to discuss requirements, be sure that someone takes detailed meeting minutes. This will pay dividends later.
- Some sort of "audit trail" is important so that details are available indicating who changed the requirement each time a change is made.

Needs That Are Useful But Not Essential

Some information from stakeholders, while not essential or required, can still prove very helpful. Such information includes the following:

- It is useful to be able to create charts or graphs that indicate counts of requirement requests against stakeholders. This is useful to share with management of the outsourcing organization. It also identifies users who have not made significant numbers of requests. Sometimes, in group meetings, one or two users monopolize the meeting. Other users may not feel comfortable speaking in group settings. The counts will help you identify users you may consider approaching outside the group to gain additional input.
- Another useful capability is a graph plotting new features obtained over time. After you have met with all the users a few times, it is reasonable to expect the number of new requests to decrease over time.
- Similarly, it is useful to track requested changes to requirement requests over time. If both new requests and changes decrease, this is a sign that the requirements are stabilizing.

There are many benefits to storing requirements and associated information in an automated tool. The key is to store information that normally resides in the project analysts' memory in the tool instead. The benefits are as follows:

- Requirements information can be searched, and each member of the project team can obtain answers to questions about the requirements without depending on asking someone. This reduces dependency on one person.
- Development progress can be measured against the requirements, with each requirement "checked off" as it passes testing. This provides a clear measurement of progress toward completion.
- New members of the project team can use this "storehouse of knowledge" to become familiar with the project requirements.
- The project is less affected by personnel turnover, because more information is kept in the tools instead of in someone's head.
- When planning iterations, it is easier to group requirements so that they can be sorted by the iteration in which they will be implemented.

- Dependencies between different types of requirements can be established and tracked.

- When managing issues related to scope, it is easier to investigate what-if scenarios for planning purposes by examining and manipulating dependencies between requirements.

MEETING WITH STAKEHOLDERS

You've made sure no contractual barriers exist to interacting with the stakeholders. You've had an initial meeting with the stakeholders, and you convinced them of the value of investing their time. Great! But keep in mind the following points:

- Not all stakeholders who participate in the meetings will be enthusiastic about doing so. In fact, some may prefer not to be involved but were told by their managers that they must be.

- Other stakeholders will be very enthusiastic about spending time with you. They may try to monopolize your time. Preventing this from derailing full participation by everyone requires a great deal of tact and careful customer management.

- Show respect for the stakeholders' time by giving them advance notice of meetings, and indicate the main topics to be discussed. This sets their expectations and allows them to collect their thoughts and any needed artifacts so that they can come to the meeting prepared.

- After each meeting, prepare detailed meeting minutes, summarizing any decisions and topics discussed. Circulate them to all meeting attendees. This gives the stakeholders an opportunity to review the topics discussed and clarify their position.

- It is not uncommon for disagreements to occur among the stakeholders when discussing issues of business process. Honest disagreement and lively discussion are useful, but personal attacks are not welcome. If you see this happening, you must defuse the situation, or the meeting will cease to be useful. Consider tabling the current issue and moving on to the next.

- Not everyone is comfortable expressing her opinion in meetings. If one participant seems very quiet, consider approaching her after the meeting. You may find that she opens up with a lot of useful information. Or perhaps she is not the right attendee for the topic being discussed. Either way, you will have learned an important piece of information, and the person will respect the fact that you valued her opinion enough to approach her specifically.

- Employ best practices for meetings discussing business process and requirements. In particular, ensure that the attendees are appropriate for the topics being discussed. Keep the meeting to three to five attendees. Refer to Leffingwell and Widrig's book (see the bibliography) for comprehensive information on these best practices.

- I have found that it works well to have two attendees from the contractor. One asks the questions and manages the discussion, and the other writes minutes, helps clarify and summarize the discussions, and records future action items.

Refer to the bibliography for excellent references on best practices for conducting business process and requirements elicitation meetings.

A SHORT STORY OF TWO EXTREMES

On one project, I managed a group that was to develop an enterprise-based system for workflow management. The product was heavily involved with the organization's business processes. Accordingly, we asked the project manager of the outsourcing organization to set up meetings with representatives of their user community. At the first meeting, only one person showed up. At the second meeting, no one showed up! I then explained to the project manager the importance of these meetings and why they were vital to getting a good result. Apparently, this discussion made an impression. At the next meeting, over 30 people showed up, far too many for a business process discussion! Eventually, we were able to get proper representation of the user community with only three or four users.

Considerations for Offshore and Other Long-Distance Projects

As I was articulating ideas for this chapter to a colleague, he complained about the continued emphasis placed on frequent contact between the development team and the potential end users and related stakeholders on the project. He said, "This just isn't possible in an offshore situation." Certain realities in software development cannot be ignored. The act of requirements gathering and elicitation is a process involving frequent communication between two organizations. However, there are some ways to meet this challenge. One approach is to look for ways to increase communication and collaboration opportunities. Another goal to pursue is understanding any cultural differences that may create communication barriers.

Looking for Communication Opportunities

Explore one or more of these approaches to opening lines of communication with the potential end users and other stakeholders:

- Exploit more-advanced telecommunications technologies, such as videoconferencing, electronic whiteboards, and even reliable high-quality audioconferencing. High-bandwidth Internet connections are also helpful.

- When choosing tools for the software development environment, emphasize those that have Web interfaces and can be used over the Internet. Chapter 6 discusses other factors to consider when choosing tools.

- Consider exchanging people between the outsourcing organization and the contractor for periods of time. Organizations such as World Bank have used this strategy successfully.

- For the contractor organization, consider locating and employing a subject matter expert—someone who has extensive experience as a user of systems similar to the one you are building or who thoroughly understands the problem domain.

- More-conventional tools also exist, such as phone calls and e-mail. It's a good idea to publish throughout the team any discussions that clarify requirements, deadlines, issues, and so on.

Understanding Cultural Differences for Offshore Projects

Differences in culture between organizations manifest themselves in several ways:

- Understanding the problem domain. Beware of hidden assumptions about business processes used by the system to be developed. For example, if you are outsourcing the development of a system that processes mortgages, does the country to which the project is outsourced even use mortgages to acquire property? If not, a thorough, generic explanation of what mortgages are and how they work is needed in addition to specific requirements.

- Differences in communication style. Some cultures, such as Asian, strictly adhere to organizational hierarchies. In the American culture, more emphasis is placed on individual empowerment. Erran Carmel in *Global Software Teams* states, "When tensions mount in an East Asian group, members of this collectivist culture will be evasive rather than confrontative. This is insulting to an individualist, who expects to be told honestly what is the matter."[3] Many other differences in cultures illustrate how communication styles differ.

- Differing values placed on quality versus time. On most projects performed by American companies, strict adherence to schedule is often placed above all else in importance. This means that when a delivery deadline approaches, an American company typically prioritizes the most severe defects, corrects as many as possible until the deadline is reached, and then delivers the product. In other cultures, emphasis is placed on correcting all defects first, even if this means missing a deadline.

- Contractual differences and the meaning of requirements. Carmel states in *Global Software Teams*, "Particularly for contract work, Americans expect requirements to be in contract style with every deviation from contract to be subject to additional charges. In contrast, in Japan it is not the custom to charge for small changes. The customer-supplier relationship can be seen as a gentlemen's agreement that takes priority over the contract. The Japanese customer would view it as a deviation to contract if enhancements were treated as additional charges!"[4]

Many other important differences are essential to understand. Carmel's book is an excellent reference—particularly Chapter 5, "Best Practices for Staffing the Contractor's Software Project Team," which discusses cultural differences. Cultural sensitivity training is encouraged and recommended for all organizations involved in global outsourcing.

Modeling the Business Process

Successful projects involve close collaboration between the development organization and the contractor. One of the first activities in this collaboration is for the contractor to thoroughly understand the business process.

---

[3] From *Global Software Teams* by Erran Carmel. Reused with permission.

[4] Ibid

You're the Expert

I once asked the manager of an outsourcing organization about his user requirements. He said, "You're the expert. You tell us how the software should work." I replied, "Well, yes and no. It's true we're very knowledgeable about software development and associated technologies. However, you're the expert on your business. In fact, no one knows more about your business than you and the people in your organization. We need your help so that we can become as knowledgeable as you."

To ensure a proper set of requirements, the development organization should learn everything it can about the outsourcing organization's business. There is more to this than simply reading piles of documents. There is no substitute for spending lots of face time with your customers. Learn everything you can about how they conduct their business. Take tours of the facilities where they conduct their business, if possible. Meet everyone you can who is involved with the business process the software will affect. Obtain their contact information and store along with it their titles, to whom they report, and who reports to them, and indicate what aspects of the business process they are involved with. As the requirements elicitation process takes place, you will have lots of questions, and this list of contacts will prove invaluable.

Definition of Business Modeling

Business modeling is the process of discovering and documenting the processes an organization uses to achieve a certain goal or objective. The key is to do this completely from the business perspective, without regard for the fact that you may be automating some or all of this process with a software system. The business could even use the artifacts produced by this process to train new employees. In this activity, the stakeholders do all the talking. Your role as contractor is to initiate the discussion. It is important to stress to the users not to get ahead of themselves by thinking of the system to be built. The emphasis at this point is only on the business processes. In other words, the participants need to talk about their jobs as they relate to the areas that will eventually be implemented by the system to be built. Activity diagrams are very useful for documenting these processes. For each business process diagram produced, you may find that you need several sessions with the stakeholders, initially identifying and documenting the business flow and conducting meetings to review the artifacts produced to validate that you have correctly captured the information.

A strong understanding of the business process is essential to producing software that the stakeholders will find useful. However, in some scenarios business modeling is not needed. The following examples illustrate how to recognize projects that are candidates for business modeling and projects that may not need it.

Indicators That a System Will Benefit from Business Modeling

Situations that would benefit from business modeling include the following:

- Any system that involves processing or tracking some sort of the business entity. Examples include company sales, contacts, assets, and information.

- Any system that tracks information or assets that involve levels of approval or concurrence in the organization.

- Any system involving workflow management.

- Any system that has significant interaction with users where the users have multiple roles.

- Any project involving migration of legacy systems to new software architecture frameworks. The associated business processes may benefit from Business Process Reengineering (BPR), depending on the users' needs.

Examples of Systems That May Not Need Business Modeling

Situations that may not benefit from business modeling include the following:

- Systems that have little or no user interaction (integration software, embedded systems, hardware controllers, and so on).

- Adapting existing systems to work with new hardware, operating systems, and so on.

- Modifying an existing system to accommodate a new feature.

Use Cases: A Best Practice for Capturing Business Processes and Functional Requirements

For each major business process that is identified, typically an actor initiates some transaction, followed by various flows illustrating who performs an activity and when. This is what activity diagrams illustrate. It is important to remember that these actors are roles defined in the business and are not necessarily tied to an individual. It is not unusual for a single individual to have multiple roles and therefore to be represented as multiple actors. This can be misleading for the stakeholders and should be clarified in the beginning. The collection of actors, the flows, and the sequence of events can be written as a business use case. The business use case is written completely from the perspective of the business, without regard for any implementation concerns. Business use cases are a high-level representation of the business activities identified for the new system. If any misunderstandings, disagreements, or concerns occur among the stakeholders on the business use cases, it is important to discuss and resolve these before the subsequent system use cases are identified.

When a strong understanding of the business processes, actors, flows, and so on is established, the focus can start turning toward identifying the system use cases. The system use cases represent a shift in perspective from business use cases. Whereas business use cases focus only on business processes, system use cases identify how an actor interacts with a *system* that implements the business processes. Instead of going into detail on the art of writing business and system use cases and how to transition between them, I'll refer you to several of the references in the bibliography. I will focus on the role and importance of use cases when working on outsourced projects. Use cases are such an important and useful tool that it is imperative that you understand and use them.

Transitioning to System Use Cases

After the stakeholders have documented, reviewed, and approved the business process, the task of identifying and writing the system use cases begins. While the business modeling activities are completely from the perspective of the business itself (without regard for the fact that you may be automating all or part of the business process with a software system), the system use cases describe how the end users will interact with the system to be built. The developers use these to develop the system; therefore, it is important that care be taken to describe all-important interactions with the system fully and completely.

The system use cases are perhaps the most important artifact produced in the RUP. The reason is that so much depends on the system use cases being correctly and completely defined. The following is a list of work products and activities that depend on the system use cases:

- Class diagrams, state diagrams, sequence/collaboration diagrams
- System architecture (for the architecturally significant use cases)
- All code produced based on the diagrams
- Test cases and associated test scripts, test requirements, and so on
- User documentation
- User training materials
- Iteration plans and schedules
- Project tracking
- Project estimation and planning (some estimation tools utilize use cases and scenarios/flows to estimate project resources needed)

If the use cases are incomplete, or wrong, there is a good chance that these work artifacts and activities are wrong as well. On the other hand, if a team has done a good job of identifying and detailing the system use cases, *and* they have been validated and verified by the stakeholders, confidence in the ability to execute the project to successful completion increases.

Note that the notion of what constitutes *complete* varies from project to project and from one situation to another. For example, on one government project in which users were very concerned about security, we had a system use case to describe how the user logs into the system. For this customer, we described many alternative flows, including flows for aging and changing passwords. If the password were changed, we verified that the new password conformed to a series of rules regarding password length, composition, and whether the same password had been used before. On the other hand, a similar use case for a client with little interest in security would not be nearly as detailed. The key is to ask your customer what is important to them. Most customers are happy to discuss this.

I am a big fan of using rapid user interface development tools to help define and validate use cases. Technically, use cases should not contain any implementation-specific constructs. In other words, when specifying a user's interaction with a system, the use case should not refer to how the user interface is designed. In most cases, the user expects, and the contractor plans, to employ the use of graphical user interface (GUI) screens to implement a system. If this is known and expected, there is no reason not to use them in use cases to the best advantage.

SOMETHING TO SHOW THE USERS BESIDES USE CASES

Several years ago, I worked with a client during a large business process modeling effort. Most of the stakeholders attending were attorneys who knew very little about software development (nor did they care to learn!). At the beginning of the time spent with them, I introduced them to the notion of activity diagrams. This was a painful effort, but most of them managed to learn how to read them and check them for accuracy against their business processes. In fact, some of the stakeholders began to appreciate the clarity it brought to modeling their business processes. With increasing confidence, we began to focus our attention on writing and developing the system use cases. To get the stakeholders comfortable with the process, we identified a couple of the initial use cases, wrote them in Word documents, and brought them to the next meeting for review.

Triumphantly, I said, "Look! These documents are written in English! There are no special diagrams or symbols to learn! These are even easier to review than the activity diagrams!" As we walked through the flows, only one user seemed to have any significant input. The others were quiet, only occasionally nodding. The next couple of meetings were equally uneventful. Finally, at the conclusion of one meeting, I asked one of the attendees why they were so quiet and had so little feedback. He said, "We're attorneys! All we do all day long is review documents. The last thing we want to do is come to more meetings to review more documents." I started to respond with the usual spiel about how important the use cases were, but I decided not to. It was clear that the group would not be excited about reviewing use case documents, no matter how well they were written.

Back at my office, I raised the issue in a team meeting. In the same meeting, an analyst communicated the status of a user interface prototype she was working on. In only a couple days' time, she had created a complete prototype of several screens that encompassed the use cases we were developing. "Great," I said. "We'll have something to show the users besides the use cases."

At the next meeting, we proceeded to show the users the screens. One of the users asked how the screens related to the use cases. We projected the prototype screen on the wall and began to walk them through the flows in the use case while illustrating how it would be done on the user interface prototype. The reaction amazed me. The entire group came alive with questions, comments, and useful feedback. From that point on, all the use case review meetings included an accompanying user interface prototype.

This example illustrates the usefulness of user interface prototypes. (It also illustrates how a review of software releases produced by an iterative development process can be.) If you decide to supplement use cases with user interface prototypes, you should keep in mind some important points:

- Stakeholders with little experience in software development will not understand that the user interface prototype is nothing more than a facade. The "real" work remains to be done even though the user interface looks complete. Figure 9-1 shows a humorous example illustrating this point.

- It is important to emphasize the kind of feedback that is useful. Although you are happy to take comments regarding screen color, placement of buttons, and so on, these issues are not your primary focus. What you actually want to hear about are issues such as the following:

  - Have all required data items been accounted for on the user interface?
  - Is any data missing?
  - When a function is invoked on the user interface, are any prerequisite actions required first?
  - Have business rules regarding security, roles, and so on been accounted for in the flows of the corresponding use case?
  - Is any functionality missing?
  - Can you envision using a tool with this user interface to accomplish your job function? Why or why not?

RUBES ®   **By Leigh Rubin**

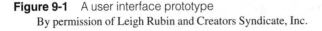

"Excellent! Pharaoh will be quite pleased
to learn that you've completed construction
under budget and ahead of schedule."

Figure 9-1   A user interface prototype
By permission of Leigh Rubin and Creators Syndicate, Inc.

I generally like to walk through the user interface prototype by reading the various use case flows. Of course, the functionality behind the user interface buttons is not operational, but it is enough to give the stakeholders an idea of what the system will be like.

There is one caveat to using user interface prototypes. When the project you are working on involves replacing a legacy system, particularly one that has been in service for many years, it is difficult for the users to "forget" about their current system while helping design the new one. If the user interface of the legacy system is well-liked by most of the stakeholders, it may not be necessary to utilize user interface prototyping. On the other hand, if you are creating an entirely new user interface, exercise care when introducing it to the end users. Although the users may dislike the legacy system's user interface, they will tend to reject an entirely new user interface, simply because it is unfamiliar to them.

When the Requirements Process Goes Wrong

Many things can go wrong in a project's business modeling and requirements activities. Fortunately, in most cases, these problems can be fixed if they are caught in time. Unfortunately, some situations are not easily recoverable. I have seen such situations occur on multiple projects. What makes these situations especially dangerous are that they are motivated by seemingly reasonable or understandable circumstances, but beware—they can derail a project.

This section describes situations in which you should exercise extra caution.

They Tell You That the Requirements Analysis Is Already Finished

I have seen many Requests for Proposals (RFPs) explaining that the requirements have already been collected and analyzed. This situation seems to occur frequently. The RFP then proceeds to request a quote for the cost of implementing the requirements that have already been collected. Understanding why the requirements analysis is said to be complete is vital to determining the proper response. Possible motivations are as follows:

- This may be an attempt to save money by eliminating the process of the contractor meeting with the stakeholders and eliciting a complete set of requirements.

- It may be an attempt to save time by directing the contractor to begin implementation immediately, before the requirements are fully collected or understood. Perhaps the system is urgently needed and time is at a premium.

- In an outsourcing situation where the contractor is separated by great distance from the outsourcing organization, it is an attempt to save time and money by avoiding the need to gather the stakeholders and contractors in the same place.

- A previous contractor performed the business modeling and requirements analysis, and your organization is being considered for the follow-on implementation.

Let's discuss each of these in detail:

- If this appears to be an attempt to conserve funds by the outsourcing organization, before bidding or committing to a project with this stipulation, ask to examine the requirement artifacts. Few organizations with little or no software development expertise can perform a thorough job of business modeling and requirements elicitation. If they are willing to share these artifacts with you, examine them for quality. Are they complete? Are the requirements testable? Do they truly represent the needs of the end users? Can the developers obtain a clear picture of what they must accomplish to satisfy the outsourcing organization? Is the system's scope clearly delineated? If this examination yields less-than-positive results, the outsourcing organization may be willing to work with you to strengthen these artifacts before submitting a bid to develop the system. Even if the artifacts appear to be in excellent shape, remember that the contractor staff will require time to examine the artifacts fully and ask questions of the stakeholders to clarify their understanding. If the outsourcing organization cites concerns over giving your organization a competitive advantage by showing you the artifacts, suggest that they make these artifacts available to all potential bidders. At any rate, avoid bidding for the development for such a project until you have had an opportunity to review the requirements artifacts and discover their quality.

- If this is an attempt by the outsourcing organization to save time, be extra careful. I am amazed that this situation continues to occur, given the plethora of literature and experts available showing that this is perhaps the worst way to save time fielding a system. If shortening the time to fielding a system is truly the motivation (perhaps it is an emergency situation), consider these alternatives:

  - Suggest to the outsourcing organization that a prototype be developed and fielded. If this is acceptable to the outsourcing organization, emphasize that this is an evolutionary, intermediate step toward building the real system. Its primary purpose is to get something in the field as quickly as possible, so it will not be a polished solution. It will also help with understanding user needs for the subsequent version of the system to be developed. This can be a risky solution, so it is best reserved for true emergencies.

  - A better solution is to leverage the advantages of iterative development. After some initial discussion of requirements relating to the selection of a proper architecture, a framework can be developed that allows the contractor to focus on the most urgently needed functionality first. These early versions would not have all the features needed by the stakeholders, but they would have enough functionality to enable the users to perform their work.

    I know of no way to eliminate meeting with the stakeholders to discover their true needs. This takes time. The suggestions given here are only ways to move forward when the situation is inflexible.

- Sometimes, the contractor and the outsourcing organization are separated by great distance. This is generally true when projects are outsourced overseas. The outsourcing organization attempts to mitigate the additional cost and time by reducing the need for the contractor representatives to meet with the stakeholders. Review the first response in this list. Examine the artifacts thoroughly, and set up some sort of process for getting questions answered as needed. In general, I recommend not outsourcing projects that require extensive business modeling and requirements elicitation by distant contractors unless the inherent delays and costs associated with travel are acceptable.

- If a previous contractor performed the business modeling and most of the requirements elicitation, find out if that contractor is being invited to bid on the follow-on implementation as well. If not, is this because the outsourcing organization was dissatisfied with that contractor's performance? In that case, perhaps it did a poor job with the business modeling and requirement elicitation. Make this determination by following the suggestions in the first response in this list. If the previous contractor is being invited to bid, this is probably a good sign, unless it is "lip service" by letting that contractor bid even though it has no chance of winning the follow-on bid. Unless you have contacts at the outsourcing organization, you may not be able to easily determine if this is indeed the situation. If the previous contractor is in good standing with the outsourcing organization, it is prudent to examine the requirements artifacts you will need to work with. If everything appears to be in order, you may be up against formidable competition for winning this bid. In addition to understanding the existing artifacts, the incumbent contractor has already established a relationship with the outsourcing organization and may have additional insider information that lets it make its bid more competitive.

INSUFFICIENT USE CASES

I was hired by a contractor to manage a project that had recently been won. The outsourcing organization said that the requirements elicitation was finished, with a complete set of system use cases developed. After the project kick-off meeting, we rolled up our sleeves and began working. It was immediately clear that the use cases were in terrible shape. They lacked detail. In some cases, the use cases were nothing more than a template with the name of the use case replaced and none of the sections filled in. I raised this issue with the project manager of the outsourcing organization, indicating that the use cases were of insufficient quality to begin development. The response was very reasonable. We were directed to do what was necessary to "clean up" the use cases and make them proper and to validate the existing requirements with the stakeholders. This is when the trouble began. Our first discovery was that few stakeholders had been consulted in the development of these use cases. It was simply one user's view of how the system should work. Second, there was disagreement over some of the business processes among the stakeholders. After expending much effort and time correcting these deficiencies, we began to realize that the system's scope went far beyond our ability to deliver under the terms of our original contract. We eventually worked through most of these issues, but not without considerable angst and gnashing of teeth on both sides.

The bottom line is that if the outsourcing organization claims that the business modeling and requirements elicitation and associated analysis are complete, insist on seeing this information to prepare a proper bid. Explain that your interest in seeing these artifacts is to better understand the problem so that you may prepare the best bid possible. If the outsourcing organization refuses, don't bid. In other disciplines, this situation is unthinkable. Imagine a civil engineer being asked to bid on construction of a building without knowing any of the requirements. A bid produced under those circumstances would not be considered valid.

Lack of Agreement on the Business Process in the Outsourcing Organization

This problem is very difficult to overcome. If there is disagreement on the business process, there is no way a system can be built to satisfy all the stakeholders. This is a sign of a dysfunctional organization. Any system use cases that are developed under these circumstances are likely to be unacceptable to some of the stakeholders. Forging ahead with developing a system in such a situation may lead to considerable angst during the customer acceptance test, when the disagreements will rise to the surface again. Note that some disagreement is normal, perhaps even healthy. But it should be overcome after some discussion. If meetings to discuss business process frequently degrade into chaos, it is time to call a halt to the meetings to determine the underlying cause. Meet with the management of the outsourcing organization and the key stakeholders in question. If no constructive outcome can be determined, it may be wise to pull the plug on such a project until the organization gets a handle on its business process.

A variation on this problem happens when you discover upon meeting with the stakeholders that no one has ever discussed or documented the business process in the stakeholders' organization. Remember that it is possible to succeed in this environment, but ironing out the kinks will take longer than the normal business modeling effort. I consider this effort beyond the scope of most contractors. Your organization may not have the expertise in the company's business to lead it through this effort. Proceed in such situations very carefully.

Avoiding Unbounded Growth in Requirements, or Requirements "Churn"

In the traditional Waterfall lifecycle process, requirements are "frozen" at some point, where design begins, followed by implementation. Iterative processes such as the RUP assume that it is impractical to "freeze" requirements at any point in time. Instead, requirements are discovered through a process of learning, and as these new requirements are discovered, they are prioritized with the other remaining requirements. However, the discovery of new or changed requirements should taper off and trend downward as Elaboration nears completion. I prefer to be able to confidently state by the end of the Elaboration phase that all requirements affecting the architecture have been discovered by that point (with the architecturally significant ones implemented), plus 80% of the end user functionality. In other words, all the complex, risky-to-implement requirements have been discovered by that point.

The reality of contracts (finite time and resources, funding, and so on) catches up to you at some point. The wise contractor monitors requirements growth closely and gives the outsourcing organization advance warning when the number of requirements to be implemented is reaching a point where they cannot all be completed within the existing contractual framework. In other words, the contractor has to start saying no to the outsourcing organization, or it risks failing to complete the project on time and within budget.

It is possible to offer an alternative to the outsourcing organization. This assumes that the contractor has been wisely tracking the priority of each requirement as it has been elicited. Instead of giving a flat-out no answer to a request for a new requirement, offer the notion of eliminating or deferring an existing low-priority requirement to accommodate the request for the new requirement. In this way, the set of yet-to-be-implemented requirements remains stable, and you avoid having to say no to your customer.

It is also wise to counsel contractor analysts not to make commitments to stakeholders during requirements meetings. Instead, advise them to carefully note each request, along with the contact information of the person requesting it, and the level of importance (priority) to the requestor. The contractor can review the requests during its internal planning sessions, determining whether each request is within scope. Usually, especially in the early stages of requirements elicitation, most requests are within scope. When you encounter requests that may be out of scope, you can review them with the project manager and lead user representative of the outsourcing organization. The key in this process is to avoid making a commitment directly to the end user organization that later has to be retracted due to issues of scope or funding. Failure to avoid this can mean that the stakeholder meetings become less productive as the stakeholders lose confidence in the process and the contractor.

SAYING NO TO END USERS

One weakness some contractors seem to have is a reluctance to tell a customer no. Many otherwise good projects can spiral out of control due to this weakness, where the contractor commits beyond what can be reasonably accomplished within the time and budget given. When this happens, projects get behind schedule and go over budget, and stakeholders lose confidence. To avoid this problem, instruct the contractor not to make commitments directly to the end users. Instead, management from both organizations should review requests for requirements together and make decisions jointly. For requirements determined to be out of scope or beyond the ability to be met within the time and budget, you need to manage this within your organization, particularly the lead user representatives. Emphasize to the users that although all requests are important, some have to be postponed or deferred to protect the ability to get the existing requirements implemented and make them available on time. Avoid putting the contractor in a position where it has to manage the end users' expectations by itself. Some organizations perform this function as part of a Change Control Board (CCB).

Multiple Contractors and "Forgotten" Stakeholders

So far, this chapter has used the term "stakeholder" almost interchangeably with "end user." It is important to note that although all end users are stakeholders, not all stakeholders are end users. Early in this chapter, it was noted that some projects involve interfacing to other systems, either legacy systems or newly developed systems. If your system to be developed falls into this category, consider the nature of the interface between the systems. Will an application programming interface (API) need to be built? If so, who will build it? Do the existing contractual mechanisms permit allocation of resources to solve the issues? If the application to be interfaced is a legacy application, are the original developers of that system still available? If not, does your group have the expertise to develop the API needed? Do you have access to source code and documentation for the legacy system? These questions need to be addressed early in the project, or they risk becoming expensive showstoppers later.

Another "forgotten" stakeholder is the IT department of the outsourcing organization. Does your customer's IT department have any initiatives under way that affect how your project should be implemented? A common example is the increasing use of Service-Oriented Architectures (SOAs).

One function of an SOA is to provide "services" in the form of software that can be referenced or "called" from multiple applications. The value is that tasks common to many systems can be designed, implemented, and tested once and then reused across all newly implemented systems. An example of an SOA service might be a login service that implements the organization's business rules for login security. Other examples might involve logging transactions, searching, and auditing.

Finally, the organization may have standards for user interface design. This is common with companies that outsource many of their systems. Without these standards, every system's user interface might have an entirely different look and feel.

During the project's Inception phase, part of the requirements elicitation activity should be to seek out and identify these types of requirements. Obtain the documentation for the application interface if appropriate. Incorporate the organization's user interface standards into your requirements repository for the project.

Summary

- Ensure that all contractual commitments allow adequate contact between end users and requirements analysts.
- If the outsourcing organization and the contracting organization are geographically separated, use tools such as audio and videoconferencing, high-bandwidth network connections between sites, and exchange of project personnel where possible.
- For projects involving global outsourcing, implement cultural sensitivity training, including all team members.

- Give advance notice to management of the outsourcing organization that you will require significant amounts of time from the organization's end users and business process experts.

- The contractor team should create a contact list of all personnel in the user community, including name, e-mail address, phone number, role in the organization, and so on.

- When using user interface prototypes, be sure to caution users that the interface is only a facade. The real work remains to be done.

- Be sure to monitor requirements growth and revisit it regularly, and be sure that existing requirements can be implemented within the allotted time and funding.

What's Next?

The next chapter discusses issues in the Construction phase. First, how can you tell if your project has successfully concluded the Elaboration phase and is ready for Construction? How long should an iteration be? What can the team expect in Construction? What are some of the common pitfalls experienced during a project's Construction phase? Developers, project managers, and test professionals will benefit the most from reading the next chapter.

CHAPTER 10

Construction Iterations: Staying on Target

In the Construction phase, the project's emphasis shifts away from Requirements Elicitation and more toward Implementation. Indeed, the major goal of the Construction phase is to reach the Initial Operational Capability (IOC) milestone. This represents a point where the product has most of the key requirements implemented. The prime features requested by the users are functional and can be demonstrated to the users. At the conclusion of the Construction phase, the product is suitable for beta testing or end user testing. This chapter includes checklists for determining whether the project is ready to move into the Construction phase. This chapter also discusses some of the common mistakes made by projects moving into the Construction phase and what you can expect from your customers and project team.

How Can You Tell if the Project Is Ready for Construction?

A project's readiness for the Construction phase is largely determined by what happened in the Elaboration phase. In some respects, the shift from the Elaboration phase to the Construction phase is subtle. In other respects, it is a major change in emphasis. Simply stated, during Elaboration, risk reduction is emphasized. This task is accomplished through choosing a suitable architecture for the system and testing it by implementing the requirements that affect the architecture. The project is ready to move into the Construction phase after the following two things happen:

- The team is convinced that the chosen architecture can accommodate all the prime system requirements, especially attributes such as response time, throughput, capacity, security, and reliability.

- Their conviction is proven through demonstration of the implementation of the key requirements.

Staffing-wise, Construction is the phase in which the bulk of the product funds and resources are consumed. If the project is truly ready for the Construction phase, the team will settle into a smooth, rhythmic pattern, somewhat resembling an assembly line. If the project and team are not ready for Construction, they lose forward momentum while their "burn rate" (the rate at which money and resources are being consumed) is at its highest. This is a difficult situation from which to recover.

Although the architecture is perhaps the most significant risk that must be mitigated during Elaboration, it is by no means the only risk. For example, is the project infrastructure ready to support the Construction phase? Is the entire team in place, and have they received any applicable training? What about the software development environment and associated tools?

Assessing Project Readiness for Construction: Checklists

When the project is believed to be approaching the end of the Elaboration phase, it is useful to hold a group meeting. The people in the following roles should be present:

- Project manager
- Software architect
- Lead developer or technical lead
- Lead requirements analyst
- Testing lead

The key topic of the meeting is to determine whether the objectives and exit criteria of the Elaboration phase have been reached. During the meeting, discuss the items in the following checklists.

Checklist for the Product in Development

✓ Has the system's candidate architecture been established?

✓ Have the functional requirements that affect the architecture been implemented and successfully tested?

✓ Has the architecture been validated against the system's supplemental requirements? For example, if there is a requirement that the system must support 1,000 users, and that response time with 1,000 users must be within 2 seconds, has the architecture been demonstrably proven to meet the requirement?

✓ Is the system suitable for partitioning development in such a way that portions of its development can easily be allocated to groups of developers?

✓ Have all other risks, in addition to the system's architecture, been identified and mitigated? At the very least, a plan should exist for any significant risks that are not mitigated by the conclusion of Elaboration.

Checklist for the Project Environment and Staffing

✓ Is all of the required staff (developers, testers, and so on) available to staff the project?

✓ Have all the necessary software development tools been acquired and installed?

✓ Is the staff proficient with the tools and technologies used on the project, or have they received training?

✓ Is any Commercial Off-The-Shelf (COTS) software required? If so, has it been acquired and set up? For some COTS software, setup and configuration may not be trivial. The software should be ready for use so that the team can be productive with it.

✓ Has a viable test plan been created, and are testing resources in place?

Checklist for the Customer

✓ Has the customer reviewed the project's status?

✓ Is the customer satisfied with the project's progress in terms of the schedule and budget?

✓ Have projections to completion been made, and is the customer comfortable with these projections?

✓ Have the end users reviewed the system's major artifacts, such as the user interface design? Have they signed off, signifying their approval?

These checklists are not exhaustive, but they cover the major areas. The importance of performing a thorough, accurate self-assessment cannot be overemphasized. Resist the temptation to plunge into the Construction phase until you know the status of these issues.

Iteration Planning, Execution, and Assessment

Your assessment of your project's readiness for Construction has yielded results that say it is time to go ahead. What do you do next? You move on to managing the project iterations. Before you begin Construction, you need to think about some general things in terms of the iterative process. After you begin the Construction phase, detailed planning can begin for the next iteration. As each iteration draws to a conclusion, the detailed plan for the next iteration begins.

How Long Should Iterations Be?

Loosely explained, an iteration should be long enough to get something useful accomplished, but short enough to maintain a sense of urgency on the development team. The exact length depends in large part on the size of the development team. The larger the development team, the longer your iterations should be. Smaller teams can (and should!) have significantly shorter iterations. For example, an iteration length of about 6 weeks is appropriate for a team with six to ten developers. Small teams with two or three developers might have iterations 1 to 2 weeks long. For very large teams, with perhaps 20 to 30 developers or more, iterations 2 to 3 months long may be indicated. This figure could grow even larger for projects with multiple contractors and dozens of developers.

Determining the Content of Iterations

With some projects having thousands of requirements, how do you determine what requirements to assign to each iteration? I generally use five criteria to identify the contents of each iteration:

- Requirements that are particularly risky get scheduled first. Although the biggest risks should hopefully have been driven out during the Elaboration phase, some implementation risks may remain. Some examples might be requirements that specify interfaces to legacy systems, requirements involving very complex algorithms, and requirements that the developers are not sure how to implement. The point is to embrace risk and face it head on. Don't save the hardest requirements for later. This just delays risk mitigation and can derail the project later. A project manager who consulted with me once complained that his project was in danger of cancellation if his team didn't show something working soon. He also said my recommendation to schedule risky items first could cause his project to be canceled. If this is the case, project cancellation is certainly an important risk to mitigate. I suggested that the project manager schedule some high-risk requirements early but mix in some key, easy-to-implement, easy-to-demonstrate requirements. Also, note that your assessment of "risky" requirements may change as time progresses. In each iteration, you learn more about the application, the environment, and various other areas. Your assessment of areas previously considered risky may change. Likewise, you may identify new risks that were previously unknown.

- Items that were planned for earlier iterations but were not completed should be reviewed for possible inclusion in the iteration.

- Components that represent functionality needed by subsequent code. These components must be identified and scheduled for coding and testing before they are needed for the rest of development.

- Requirements that represent functionality of particular importance to the users or customer should be scheduled in the earlier iterations. By scheduling these in the earlier iterations, you can demonstrate this important functionality to users earlier in the project. This helps you maintain the customer's interest in the project.

- High-priority defects discovered through demonstration of earlier iterations. This is an often-forgotten aspect of planning the scope of the Construction phase. Don't forget to give the developers some time to correct any defects found along the way. Hopefully, these will be few, but there may be enough to distract the developers from working on implementing new requirements.

Construction Phase Iteration Planning

Toward the end of the Elaboration phase, it's appropriate and important to determine how many iterations will be needed to implement the project. This helps determine the total length needed for the Construction phase. You should also perform detailed planning for the first iteration in the Construction phase. What constitutes detailed planning? Let's take a closer look:

Detailed Planning of Iterations in the Construction Phase

What does detailed planning of an iteration involve? For each iteration, a plan should be prepared that takes into account the following points:

- What is the iteration's main purpose? Are you trying to mitigate a particular risk or complete a specific set of functionality? Having a high-level goal set for each iteration helps set the iteration's context. That way, if problems surface, you can make decisions in the context of the goal. If the iteration's deadline is approaching and you determine that you cannot accomplish everything, this high-level goal will help you decide which requirements you can drop while still achieving the iteration's main goal.

- What staff is available to develop the functionality? Each developer should be assigned to develop a portion of the functionality for the iteration. You need to work with the developers carefully to estimate each item assigned to the iteration. Ideally, each iteration should be a bit of a challenge to get completed on time but should definitely be achievable. Developers should experience a sense of accomplishment at the conclusion of the iteration. On the other hand, developers should be challenged enough that they do not finish too early. This is a delicate balancing act that is awkward at first, but you get better with practice.

Other Aspects of Iterations

In addition to careful planning, consider the following points when conducting each iteration:

- Each iteration is time-boxed. It is important to end each iteration on time. Sometimes, this means that some planned functionality may have to be deferred to subsequent iterations.

- Each iteration should produce a demonstrable, stable, executable release. Not all of these releases necessarily need to be demonstrated to the customer or end users, but this is important as a goal. This helps ensure and verify that all functionality was implemented and that all aspects of the process (including integration) were exercised.

- The code and artifacts for each iteration should be baselined in some sort of configuration management tool. The baseline should be easily produced on demand and should be isolated from ongoing development. This ensures that the results of the iteration can be inspected or demonstrated at any point in time. It also provides a stable code base on which testing can proceed.

- Testing of the code produced in an iteration, together with regression testing of code produced by previous iterations, should be completed by the end of each iteration. This is another key advantage of iterative development, because testing can begin very early, even in the Elaboration phase. In contrast, projects conducted with the Waterfall lifecycle process do not begin testing until very late in the project's lifecycle.

This process is illustrated in Figure 10-1. Note that progress does not begin at 0%, because some functionality should have been completed in earlier phases. The percentage complete graph indicates progress toward the Initial Operational Capability (IOC). Some additional development may still be needed in the Transition phase to complete the product.

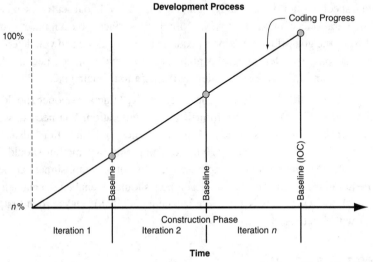

Figure 10-1   Progress during the Construction phase

Assessing the Results of an Iteration

One of the keys to a successful application of the iterative development method is careful assessment of the results of each iteration. This assessment is an opportunity to evaluate progress against objectives and adjust the course of the next iteration accordingly. This is one of the advantages of iterative development. Adapting to lessons learned as you execute the process hones the team's direction and the likelihood of achieving a successful conclusion to the project. At the end of each iteration, consider the following questions:

- Review the main purpose and goals you identified before the iteration began. Were the goals achieved?
- Of the functionality assigned to this iteration, was any not completed?
- Were any risks to be investigated or mitigated during the iteration successfully overcome?
- Were any new risks or problems identified?
- Have you received any feedback from prior iterations from the customer that might suggest a change in direction?

- Have any new events occurred that might change the project's focus, such as the final due date or project funding? Have there been any changes in the customer's staffing or changes among the key users? If so, this might suggest changes in the users' wants and needs.

- Are there any issues in project staffing (such as a team member who is having difficulty completing functionality) or problems with the development environment?

Based on the answers to these questions, you can begin planning the next iteration. The most important points in the assessment involve whether the iteration's main purpose and goals were achieved, and whether any risks assigned to the iteration can be retired. If not, a more extensive evaluation, possibly involving project management, should be undertaken. Why were the assigned risks not resolved? How serious is this risk? If it is significantly serious, you need to determine whether the project should continue.

The remaining issues (such as whether any functionality had to be deferred) may simply be a matter of adjusting the amount of assigned functionality to a more realistic amount that can be accomplished by the team given the time allotted for the iteration.

Demonstrating the Results of an Iteration

During the Construction phase, the emphasis shifts from eliciting and defining requirements and identifying and mitigating risks toward implementing the functionality. During this time, interaction with the customer tends to reach a low point, with the exception of demonstrations of releases. The requirements have mostly been defined (perhaps at the 80% level), and the developers are busy implementing functionality. The testers are hard at work testing. Ironically, this occurs when the burn rate is at its highest. Accordingly, it is worthwhile to demonstrate selected iterations to your customer and end users. This helps maintain customer interest and involvement and, more importantly, allows them to give you feedback.

The notion of periodic demonstrations requiring customer involvement may be new to some customers. It is important to set expectations with the customer and to ask that they be available periodically for review of and comment on these releases. Depending on the customer, this may take some convincing. In fact, the process of demonstrating releases to the customer and eliciting their feedback may need to be executed a few times before it goes smoothly and the customer begins to recognize the value.

Although all iterations should produce an executable, demonstrable release, it may not make sense to demonstrate every iteration to the customer. If possible, demonstrations should be kept low-key and informal to minimize the preparation time. In some cases, preparation for formal demonstrations may take more time. You might need to prepare a demonstration script, sample data, and so on. Furthermore, unless the product is primarily a Web-based interface that could be accessed over the Internet, significant logistics might be involved, such as transporting servers to the location for the demonstration. Ideally, demonstrations should take place at the contracting location. This way, if a problem occurs during the demonstration, the entire development staff is available to help. Also, a demonstration conducted in the same environment in which it is developed minimizes setup and preparation time. Finally, although the iteration is executable, the functionality may be of little interest to the end users, particularly in the earlier iterations. For example, an earlier iteration may consist of implementing a complete thread of entering some value in a screen, processing it according to certain business rules, and storing the data in a database. Although the first time this is accomplished may be a significant technical achievement, it's hardly satisfying to see from a casual observer's perspective. In general, because these demonstrations should be conducted numerous times over a project's duration, the ceremony and preparation should be kept to a minimum. This may also involve some expectation-setting for the customer, who may not understand that these demonstrations are meant to be a work in progress and not necessarily the final, finished product.

Eventually, functionality is implemented that connects the presentation layer, or user interface, with significant implemented functionality that performs some useful function. Functionality involving successful implementation of business rules that can be observed through the user interface will be of particular interest to the users. If you cannot demonstrate every release, these are the releases you will want to focus on demonstrating to the customer.

Because your team has been intimately involved with developing the application, they know exactly what it does. However, at the demonstration, you need to tell the users exactly what will be demonstrated. Users should also be cautioned that the demonstration is a work in progress, so they may experience some bugs during the demo.

It's also wise to have a plan in place for collecting defect and change requests during the demonstration. I prefer to ask the users to make note of minor issues they observe and to voice any major issues they see. Depending on the personalities and interests of the people in attendance, you may hear a significant number of requests, or very few. I also like to set the users' expectations carefully regarding the implementation of any change requests. A brief (5-minute) explanation of the change request process may be indicated. Explain that any serious problems will receive immediate attention, but minor issues may be deferred so that the team can focus on implementing new functionality. If possible, before the demonstration, ask the project manager of the outsourcing organization to work with the people in attendance at the demonstration to set the final priorities on the change requests. If you make this arrangement before the meeting, you can then explain that the development team will work with the project manager of the outsourcing organization to set priorities. This takes some of the pressure off the team so that the users will communicate their issues regarding priorities to the project manager of the outsourcing organization.

When giving the demonstration, I always like to have at least three people available to perform the demonstration. The first person manipulates the keyboard and user interface. The second person speaks to the audience and explains what the user is doing as well as what the system is doing. Finally, I prefer to have a third person off to the side observing the audience closely and monitoring their reactions. You may want to have a fourth person in attendance at the demonstration solely for the purpose of documenting any voiced change requests. Let the customer have some time for exercising and trying out the release as well.

Regrouping After the Demonstration

It is quite possible that you will receive many change requests during the demonstration. This is not necessarily bad. On the contrary, it indicates serious interest from the attendees. I like to convene a meeting following a demonstration to discuss the results. The following attendees are suggested:

- The project manager of the outsourcing organization
- The project manager of the contracting organization
- The lead user representative and internal project champion
- The technical lead of the contracting organization

The purpose of this meeting is to discuss and prioritize the change requests received during the demonstration and to assess and evaluate the reaction of the attendees. As a start, the following are examples of discussions:

- What is the meeting's general consensus? Was the demonstration well received?
- If few or no change requests were received, why? Is it because the demonstrated functionality was exactly what the attendees expected? Could it be because the wrong people attended the meeting?
- If many change requests were received, why? Does this mean the demonstrated functionality was not what the attendees expected? Or is it simply a reflection of intense interest on the part of the attendees? Sometimes, users are so enthusiastic at a demonstration that they get carried away with minor change requests. This is a key evaluation parameter. You need to determine if any adjustments in the project's direction are needed or whether to continue in the same direction.

Contractual Issues Revisited

Earlier in this chapter, it was stated that toward the end of the Elaboration phase, the overall scope and length of the Construction phase are determined, including the number and length of iterations. This implies that the contractor can set the date of the IOC according to the project's needs. In an outsourcing situation, this is often not the case. A delivery date for the IOC may have been set contractually long before the Construction phase was set to begin. This could mean that you do not have sufficient time for enough iterations to completely deliver all intended functionality in the IOC. Although this is not an ideal situation, it is manageable. You have three alternatives:

- Convince the customer to accept the IOC without all the intended functionality. Renegotiate the priorities of the functionality to be implemented so that the most important functionality gets completed for the IOC. Explain that the remaining functionality can be delivered during the Transition phase releases.
- Convince the customer to push out the date for the IOC to allow enough time for iterations to deliver the needed functionality for the IOC.

- Descope the requirements or defer them to another time.

The point is that some flexibility from the client is required.

Common Mistakes Implementing Iterative Development in the Construction Phase

In my consulting experience with projects implementing iterative development, I have witnessed five mistakes that seem common to practitioners implementing iterative development.

Mistake 1: Plunging into Construction Before the Project Is Ready

This mistake is common for those accustomed to Waterfall-style methods. Those who focus primarily on requirements elicitation and analysis seem particularly predisposed to this. You cannot move into the Construction phase simply because you have collected most or all the requirements. Although perhaps 80% of the requirements have been collected when Construction begins, this is a correlation, not a cause.

The key is to focus on the system architecture and other major risks that have been identified before the Construction phase begins. The primary requirements receiving the most attention during the Elaboration phase are those that exercise and prove the system architecture. Without proof of a stable, viable architecture, a move into the Construction phase diverts attention from risk mitigation. This can have disastrous effects later, because the failure to mitigate these risks early results in serious problems toward the end of the Construction phase, when an inadequate architecture becomes evident. By that time, much of the funding and resources on the project have been expended. You might be lucky and find that the architecture happens to be suitable, but why leave this to chance?

Mistake 2: Iterations of an Inappropriate Length

One project I worked on had six developers. When I looked at their schedule, they had iterations that were several months long. This dilutes some of the benefits of iterative development. For a small group of six developers, iteration lengths of 3 to 6 weeks are more appropriate. The idea is to exercise the complete lifecycle multiple times at frequent intervals. As development groups become very large (20 to 30 developers or more), iterations of 2 to 3 months may make sense. Larger groups are more difficult to control than small ones. Remember that iterations should be long enough to get something useful done, but short enough to create a sense of urgency in the development group.

Mistake 3: Iterations with No Stated Purpose

A project manager had determined the total length of time available to develop the system. He then chopped up the amount of time into equal-length periods and divided the requirements to be developed evenly across the periods. Then, he proudly proclaimed he was implementing iterative development.

Not by a long shot! Each iteration should have a specific purpose (usually determined by the risks remaining), and the requirements should be allocated to an iteration according to the criteria discussed earlier in this chapter. The success and lessons learned from an iteration are then used as input to help determine which items receive attention in the next iteration. Thus, you have the opportunity to make "course corrections" between iterations.

Mistake 4: Getting Derailed by Change Requests

Projects can become a victim of their own success. Sometimes, particularly after a demonstration, the customer and users flood the project with numerous change and enhancement requests. The development team, in an effort to be responsive to the customer, begins devoting more time to working on the change requests than developing the requirements. Actually, this may or may not be a mistake. The key is to stop and evaluate the reasons for the change requests. Are they mostly cosmetic requests? Are the users simply trying one last time to sneak in features that were rejected during requirements elicitation? If this is the case, the best course of action is to collect all these change requests and track them in some formal tracking system. Then, you can give your customer choices. Given limited time and resources, you can continue along the original path and deliver the IOC on time, but without all the change requests implemented. Or you can delay the IOC delivery and incorporate more of the change requests. Most customers will understand that last-minute change requests delay the implementation of new functionality. As a compromise, you can implement just a few of the change requests with each successive iteration.

If the team receives numerous change requests because the users are not seeing the functionality they expected, you have a more serious problem to solve. You might need to re-evaluate the requirements and review whether the project is headed in the right direction.

Mistake 5: Trying to Plan All Iterations in Detail Up Front

The whole point of iterative development is to use the lessons learned from one iteration to plan the next one. Based on the experiences of one iteration, you may learn or discover new information that causes you to alter what you had planned for the subsequent iteration. Because of this, it is usually a waste of time to plan every detail of every iteration up front. In all likelihood, the iteration will change anyway. A fine-grained, detailed plan is best used with the next iteration.

Anecdotal Observations from Development Teams Using Iterative Techniques Versus Waterfall Techniques

I have worked with a number of teams who have made the transition from applying Waterfall-style methods to applying iterative methods. In addition to all the advantages of iterative techniques we have already discussed, I have noticed one other interesting phenomenon—observing the general stress levels of the development staff.

Figure 10-2 plots my experiences concerning general trends of team stress for projects using Waterfall versus iterative techniques. This is not based on scientific research, but on my own observations across many projects. I interviewed a number of development teams at the conclusion of various projects and asked how they felt about the experience.

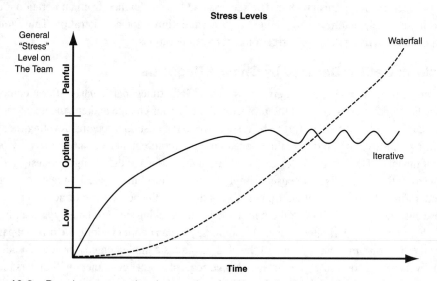

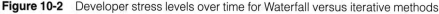

Figure 10-2   Developer stress levels over time for Waterfall versus iterative methods

For Waterfall projects, the developer stress level starts out very low and tends to stay low for quite some time. Usually after Critical Design Review (CDR), stress levels rise rapidly as implementation suddenly begins (after months of doing some design work and producing documentation). Initially, developers are quite happy and morale is high as they finally begin the work they really like to do—developing code. After a time, when the delayed risk reduction begins to hurt forward progress, developers start working overtime as they rush to solve unforeseen problems. On some projects, panic sets in. Testing often ceases. There generally isn't much time for testing as resources are diverted to fight the inevitable brush fires. If the project makes it to its deadline, the result is often riddled with bugs, morale is low, and development personnel and management are frustrated.

For iterative projects, the team stress level seems to rise almost instantly. This makes sense, because the developers begin work almost right away, designing architectures, testing, developing, and having to meet deadlines that are seldom more than a few weeks away. Then an interesting thing happens—the stress level seems to stabilize and fall into a rhythmic pattern. This coincides with the beginning and end of iterations. However, "panic mode" seldom seems to occur.

I'll never forget the first major project I managed using iterative development. I had become accustomed to the normal "panic" stages that always seemed to occur on Waterfall-based projects. It was very common to work evenings and weekends on those projects. As my new project entered the Construction phase, I assumed it would be the same—lots of overtime. I designated every Wednesday as the night the entire team would work late (I bought the pizza). We did this twice before we decided it simply wasn't needed. Selected team members occasionally worked overtime, but it did not seem to be needed for the entire team. I scheduled the final iteration to end the day before a holiday weekend, knowing that if the team got in trouble, they would work over that long weekend to catch up. This elicited many groans from the team. However, when the time came, not a single developer had to work over the weekend.

I would much rather manage a group using these iterative techniques. Just judging from the stress level alone, it's much easier to manage a group where there is some stress, but it is fairly constant and stays at a healthy level.

Summary

Not every project (even iterative) goes as well as the one in the preceding example, but it's much more likely to be this way with an iterative lifecycle model. Keep in mind the following points:

- Iterations are carefully planned only one step at a time.
- Use the lessons learned from each iteration to adjust the project plan for the next iteration.
- Be sure to examine the exit criteria from the Elaboration phase before moving the project into the Construction phase. Be honest with yourself and the team. Is the architecture really stable? Can it meet all the supplemental requirements levied on it?
- Demonstrate iterations to your customer carefully. Be prepared to deal with the change requests resulting from them.

What's Next?

The next chapter tackles the subject of testing. Although those who perform test and quality assurance roles are the obvious audience for this chapter, the notion of testing with iterative processes is different enough that developers and project managers may want to peruse it as well. I discuss how testing differs from traditional lifecycle models. I also address issues common in some outsourcing situations, such as the testing team being in a separate organizational group from the development team.

CHAPTER 11

Testing

The use of iterative development methods enables significant improvements in the testing process. When combined with best practices for testing and modern testing tools, the result is applications that are reliable, perform well, and improve the contractor's reputation.

This chapter describes the problems relating to testing when using the Waterfall lifecycle model. It also discusses how testing differs when iterative lifecycle models such as the IBM Rational Unified Process are employed. Some best practices for staffing the roles relating to testing follow. The different types of testing are discussed, and the importance of each kind of testing is explained. Integrating the testing process with the iterative development process is discussed. Finally, some examples of improper testing efforts are given.

How Traditional Waterfall Lifecycle Models Inhibit Testing

Chapter 2, :"Overview of the Rational Unified Process," identified the four phases of the Waterfall lifecycle: Requirements Elicitation and Analysis, Design, Implementation, and Integration and Test (see Figure 11-1). Each phase has specific activities and skills that are conducted and applied. Although test planning and documentation are typically performed in the earlier phases, the main goal of proving adherence to requirements does not begin until the fourth and last phase—Integration and Test. Although the Waterfall lifecycle process is conceptually clear, in practice this approach can cause problems with the testing process. The main disadvantages of testing in the Waterfall lifecycle are as follows:

- As illustrated in Figure 11-1, less than one-half of the project's time is available for testing. No testing can be done during the Requirements Elicitation and Analysis and Design phases, because no development is performed during these phases. Some unit testing can be done during the Implementation phase as coding progresses. However, no system testing, load testing, or stress testing is possible, because no complete, executable release is available for testing. This means that some of the most meaningful tests that are conducted must be completed entirely within the last, final phase of the lifecycle.

- Because testing occurs at the very end, in one intense "burst," testing personnel have no opportunity to become more proficient with the tools or to easily apply lessons learned to the testing process. They must get all the testing done in one short amount of time.

- The usefulness of some automated testing tools can be reduced depending on how the code is implemented. If the developers use a technique or method to implement the code (particularly the user interface) that is incompatible with the testing tools, this may not be discovered until testing begins in the Integration and Test phase. Because the majority of the code is already implemented, going back and changing the code's design to make it more compatible with the test tools may be impractical. Changing the test tool at this point means that the investment in the first tool, in terms of both training and the cost of the tool itself, is lost.

- Many system-level testing tools produce their greatest Return on Investment (ROI) when tests are run in regression fashion, which is difficult to do in a Waterfall approach.

- The testing occurs during the project's most hectic phase. As discussed in Chapter 2, the discovery of risks in the Waterfall lifecycle model tends to be deferred to the later phases, especially the Integration and Test phase. This is because the final phase is the first time a complete, executable release is created. As a result, testing begins at the same time significant risks are discovered and begin affecting the project. If the risks encountered are serious, the project's focus changes. Instead of getting the system ready to be placed into production, efforts are diverted to solving the problems that crop up during system integration. In fact, it is not unheard of for testing to cease entirely. This is the most stressful time on the project. Team members may even come to view testing as an impediment to project completion. Usually, some testing is done to be able to claim that testing was performed, but the testing is spotty and incomplete at best.

- If the risks discovered during Integration and Test are severe, defects uncovered by testing efforts receive little attention from the developers. It may not be possible to correct all the bugs discovered before release to the users. At that point, the only choices are to delay the project's release or release it before thorough testing is completed. Unfortunately, this situation reflects poorly on the testers, even though they are not at fault. This is an example of a process problem.

- Waterfall-based lifecycles do not provide enough flexibility for early deployments of the product being built to have received significant attention through testing. Early releases are, therefore, likely to contain many defects, even if the project is running on schedule overall.

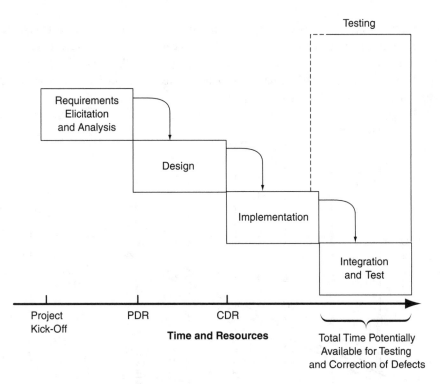

Figure 11-1   Testing in the Waterfall lifecycle model

As a result of these disadvantages, testing on projects using Waterfall lifecycle models often falls short. When a project runs into schedule difficulties, testing is often the first activity to be compromised, partly because of its position in the lifecycle. This is a process problem, not necessarily a weakness of the project personnel, who often work significant overtime to get the project completed on time. When project managers must choose between testing completely and thoroughly versus missing a contractually required completion date, the decision is easy. It's certainly not a good situation, because the failure to get the testing done reflects poorly on the project team. The result may be a project that is delivered on time (or perhaps it is still late despite reducing or eliminating testing) but that performs so poorly it is considered unusable. By the time this discovery is made, the project funding has been consumed. The users of the software then must decide whether they can salvage the project or need to start over.

Testing with Iterative Lifecycle Models

Testing with iterative lifecycle models, such as the Rational Unified Process, occurs during, and especially near the end of, each iteration. As explained in Chapter 2, each iteration produces a specific, tested, executable release that addresses specific risks and requirements. These releases are then baselined in a configuration management tool. As testing progresses, defects are entered into a defect-tracking tool. The defects are prioritized and, in most cases, corrected and retested by the end of that iteration. Some lower-priority defects can be deferred to subsequent iterations. Figure 11-2 illustrates this process. Coding begins in iteration 1. Testing begins during the iteration and concludes by the end of the iteration. Defect correction begins near the end of the iteration. The process continues for each subsequent iteration.

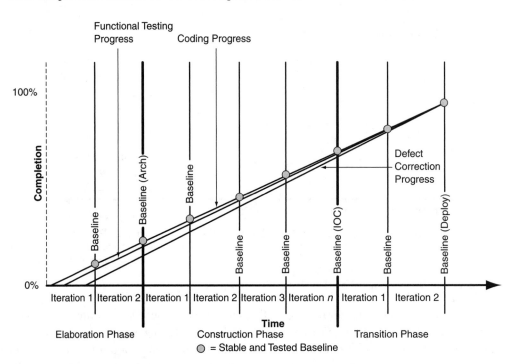

Figure 11-2   Testing and defect correction progress during iterations

Advantages of Testing with Iterative Development

Numerous improvements to the testing process are made possible through the use of iterative development. The following list explains each of these advantages:

- Testing begins much earlier in the project lifecycle compared with traditional Waterfall lifecycle methods. Testing could even begin with the first executable baselined iteration in the Inception phase. In most cases, testing is more likely to begin in the Elaboration phase, since Inception phase iterations are the only ones that may not have an executable release. Testing so early in the lifecycle creates the following benefits:
  - Testing can proceed at a deliberate, sustainable pace. In the first few iterations, the amount of testing is quite light. Each iteration implements a subset of new requirements. Thus, testing for each iteration is composed of functional testing of all the

new requirements implemented in that iteration, plus regression testing on requirements implemented in prior iterations. Because early iterations require little regression testing, testing can easily be accomplished in the iteration's time frame. As the project's lifecycle progresses, testing requires more resources as the amount of functionality that must be regression-tested increases.

- As testing begins and slowly ramps up, the testing personnel gain experience with the tools and testing process. They can then apply this knowledge to the testing of subsequent iterations. They can fine-tune the process and use of the tools to be more effective as a result.

- Early product deployment is easier, because testing begins so early in the project lifecycle. If a decision is made during the project to deploy early, the majority of the functionality developed at any one point has already been tested. The result is a higher-quality product. Or, at the very least, the problems are known, and users can be forewarned.

- As explained in Chapter 2, iterative development lets you develop "riskier" requirements first. Therefore, requirements that represent significant technical risks are implemented and tested in the earlier iterations. Accordingly, this means that requirements that are particularly difficult and complex to implement are afforded a longer period of time to correct the defects discovered.

- Because the testing process is repeated for each iteration, the testing team can give feedback to the development team. The development team can then incorporate the feedback into the process. For example, if the development team is using constructs in implemented code that are incompatible with automated testing tools, this is discovered early, and adjustments are made. If certain types of errors are discovered frequently, the cause can be determined and the process adjusted to prevent them from reoccurring.

Prerequisites for Testing with Iterative Lifecycle Models

Before implementing a testing process on projects that use iterative lifecycle models such as the RUP, the practitioner should be aware of the testing team's needs. These needs do not differ significantly from testing teams on Waterfall lifecycle projects, but some needs take on an increased level of urgency.

Requirements Management

For each iteration, only a subset of the complete set of functional requirements are implemented and tested. Furthermore, at the conclusion of each iteration, while planning the next iteration, the requirements assigned to subsequent iterations may change. Finally, requirements themselves can change. In Waterfall-based processes, from a testing perspective, this is not a problem, because all functional requirements are considered ready for testing all at once—after they are all implemented and integrated to create the complete system. For an iterative lifecycle model, this requires careful tracking of requirements. Because testing begins earlier in the project lifecycle, requirements are more likely to change. Also, it's important to know for each given iteration exactly which requirements have been implemented and which ones have not.

This means that iterative lifecycle models require some sort of automated requirements management tool. Testing personnel need to quickly determine which requirements are implemented for each iteration. They need to know this information as soon as it is available so that test plans and scripts can be finalized. They need to be informed quickly if any requirements change so that they can review any test artifacts to determine how the change affects the artifacts and make any adjustments to the test artifacts if needed.

I also like to use the requirements management tool to track, for each functional requirement, which requirements have been implemented and which have passed testing. As the iterations progress, I often find it helpful to post graphs and charts of the progress in some common area where project members can see them. They can even be used as input to calculate Earned Value if your project uses it.

Configuration Management

It's also vital to have robust configuration management tools and processes in place for testing with iterative lifecycles. This includes workspace management. Because testing and development occur simultaneously, the configuration management tools and processes must do the following easily and intuitively:

- A complete, identifiable baseline of the just-completed build, including all the executables produced, needs to be created and maintained. This provides a stable release for the testing personnel to work with.

- Ongoing new development for the subsequent iteration must be isolated from the previous baseline. Developers need freedom to perform their work without fear of disrupting the test process. The test team must have a stable baseline that is completely frozen from any changes.

- The test team needs to determine exactly which requirements were delivered in the baselined build, as well as which defects (if any) were supposedly fixed in that baselined build.

- Depending on the organization's process, it may be important for developers to make emergency bug fixes to the baselined build without actually changing the baseline itself or mixing in newly developed functionality from the subsequent build. In most configuration management tools, this is called a branching capability. Some organizations choose to simply complete as many tests as possible and fix them late in the iteration.

Change Management

A defect tracking system that is easily accessed by testing personnel and developers must be in place. It should track all information related to the defect, including how it is reproduced. In particular, it should identify the baselined build in which the defect was discovered, along with an estimate, or rating, of the defect's severity.

It's important for the testing personnel to thoroughly document the exact steps needed to reproduce the problem. Screenshots of any error messages or screen settings are also useful. When the testers enter a defect into a defect tracking system, they should word the defect's headline or title carefully. The tester should use the headline or title to capture the essence of the problem and also get the team's attention. You don't want the developers to be unable to reproduce the defect because the description is too vague. This wastes the time of both testing personnel and developers.

Staffing

Testing personnel are needed much earlier on projects that use iterative lifecycle models. However, unlike the "big bang" of the Integration and Test phase of the Waterfall lifecycle, staffing can ramp up more slowly, starting with senior test personnel for planning the testing process. As more iterations are completed, more test personnel can be added as the amount of code to be tested increases. This may be alleviated somewhat through the use of automated testing tools, which are discussed a little later in this chapter.

Because testing begins much earlier in an iterative lifecycle, testing personnel and developers work together closely for much of the project. It is vital that these two groups work well together. It's not uncommon for testing personnel to need assistance from the developers while they are testing an iteration. This informal communication is good and should be encouraged. However, the testing personnel need to remember that the developers are on fairly tight deadlines as they work to produce the next iteration.

Feedback for the Iteration Planning Process

As the testing results become available for a given iteration, the project manager should examine the defect reports that are available from the testing. As part of planning the iterations, the project manager should allow some time to correct bugs as well as test and implement another subset of the requirements. It may be unrealistic to expect to have enough resources to fix every bug. In that case, the severity rating on each defect report can be used to prioritize which ones will receive attention in the next iteration. Maintaining a "queue" of the remainder of the defects can be useful if a developer finishes his work for an iteration early, or an extra person becomes available. This keeps everyone busy and uses staff more efficiently. It also reduces or eliminates an extensive "cleanup" or defect correction activity later in the project lifecycle. Any defects that did not receive attention due to time constraints should be documented in the product's release notes. Although defects are undesirable, the fact that they are documented tells the customer that you've already tested the product and are at least aware of them.

To illustrate this process, consider Figure 11-2, shown earlier. During iteration 1, a build becomes available containing functionality that can be tested. The testing begins, and defect reports are submitted into a tracking tool. Toward the end of iteration 1, defects are prioritized, and correction and retesting begin. Any defects not corrected are examined, prioritized, and scheduled for correction in the next iteration. In the next and subsequent iterations, the process repeats until the end of the project.

The Different Types of Testing

There are nearly as many ways to test software as there are ways to develop it. In an ideal world, developers would write perfect code, and testing would be unnecessary. Because the technology does not yet exist to write error-free code, you must test carefully to discover and repair the defects found before the customer discovers them.

Given that you cannot produce error-free code, the goal of testing is to catch as many defects as possible. Of course, your resources are finite. Even with nearly unlimited time and resources, it is nearly impossible to exercise a system to the point where you can guarantee that all bugs are removed from it. But for most projects, you cannot allocate that many resources to testing (see Figure 11-3). The best you can do is obtain the best testing coverage possible and leverage the resources available in the most effective way possible. Customers are willing to accept some level of defects if the overall product is of an acceptable quality level.

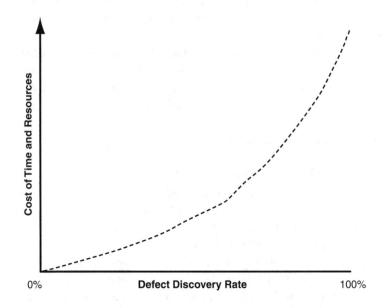

Figure 11-3   Resources and defect discovery rates

The key to a successful testing effort is determining a point on the curve illustrated in Figure 11-3 that is acceptable to both the customer and end users and that can be accommodated by the number of people available for testing on the project.

To help identify this point on the curve, it is important to review the project requirements (especially the supplemental requirements). The Vision Statement may also have clues as to the customer's expectations. Is this system mission-critical? Will the safety of lives and property depend on the system's functioning correctly? If so, you will no doubt want to devote considerably more resources to the testing effort than if the system had none of these qualities.

The following sections cover the different types of testing that are common on outsourced projects. The advantages and disadvantages of each type are discussed. For projects that have severe resource constraints, types of testing that are particularly economical (in terms of resources expended per defect found) are identified.

Functional Testing

Functional testing is the most common type of testing. It is the process of verifying that the product meets its functional requirements. If a project performs only one type of testing, it is probably functional testing. Functional testing is often used to prove to a customer that the system meets all the functional requirements. After a system is delivered to the customer, some customers simply want to see all the functional tests executed. A witness, usually part of the customer organization, signs off after agreeing that the tests have passed. Functional testing performed in this scenario is generally called acceptance testing.

With iterative development, functional testing consists of testing all the newly implemented requirements, plus the requirements previously tested on earlier iterations. As more iterations are completed, the number of previously tested requirements grows as more and more of the system is progressively implemented. It is necessary to retest these requirements. As the code base changes and new code is added, it is quite possible that previously working functionality may cease working. The process of retesting previously tested requirements is known as regression testing. Functional testing is an arduous task when performed manually. Systems with extensive user interfaces might need hundreds of tests. Each test may contain dozens of steps that must be followed in the correct order. As a result, the process can be error-prone and time-consuming.

Automated Functional Testing

A number of companies offer automated functional testing tools. Most of these tools are of the capture-replay variety. These tools record all mouse movements, mouse clicks, keystrokes, and so on. They can start an application, perform the necessary steps in the correct order, compare the application's response with the expected results, and produce an error log for any responses from the application under test that are not equivalent to the expected results. This provides an obvious increase in productivity and reduces the number of manual steps that have to be performed.

Careful consideration should occur before you invest in automated testing tools. Although the advantages are real, preparing a suite of automated tests takes more time than preparing a suite of manual tests. In a Waterfall lifecycle model, where the tests are performed once, or perhaps twice, the extra time involved in creating automated tests may not be recouped. It may make more sense in these situations to use manual tests.

Iterative development and automated functional testing are an excellent match. Because regression tests on previously tested functionality are performed at the conclusion of each iteration, there is a greater chance that the upfront investment in developing the automated scripts will be advantageous in the long run.

Precautions to Follow When Considering Automated Testing

Although advances in test tool technology have been tremendously useful, you should follow some precautions before making the investment:

- Try before you buy! Each vendor's tool uses different techniques to recognize graphical user interface (GUI) objects on the screen. Sometimes, the constructs and methods used on a specific user interface are incompatible with a specific tool. If you discover this too late, you may have invested in tools that are essentially useless.

- Take the time to understand how the vendor recognizes the GUI objects on the screen. Some tools are more resilient to minor changes in the user interface than others. It should not be necessary to record a new automated test script simply because the color or position of an existing button widget changes on the screen. Otherwise, you may lose a significant amount of time if the user interfaces change from release to release.

- Don't try to automate everything. Some tests simply lend themselves better to manual testing. There is nothing wrong with using a combination of manual and automated tests to test a release.

- Automated test tools are not a substitute for sound test planning and management. Make sure that the results of each test run are baselined along with the version of the code under test. All defect reports should clearly indicate the version of the code under test.

Unit Testing

Until recently, I was not a big fan of unit testing. Setting up unit tests is generally very time-consuming and tedious. Most programming languages have individual modular routines that are considered by themselves for unit testing. Some languages call them functions; others call them procedures, methods, or subroutines. Regardless, a **unit** is the smallest amount of code that performs a specific purpose. Because it is a small segment of code, it may have no user interface, or it may not perform any action externally visible to an end user.

Developers generally are the ones who perform unit tests. The reason is that individual units often require additional code to be written as test "drivers." These routines must be written, and appropriate values need to be determined to pass to the unit under test. When the unit is tested, the response from the unit under test must be determined and compared to the expected result.

As a result of the additional code that must be written, unit testing takes longer, on average, per defect found. In addition, unit tests require the developer to try to identify input values that will adequately test the unit. Although there are always exceptions, developers as a group are not highly motivated to properly perform unit tests.

Recently, a new generation of automated unit test tools has appeared in the marketplace, such as those from Agitar. These new tools can exercise code in an automated fashion, freeing the developer from having to write test drivers and running the tests manually. If your project can acquire these new testing tools, they will elevate unit testing on a project to an entirely new level. Without them, and especially if you have very limited time, a project may be better off investing more time in the other types of testing.

Reliability Testing

Some types of errors lurking in code cannot be caught through traditional functional or unit-testing techniques. The most common examples are memory leaks and similar types of storage mismanagement. When these errors are contained in developed code, they may not occur until the system has been running for many hours. Or the error might occur only when a certain sequence of functionality is used.

Although these types of errors are less common than simple functional errors, they are serious when they do occur, for the following reasons:

- They do not occur consistently. Because the errors are related to memory, many variables create the conditions that cause the error to occur. Accordingly, the error does not appear to occur at the same point in time. For example, it could depend on how long the application has been running, or how loaded the system was running other applications at the time the error occurred.

- As a consequence of the number of variables involved, the error may not be reproducible in the development environment.

- When the error is reproduced, the cause is difficult to isolate. The portion of code causing the memory leak is probably not the area where the application is failing. In other words, because of memory corruption or excessive memory consumption, the error may manifest itself in some innocuous section of code.

These types of errors are also severe because the system is probably unusable when the error occurs. The application will probably crash or present nonsensical errors randomly. It may take a long time for the developers to understand and correct the cause. As a result, these errors undermine the user's confidence in the system. If the system is mission-critical or involves the safety of lives or property, the customer may consider the entire system unacceptable.

Tools to the Rescue

Fortunately, some excellent tools are available to detect these types of errors. Perhaps the most commonly known tool is Purify, marketed by IBM/Rational, but others exist as well.

Because these tools require an intimate knowledge of the code under test, the developers, instead of the testing personnel, are the appropriate ones to use them. Many development organizations require use of these tools as part of the unit testing process. The result is an application that is more stable and less likely to suffer from unexplainable crashes.

Performance/Stress Testing

Many systems have supplemental requirements of this form: "The system shall support a concurrent load of 500 users while maintaining a response time of less than 2 seconds." How can you determine that a system under development meets this requirement? Even if you are convinced that your system can meet the requirement, how can you advise the customer what minimum system configuration (such as CPU speed and memory) is needed to meet the requirement? How many users above the 500 required could the system support before the response time exceeds 2 seconds?

The answer is to perform formal load and stress testing. Ironically, this kind of testing seems to be the most neglected type of testing today. This is unfortunate, because if the system fails to meet the requirement, the solution can be expensive. Customers should be more assertive and ask their contractor to prove it can support the required load, just as they would for any functional requirement. On the other hand, contractors should be more diligent and test systems with these kinds of requirements before formal delivery to the customer.

Until a few years ago, performance and stress testing was done by attempting to have a large group of people interact with the system and extrapolating the results to the required number of users. However, this approach has several problems:

- System performance and response time are not linear with respect to the number of users interacting with the system. In other words, extrapolating system performance based on only a few users is inaccurate.

- The logistics needed to set up a representative number of users are difficult at best. Therefore, the tests cannot be repeated on demand, such as after making a change to the system. Significant lead time would be needed to obtain the required number of users.

- The results from testing in these scenarios are not easily repeatable, because the users will not interact with the system in exactly the same way, or with the same timing each time they run through the tests.

- When a performance problem is found, it is difficult to narrow it down further.

Tools to the Rescue—Again

A number of vendors, in particular Mercury Interactive and IBM Rational, have developed tools to simulate multiuser loads very efficiently. The catch is that most vendors price their tools according to how many users are needed in the simulation. If you are building a single system that has to support 5,000 users, the cost of the tool may be too high for a single project to afford. Companies that build many systems can spread the costs among several projects or treat the purchase as a capital investment, so the cost is incorporated in the corporate overhead. One alternative is vendors that offer testing services, where you effectively rent the tools and testing personnel who are experienced with the tools. They perform a set of test runs and provide the results for a fee.

If your project is fortunate enough to have access to these load and stress testing tools, keep in mind the following points when planning a load/stress/performance testing effort:

- Understand exactly what the performance requirements are when designing the tests. For example, in the sample requirement from the preceding section, the system must support 500 users and have a response time of 2 seconds. What exactly should these 500 users be doing? Should all 500 users be actively interacting with the system, or merely logged on? Exactly how is the response time measured? This is an example of a vague requirement, although it is a typical one. It will require further analysis to define the parameters for testing.

- Further discussion with end users may be needed to identify typical and peak loading periods. Does everyone perform a certain function with the system at a particular time of day? Is usage at a peak during other periods, such as at the end of a quarter or calendar year? Or is usage completely random? The performance tools let you design certain scenarios that simulate real usage.

- One issue that is frequently overlooked when planning for automated load testing tools is the hardware required to generate the load against the system under test. If you want to simulate the load of 500 simultaneous users, you will need more than a single desktop PC. In fact, you may need multiple servers to generate the load. This is in addition to the servers required to run the system under test.

- Although costly, the most realistic performance and load tests are run on the same kind of hardware that the production system will ultimately run on. Without this, you are only guessing at how the system will perform when it does get on the production hardware.

- Don't forget to survey the IT environment where the system will ultimately be located upon delivery. Network infrastructure can have significant impact on system performance. If the system undergoes testing when the servers are located on a network with 1 Gbps bandwidth or a lightly loaded 100 Mbps bandwidth, the system will perform noticeably better than it would located in a heavily loaded 100 Mbps network.

Another advantage of performance testing tools is the ability to help identify performance bottlenecks. Figure 11-4 shows the hardware architecture for a Web-based system. Most load testing tools can record and play back the traffic between any two tiers of the system. Initially, in a system such as the one shown in Figure 11-4, the network traffic caused by interaction with the user interface is captured and played back to simulate the load of multiple end users. This corresponds to load injection point 3 in Figure 11-4. If the performance test reveals a problem, the network traffic can be recorded and played back at load injection point 2 (for the application server) or load injection point 1 (for the database server). If playing back the traffic recorded at injection point 1 shows markedly improved performance, there is an excellent chance that the performance problem is caused by either the application server or the Web server. Recording and playing back the traffic can then narrow the performance problem to the tier causing the problem. At that point, you may be able to use code-profiling tools to find the specific code module causing the problem.

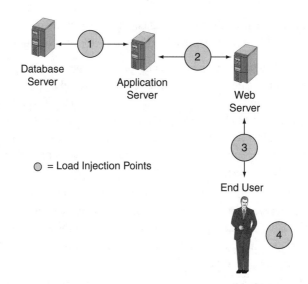

Figure 11-4   Where is the bottleneck?

Other Types of Testing

Other types of testing cannot be automated. One example is usability testing. For some projects, it may not be possible to understand the collective skill set of all the system's potential users. An example is a Commercial Off-The-Shelf (COTS) system or a product for the retail environment. For these types of products, particularly high-volume products, usability testing may be indicated. This might consist of randomly selected users placed in a room while being observed (or even filmed) while attempting to use the software. When the users experience difficulty figuring out how to interact with the system, it may be because the system is not intuitive. Correcting these types of problems beforehand can eliminate many calls for support after the system is deployed.

Other Best Practices for Testing

Several best practices, when combined with iterative development, will help achieve optimal results from testing. Note that most of these best practices are applicable regardless of the lifecycle model being used.

Involve Testing Expertise During Requirements Elicitation

Earlier, this chapter explained how iterative development enables testing earlier in the project lifecycle. Even more benefits can be realized by involving testing expertise during the requirements elicitation activity. Obtaining the perspective of an experienced tester during requirements elicitation, before the requirements are finalized, helps the project in a number of ways. A tester can examine the requirements and do the following:

- Is the requirement testable? Functional requirements (even supplemental ones) should be reviewed by someone with experience and expertise in testing. If the requirement is not easily tested, it will be difficult to prove that it is working. For example, a requirement that states "The system must be available 24 hours a day, 365 days a year" would take a full year to prove. If the requirement is written as a percentage of availability, such as "The system shall be available for use 99% of the time," it can be measured for short periods and extrapolated to longer periods.

- Is the requirement subject to multiple interpretations? Consider the requirement from earlier in this chapter: "The system shall support a concurrent load of 500 users while maintaining a response time of less than 2 seconds." This requirement could be interpreted multiple ways. Viewed conservatively, you could interpret a "concurrent load of 500 users" as 500 users logging in and then idling. Viewed aggressively, you could interpret it as 500 users simultaneously performing a computationally intense function. A more plausible scenario might be as follows: "Out of 500 users, 10% will be logging in, 20% will be performing search functions, 10% will be logging out, 30% will be running reports, 20% will be browsing items, and 10% will be idle." Even this is a little vague; for example, what reports will 30% of the users be running? The point is to clearly and succinctly define the goal. Many requirements are written or stated by users who do not have expertise in this area, so they need guidance. This is one of the ways testers can add value early.

- Getting testers involved in the requirements early gives them a "sneak preview" of what they need to test so that they can generate test ideas that will help them implement tests more rapidly as releases begin being produced.

Keep Testing Staff in the Loop

A common complaint heard from testing personnel involves changes to requirements and the project in general. As test planning takes shape, many artifacts are created that are tied to the requirements. If the requirements change, the artifacts tied to those requirements may need to change as well. Therefore, make sure that testing personnel are aware of any changes to requirements. If you are using an automated requirements management tool, this will be easier.

Replicate the Production Environment

Another important aspect of proper testing involves testing in an environment that mimics the production environment as closely as possible. If possible, the best arrangement is to test in the exact environment, including using the same machines, operating system, networking environment, and so on that will be used when the system is in production. In most cases, this is probably not possible. Therefore, a test environment must be created. It should be physically separate from the machines on which development is performed. It also must be carefully controlled to ensure that no changes to the operating system, hardware configuration, and so on, are made without being carefully documented.

Even if you believe you have created a testing environment that duplicates every possible aspect of the operational environment, you will probably find something that was overlooked when the system is placed into production. For this reason, it is a best practice to schedule some time for final testing on the actual operational environment before the new system is placed into production.

Testing Is Part of the Delivered Product

The customer that accepts delivery of the product should be assured that the product has been tested to meet its requirements. For requirements that have defects outstanding, these defects should be listed in the product's release notes. A process for reporting any new defects should be defined and communicated to the customer.

Final Thoughts and Philosophies on Staffing for the Testing Discipline

When I entered the fascinating world of software development years ago, I observed certain attitudes related to testing that I considered puzzling. Testing as a discipline was considered to have less status and importance than development. It was considered a stepping-stone to "more important" activities, such as coding. It was also where junior personnel aspiring to be developers and coders began their careers. This attitude must change.

I suspect that this attitude originated in earlier years when the software testing discipline was in its infancy and few tools or formal techniques were available. Most testing consisted of running the software and observing the output for correct results. Furthermore, software systems as a whole were far less complex and complicated than they are now. Back then, testers simply did not need much knowledge or skill.

This is no longer the case. Some systems support tens of thousands of users. Other systems are safety-critical, or perhaps downtime can cost thousands of dollars per minute. The consequences of failure are much higher.

At the same time, the complexity of software systems has grown exponentially. We have certainly moved far beyond the point where testers can merely observe the system's behavior for correct results. Today's testing tools are very sophisticated and require much knowledge, skill, and training to properly deploy and use. Some tools mentioned earlier in this chapter, such as code profiling tools, require a working knowledge of the underlying code to properly interpret the results. Some projects compensate for this by having the developers test their own code. Although this may make sense in some cases, the workload on most developers and the constant pressure to be productive runs counter to thorough and complete testing by the developers themselves. In addition to tools available for testing, a number of scripting languages, such as Perl, VBScript, and JavaScript, aid in the testing effort. These are requisite skills for modern testers.

I consider the best testing groups to be staffed by people who have the talent and skill to be developers, yet they choose to be testers. They do not view testing as a stepping-stone to other pursuits. Instead, these professionals recognize the importance of the testing discipline and the value a strong testing effort can bring to a project. These types of testers not only find the less obvious problems in a product, but they also can suggest solutions and work closely with the development team to help prevent and solve these problems. They can also add value in a proactive manner, working with the requirements team to define requirements that are easily testable and verifiable.

Fortunately, testing is increasingly being recognized as a key discipline on projects. As a result, testing is beginning to attract highly talented engineers. Enlightened companies seek out these individuals and compensate them accordingly.

Some companies separate testing and quality assurance from product development. The testing and quality assurance groups report to a different person in the organization's management chain. I consider this a wise strategy, because it reduces the chance of the testing and quality assurance group being forced to approve a release simply to meet a deadline. It also ensures that the importance of testing does not take a backseat to development.

What if a Separate Team, Perhaps Offshore, Performs the Testing?

On some large projects, particularly government projects, a different team performs testing, possibly under a separate contract. Other projects, such as some projects in the commercial domain, may outsource testing to an offshore company. The tactics for managing these two situations are quite similar.

The first tactic is to determine how the test team will become fluent and comfortable with the concept of the system. Much as with requirements elicitation, this cannot be done by simply supplying manuals and documents. The test team must understand the problem domain itself and then understand how the system to be tested solves a specific issue in the problem domain. This process is similar to the process undertaken by the development team. If possible, arrange for members of the test team to meet with selected end users of the new system, as well as members of the development team. After they understand the customer and the problem domain (and have had time to digest this information), they should view demonstrations of any proof of concept.

The second tactic is to incorporate the use of a technique in which testing of a given iteration occurs after it is delivered. On small- to medium-sized projects where the test team is colocated with the development team, an iteration should be tested during the iteration. This requires close collaboration between the test team and the development team. When testing is outsourced to a team separated by distance, this may not be practical. Instead, a technique sometimes called **pipelining** can be used. With pipelining, the release produced by an iteration is delivered to the testing team at the iteration's conclusion. Functional and performance testing is then performed by the test team while the development team begins developing the next iteration. The amount of time allocated for the test team to complete its testing should be kept the same as the length of the iteration used by the development team. Thus, when the development team completes an iteration and delivers its release, the testing team completes its testing of the previous iteration and has reported all its results. This process is illustrated in Figure 11-5.

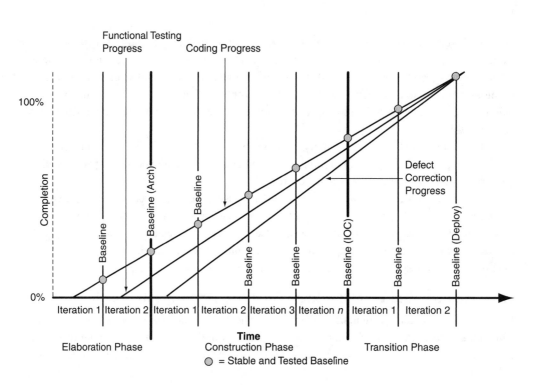

Figure 11-5   Testing progress in a "pipelined" process

For this to work efficiently, consider the following:

- Make sure that the test team has seen demonstrations and is comfortable with how the product works before they begin testing.

- Along with the release, the test team should receive an updated list of requirements, indicating which new requirements are implemented with the newly delivered release.

- A list of any bugs reported on earlier releases that are corrected in the new release should be furnished.

- To make reporting of bugs and to track status of bugs more efficiently, the test team and development team should have access to the same repository used to track this information. This suggests the use of a Web-enabled bug-tracking tool.

Provided that the test team is not left to fend for themselves in a vacuum and the practices here are employed, testing by a separate team can work effectively.

Testing Efforts Gone Awry

Unfortunately, I have been witness to many ineffective testing regimes. Worse, I have seen some testing efforts that were a complete waste of time and resources. Consider the following scenarios. Your organization will not do these things, right?

Little or No Performance/Load/Stress Testing

For any project with a requirement to support a community of users, you should have some method of proving that the system can meet the requirement. As mentioned earlier, customers should insist on seeing proof that the system can meet these requirements. I actually witnessed a group that provided this "proof" by simply having two users manually access the system simultaneously and comparing the response times with those when only one user used the system. Then, they extrapolated the results to hundreds of users, claiming this proved that the system could handle the required load. This is at best naive and at worst just plain wrong. The relationship between system response times when plotted against the number of users is seldom linear. It may be linear *part* of the time and then grow exponentially after the number of users reaches a certain point.

Succumbing to Pressure

Some organizations, when pressured by deadlines, still deliver a system, regardless of the test results. This is the "throw it over the wall" strategy. It may satisfy a short-term deadline, but in the long run, it seldom works. This often happens when the testers and quality assurance personnel report to the same managers as the development organization does. Tell the customer that you have completed development (assuming you have) but that your testing and quality assurance organization has identified issues that need to be corrected before delivery. Most reasonable customers, although perhaps initially upset, will ultimately respond positively. If you *must* deliver a system with known issues, at least document the issues and indicate that they are already known. This is better than simply hoping the customer will not find them.

Another form of succumbing to pressure is for the development organization to release a product with little or no testing. This is usually associated with testing in a Waterfall lifecycle model, because nearly all testing is performed at the tail end of the development lifecycle. When development and integration fall behind schedule, testing is severely curtailed or eliminated to meet the final deadline. Adopting an iterative lifecycle process can help prevent this.

Relying on Developers for All Testing

This is seldom a wise strategy. Most developers do not like to perform testing—that's why many of them became developers in the first place. Furthermore, developers' natural response to schedule pressure is to skimp on testing and get the development done first. Furthermore, you lose the independent perspective that formal testing provides. Without a second set of eyes looking at the problem, bugs can slip through the cracks.

Ineffective Third-Party Testing

Some customers believe they can obtain independent, unbiased results by having a third party handle testing. In fact, some contractors specialize in these and related activities, known as Independent Validation and Verification (IV&V). Although this may provide the customer with an added level of assurance, they must remember that these third parties will require that a complete and extensive set of documentation be delivered to them long before testing begins. If this third-party contractor is offshore, the need for this documentation is even more important. Here are some examples of the documentation that would be needed:

- Installation and configuration documentation
- User manuals and instructions
- The complete set of requirements, including functional and supplemental requirements
- The project's vision document, known in some projects as a Concept of Operations document
- Design documentation

The contractor also needs to replicate the production environment and, therefore, needs instances of the hardware and software to create the testing environment. Make sure the IV&V contractor has these and any other resources it needs to be successful.

Summary

A successful testing effort is the "project within the project." It involves much planning, coordination, and talent. The result can increase the chances of success and customer satisfaction. The following are the major points from this chapter:

- Understand the customer's expectations to help guide you where to focus testing efforts. On any project, with the proliferation of testing tools and techniques, you cannot do it all. You must focus on the areas of most importance to the customer.
- Any enterprise-wide system that must support many users needs some method of proving that the system can support the required load. Testing this for the first time after system delivery is not a valid success strategy.
- Automated load testing tools are expensive to acquire. The project manager needs some resourcefulness to ensure that the project has these tools or services available.
- Involve individuals who have test expertise early in the lifecycle, and put them in a position where they can influence the writing of requirements.
- Test teams no longer work in a vacuum. They collaborate heavily with developers, configuration managers, quality assurance, and requirements analysts. Staff the team with testing personnel who can work well in a team environment.
- Be sure to try test tools in the specific environment before committing to purchase.
- Try to staff the testing team with people who recognize and believe in the importance of thorough testing.
- Consider adjusting development methods and techniques as needed to ensure compatibility with automated test tools.

What's Next?

The next chapter assumes that you've reached the end of the Construction phase and that an Initial Operational Capability (IOC) has been created. It's time to shift into the Transition phase of the Rational Unified Process. The next chapter covers many of the activities that are common in the Transition phase, including data migration, user acceptance testing, and other activities performed by the development team.

CHAPTER 12

Transitioning a System into Service

Your project team has been working hard for months, perhaps even years, and the system under development is taking shape. Perhaps, you've even demonstrated some releases to your customer, which have been well received. As you approach the end of the Construction phase, the Initial Operational Capability (IOC) milestone seems easily within your grasp.

This is definitely a major achievement from the perspective of the development team. But from the perspective of the user, the work is far from finished. Indeed, several important tasks remain as the project enters the Transition phase. This chapter discusses the major tasks that receive attention in the Transition phase. It begins by discussing staffing considerations. Another activity may be a partial deployment of the IOC. The chapter continues with the kinds of development tasks that are typically performed during the Transition phase. This includes data migration, which is often a major task when the new system replaces a legacy system. We will discuss managing end-user expectations at this critical point in the project lifecycle. This involves leveraging the relationships developed during requirements elicitation to ease the system into production. Finally, training of end users is discussed.

Staffing Considerations in the Transition Phase

As a project enters the Transition phase, all the major challenges and risks on the project have been met and resolved. The project's staffing needs to begin to decline, particularly for developers. Developers are an interesting group. They often thrive on solving difficult technical challenges. As the Transition phase begins, the most challenging tasks have already been accomplished. The tasks that remain, while no less important to the project's success, are not the serious technical challenges many developers enjoy. It is not surprising that some of the development team have begun thinking about their next project by this time. As a project manager, your goal is to recognize this and to begin destaffing the project in the least-disruptive way possible. The project must still retain the resources it needs to accomplish the remaining tasks.

A development team, particularly on a project that has been conducted for many months, or even years, is much like a family. Friendships often develop between team members. Even for the people who prefer to remain on the project, observing the group's dissolution is an unsettling experience. Although the team will still be hard at work, the team members planning to remain will closely monitor the placement of the people who leave. Project managers should consider the following points:

- Evaluate the remaining tasks, and determine the people best suited for accomplishing these tasks. Few developers, for example, enjoy writing documentation and installation scripts, but some are more amenable to it than others. Those chosen to remain should be detail-oriented and have a record of running tasks through to completion.

- Help reassure the team personnel remaining that they will be taken care of when it is time for them to leave the project. Do everything you can to place the earlier departures from the team in opportunities that are desirable to them. Without this extra effort, the entire team will quickly realize they are on their own when it comes to finding their next opportunity. This means everyone will quickly begin seeking other opportunities, even the people you prefer to remain to finish the various tasks. If your team has internal recruiters or a Human Resources department, work with them to find other opportunities. Be sure to follow through on any promises you made to the team members who remain.

- If projects at your company have a track record of "mass exodus" before completion, or if no one on the team relishes performing the remaining tasks, consider completion bonuses for the team. Team members who remain until the project manager determines that their work is complete receive a predetermined bonus. If someone leaves the project early due to events beyond her control, such as the management moving her to another project earlier than expected, she can receive a prorated bonus for the amount of time she remained.

- After the team is resized and the early departures take place, recognize that the remaining team members will experience a sense of loss. Remember to motivate and reassure the remaining team appropriately. One idea is to state the importance of the work in the Transition phase. Although the work remaining may not be the most technically challenging, from the user's perspective the work performed in the Transition phase plays a key role in shaping how the users view the project's success. If the customer cannot easily install the product, understand the user manual, or see their change requests reflected in the product, the work will be perceived negatively. All the technical challenges solved in the product's architecture or code are not directly visible to the users, and, therefore, the quality of that work is imperceptible. Placing the finishing touches on the product ensures that the product is well received by its end users.

After you address the staffing needs in the Transition phase, you can turn your full attention to the remaining tasks.

Project Tasks in the Transition Phase

As the project heads into the Transition phase, a number of development tasks remain. These include deploying the IOC, online help, installation scripts, final change requests, and data migration. Other tasks, such as training and acceptance testing, remain as well. I will discuss each of these separately.

Deploying the IOC

When the IOC milestone is reached and the Transition phase begins, the goal is to make the deployment of the new system as painless and smooth as possible. A major risk-reduction activity during the Transition phase is an **early deployment** of the IOC. This is often called a beta release. The following summarizes the goals and purposes of deploying a beta release:

- The primary purpose of early deployment is risk reduction. Early deployment provides the opportunity to discover problems that may not be found in the development environment. Issues relating to the network environment, operating system differences, hardware differences, and so on are just some of the variables encountered when moving from one environment to another. Early deployment means early detection of unexpected problems, which lets you detect and correct the problem before users depend on the system for their work.

- Early deployment allows the users to gain experience and familiarity with the system, which increases the likelihood of user acceptance.

- Early deployment permits the users to verify that the system meets their functional needs. If it is discovered that certain functionality is incorrect or missing, some time is still available to correct it before the system is placed into full production.

Although these are clearly important advantages, early deployment as a beta release does present some risks. If you plan an early deployment, be careful to monitor and plan to mitigate the following risks:

- The release must be used and exercised. Since early deployments are not "full" deployments, meaning the users do not yet depend on the product for their jobs, the users may not have a sense of urgency to try the system. In other words, using the system requires a time commitment from the users. To mitigate this risk, you should select a designated pool of interested users, which represents a subset of the user community, to participate in the testing. Preferably, they should be users who have expressed continued interest in the project and who together will exercise most of the product's functionality. The contractor should meet with the outsourcing organization's management and stress the importance of the early deployment as a risk-reduction activity that is vital to a smooth transition to production status. The customer should make sure the users have time allocated in their schedules for this activity.

- The customer may not understand and appreciate the importance of the early deployment. Be sure to explain the purpose and goals of the testing. The focus should be on finding last-minute bugs and to be sure the existing requirements have been interpreted correctly.

- Be sure to document and present to the users any functionality that is not yet implemented, such as help files and installation scripts. You do not want the customer to spend time looking for functionality that is known to be missing. It is also important to set their expectations up front by informing them of any features not yet ready.

- One risk that occasionally surfaces is users getting carried away and flooding the project team with change requests. These need to be evaluated carefully. Certainly, if the change requests pertain to valid bugs in the system, they should be corrected as soon as possible. But if the change requests are actually enhancement requests or new requirement requests, try to resist implementing them at this time unless they are absolutely required.

- Try to avoid risking production data during the early deployment. Until proper system behavior is proven, don't run the risk of disrupting the customer's business until the system is ready for full production. This may mean if the new system is replacing a legacy system, both systems will need to run in parallel for a time, until people gain confidence in the new system. Of course, if a separate copy of the production data were available, this would be ideal, as long as the users are aware that any permanent changes should still be made in the legacy system. Use of a separate copy of the legacy data should increase interest in using the early deployment, because users will be better able to observe the system behavior using data with which they are familiar.

Despite the challenges, early deployment testing is an important risk-reduction activity that should be performed.

Online Help

The first step in producing online help is to examine your system's requirements. Do the requirements specifically ask for online help? If so, what do they state? Even if you have no requirements for online help, the reality is that most users expect some form of online help to guide them in their usage of the system. Hopefully, the analysts on the project have uncovered and documented these requirements. Accordingly, the creation of online help would then be scheduled for an iteration in the Transition phase.

The Iteration phase is not the appropriate place to discover for the first time the requirements for online help. Although "online help" sounds simple enough, it can range from simply making an online copy of a user manual available from the product's user interface, to a fully functional tutorial involving sample exercises and canned demonstrations illustrating how the user interacts with and uses the product. Creating online help can, therefore, be a major task and should be planned in an iteration just like other major portions of functionality. Remember that online help is likely to be heavily used initially, until the end users become comfortable using the product. As discussed previously, this feature is highly visible to end users and will shape their experience with the product.

Installation Scripts

Installation scripts are another example of a task that is conceptually simple yet can be extremely complex to implement. Here are some considerations for determining how to structure the installation procedures:

- Who will be installing the product? If the product is a Web-based enterprise system, chances are the system administrators will perform the installation. The installation may be a one-time event, or it may take place only occasionally. If the system is a client/server-based system, the product may need to be installed by each client. If this is the case, the installation may be performed by less-knowledgeable end users, and the installation process will be repeated frequently. In the former case, it may be reasonable to make the installation less automated and involve some manual steps. In the latter case, this may be totally unacceptable. The installation process for system administrators could be a relatively simple installation procedure involving copying files into place. The installation process for client users may have to be completely automated.

- For installation procedures that are performed frequently, such as for client/server systems, what is the consistency of the end-user environment? For example, will all clients have the same kind of PC, with the same operating system, or will there be a lot of variation in the environment from client to client? If there is a lot of variation, the installation procedure should check whether the PC has enough disk space, memory, and processor speed before proceeding with the installation. Also, the installation procedure itself may have to vary, depending on the client's exact version of the operating system.

- It is strongly recommended for client workstation installations that any automated installation scripts and procedures be tested on several typical client machines in the actual environment. An infinite number of unknowns relate to the environment and are difficult to discover or anticipate. Testing in the actual environment is the only way to ensure proper operation.

Change Requests

Up until the Transition phase, the team has focused primarily on high-priority change requests. This means that lower-priority change requests, such as typographical errors and minor formatting changes on the user interface, have been accumulating. The Transition phase is the time to complete as many of these lower-priority requests as possible. These change requests are often items very visible to end users. An investment of time to correct these change requests will pay dividends in increased customer satisfaction.

Exercise caution in expending resources on change requests involving requirements that significantly alter the system's behavior or its business rules. Chances are when the system is fielded for the first time, there may be high-priority change requests, which are much higher in importance. The focus in Transition should be to make the system rollout as successful as possible, which means that a stable, bug-free release is the goal.

Data Migration

Data migration is another example of a task that is conceptually simple but that in practice is complex and tedious. Simply stated, the purpose of data migration is to move data that currently resides in legacy systems into a new system. In some cases, more than one legacy system may exist, such as when a newly developed system replaces multiple legacy systems. In most cases, this data represents core business knowledge or information that must be preserved. Often, this data represents an asset that has been built and accumulated over many years. As a consequence, the organization places a very high value on this data, and its integrity must be preserved when it is migrated to the new system.

Overview of the Steps in Migrating Data

Data migration involves a series of steps. These are summarized next and in Figure 12-1, followed by a detailed discussion of each step.

1. The data migration process is planned and prepared.

2. The legacy systems (the source of the data being migrated) must be shut down so that the data does not change during the migration. As a result, neither the legacy systems nor the new system can be used during this process. Therefore, data migration usually occurs over weekends or holidays.

3. The data is extracted, or exported, from the legacy system. The data is stored in files so that it can be viewed and possibly edited.

4. The data is examined to search for corrupt data and duplicate data and to make corrections to the data. This is known as **data cleansing**.

5. The data is analyzed to determine to which fields in the new destination system the data should be mapped.

6. Scripts are written to automate the transfer of the legacy data from the extracted, cleansed files into the destination database.

7. Testing is performed to verify the accuracy of the data migration process.

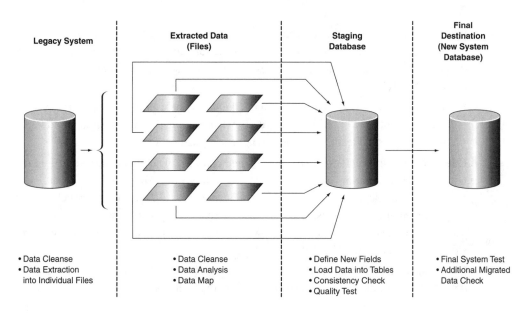

Figure 12-1 Overview of data migration steps

Details of Data Migration Steps

As just mentioned, data migration is a tedious process. The key to success in a data migration effort is careful planning and starting long before the "official" migration begins. Because of the importance of this activity, I will discuss each step in detail.

Planning a Successful Data Migration Effort

Data migration by itself is a significant project. Like any other project, it requires resources, careful planning, and the setting of client expectations. It also involves significant risks that must be mitigated. The following are important points to consider when planning a data migration effort:

- Although the steps just listed are accurate, it is vital that the planning begin during the project's Inception phase. "Planning" includes conducting at least one, and possibly several, trial runs of analyzing and migrating the data before placing the new system into production with the migrated data. This is an important risk-reduction exercise that must not be omitted. I have yet to see a data migration effort proceed without unexpected issues arising. In most cases, these issues were unforeseen and would not have been discovered without conducting trial migration efforts.

- In general, the schedule of data migration proceeds in parallel with the effort to develop the new system. But there are some points where data migration can help you develop the new system. For example, analyzing the legacy data may lead you to discover aspects of functionality not identified in the new system. For example, if a field of data in the cleansed data set cannot be mapped to a field maintained by the new system, functionality is missing in the new system. Either the functionality should be analyzed and developed in the new system, or the extraneous data should be eliminated from the cleansed data set.

- Results from successful trial runs of migrated data can be useful to test the new system with actual data that will ultimately be used when the system is placed into production. This can save the test team time when creating sample data for testing.

- Client and user expectations must be managed carefully. The client and users often do not understand the complexity of the data migration effort. It is also vital that users familiar with the legacy data be quickly available, or on call, during the data cleansing effort. During the data cleansing process, questionable data records will be discovered. This requires the assistance of users knowledgeable about the data so that a proper decision can be made on the disposition of the data.

- During the data migration effort, any problems noted in system testing using the legacy data should be captured and processed, just as with all change requests.

Shutting Down Legacy Systems to Extract Data

During off-hours, or during maintenance, a recent snapshot of the data is sufficient in most cases for trial runs. Of course, for the final migration, the legacy system needs to remain down so that changes will not be made to the data during the switchover to the new system. Depending on the use of the system, this may require months of advance notice, especially for a mission-critical system. It may also be necessary to conduct the final migration over a holiday weekend. Prepare the staff conducting the data migration accordingly. If several trial runs using recent snapshots of the legacy system have been conducted, and the system has been tested with this data, there is an excellent chance that the migration effort will proceed successfully. However, be prepared to place the legacy system back into production if the migration effort fails. The goal, of course, is to place the new system into production; however, preserve the option of returning the legacy system into production as a fallback position.

As mentioned previously, trial runs of the data migration are mandatory. Another reason for conducting trial runs is that it helps produce a reliable estimate of the total amount of time the final migration effort will take. This is key, because neither the legacy system nor the new system will be available during the final migration effort. Because this is not a trivial situation for most organizations, it is vital to know ahead of time how much time needs to be allocated for the final migration.

Extracting the Legacy Data

Depending on the type of system in which the legacy data resides, methods for extracting the data will vary. If possible, automated scripts should be developed for this purpose, because extraction of the data will probably occur multiple times. The data should be stored in files that can be viewed and examined. Note that depending on the customer and the application, significant security concerns might be involved. Be sure to discuss any concerns about security and access to the data during the migration process with the customer ahead of time. Addressing these concerns beforehand minimizes disruptions during the process.

Depending on the amount and types of data stored in the legacy database, it may be necessary to extract the data in phases.

Data Cleansing

Data cleansing involves a thorough check of the data extracted from the legacy system. The data is modified when data meeting certain attributes is located. Examples include eliminating duplicate data, deleting obsolete or unused data, and even repairing corrupted data records. Most of this effort is done from the perspective of the legacy system. In other words, no consideration is given to the ultimate destination of the final migrated data. It is simply a "cleanup" effort that yields a "purified" set of data that still works perfectly in the legacy system. You must perform this step in close collaboration with users who are familiar with the data.

Sometimes, depending on circumstances, it may make sense to perform the cleansing step before you extract the data from the legacy system. The point is to examine all data records and purge any that are unnecessary.

Analyzing the Cleansed Data

Analyzing the cleansed data is perhaps the most painstaking step of the data migration effort. Each field of data must be traced to a corresponding field in the destination database. If a data model has been created, it will become very useful in this step. During this step, the data is also analyzed for consistency.

One example of inconsistent data is illustrated in the following example, which occurred on an actual project. A Web-based system was developed that was to contain a centralized database with a Web interface that could be accessed over the organization's internal network, which reached nationwide. The system was replacing a former client/server system in which the user community was divided into separate regions. Each region contained its own database. The format and layout of the database were the same for each database across all the regions. These databases were to be consolidated into a single database for the new system. The issue happened over the disposition of a field indicating which region the data belonged to. It turned out that two different regions were using the same value to indicate the region they belonged to. Previously, this had not caused any problems, because each region had its own separate database. But when consolidating the databases, it was definitely a problem. There was no way to distinguish between the two regions after the data was consolidated.

This is a good example of data consistency. In this example, the data in both databases is perfectly valid. But during the analysis, the problem is discovered. In this situation, the solution, of course, was to change the value for one of the regions so that each region was using a unique value.

Another scenario that requires extra diligence frequently occurs when you replace a legacy system that has been running for many years. In one case, analyzing the cleansed data revealed inconsistencies in the format of the data records prior to a certain date. It turned out that the legacy system being replaced had previously replaced yet another legacy system. This occurred before most of the users joined the organization, so no one recalled this event. The lesson learned was to be sure to investigate each instance of the data that does not conform to the expected parameters.

Yet another example encountered on a project involved replacing a mainframe-based legacy system. In this system, the database contained a customer name. The mainframe database defined a single string to contain the customer's entire name. The new system defined separate fields for each component in the customer name. The data migration effort involved writing scripts to parse the string from the legacy system to place it in separate fields in the new database.

These are typical examples of issues that can arise. Of course, each migration effort is different. Be prepared to discover these sorts of scenarios.

Transferring the Legacy Data

For simple systems, cleansed, analyzed data can be imported directly into the final destination database. For most systems, the data's complexity may not permit this. In addition, consider the original system managing the legacy data. If the legacy system uses an earlier release of Oracle, and the new system also uses Oracle (albeit a newer release), you are less likely to run into data representation problems. On the other hand, if the legacy system is a database management system from a different vendor running on a completely different type of system, you should consider setting up an intermediate database to "stage" the data. For example, suppose the legacy system runs on a mainframe system running MVS and the new database system runs on UNIX. In this example, you are much more likely to run into data representation problems than in the Oracle example. Two significant variables are involved: the change in platform and the change in database vendors.

Figure 12-1 showed a staging database being used to assemble the data after it is cleansed. Each extracted table can be individually imported into the staging database, which is created on the same platform and using the same database vendor and version as the final production system. After it is loaded into the database, the data is examined to ensure that it is consistent and that the new system will interpret it correctly.

Automated scripts and utilities are recommended to load the data into the destination databases. This allows multiple runs for importing the data, which is necessary to ensure a smooth migration effort when the final migration to production occurs.

Testing the Migrated Data

At each step, the data should be examined for consistency and to ensure that it has no corrupted records or missing data. The scripts that perform the data transfer must also be tested, like any other developed code.

When the data is transferred to the final database, the database engineer should meet with a user or group of users who are familiar with the data. Together, they should spot-check several meaningful scenarios to gain confidence in the migration's success and to ensure readiness for production.

Points to Remember for the Data Migration Effort

You should now appreciate the complexity of most data migration efforts. Remember the following key points to mitigate risks during data migration:

- The database engineer performing the migration needs very fast turnaround time for answers from users concerning issues found during data cleansing and consistency checks.
- Manage user expectations carefully. Most users do not appreciate the challenges involved in the migration effort.
- Expect to encounter corrupted data, missing data, and inconsistent data. Each instance must be pursued to resolution.
- Start the migration effort as early as possible. Be sure the staff working on the migration effort communicates with the analysts and testers when developing the new system.
- Be prepared to expect the unexpected. The schedule for the migration effort should include extra time to accommodate unexpected and unforeseen problems.

Following and heeding the steps described here should ensure that your data migration effort is successful.

Training

Most projects that produce a completely new system also require training to be developed. Training development and delivery warrants its own book, so it isn't discussed here. You should refer to the many excellent books on this topic. However, you should consider some ideas specifically in the context of delivering a new software system:

- Training should involve hands-on interaction with the product. Most users simply want to be comfortable using the system to accomplish their jobs.
- Consider having separate training for administrators, users, and system maintainers. The needs and focus of each of these groups are sufficiently different to warrant separate training for each.
- For the general user population, consider having one of the project analysts present during training. The trainer should be knowledgeable about how the new product operates, but it is equally important to have someone who can tie the product's functionality to the business requirements and business process. The project requirements analysts can provide this perspective.

- To train the system's administrators and maintainers, consider having someone from the development group there to field in-depth technical questions that may arise during training.

- Be aware that you may receive questions and comments during the training about functionality that was expected in the product but not delivered. Or the functionality that was delivered might work differently than what the users had been led to believe. The end users are sometimes left out of the loop when these decisions are made. Be prepared to field these questions and, if necessary, take extended discussion of these issues offline. You do not want these discussions to derail the purpose of the training.

Acceptance Testing

Most outsourced projects have some kind of official event where a representative of the outsourcing organization's management reviews the new system's functionality and officially signs off, indicating that the contractor has fulfilled each of the new system's requirements. This is usually called acceptance testing.

Like many joint events between customer and contractor, expectations need to be set carefully ahead of time. Several considerations exist, from both the contractor and the customer's perspectives.

Contractor's Checklist for the Acceptance Test

The contractor should make the following preparations for the acceptance test:

- It is useful to have as many workstations as necessary to fully exercise the product's functionality. Depending on the size of the group attending from the outsourcing organization, consider obtaining projection equipment rather than having people crowd around the monitors. For offshoring situations where the customer and the contractor cannot be in the same location, teleconferencing software can be used to remotely display the screen contents.

- Have a workstation available in the same room with someone from the contracting team dedicated to capturing any defect reports or change requests.

- Walking through the system's use cases is an excellent way to demonstrate the system's functionality. The use cases describe all the functional requirements, and users should already have some familiarity with them.

- Be aware that with a system that has lots of functionality, it may take several days to completely walk through the acceptance test. A dry run of the acceptance test helps you estimate how long it will take, in addition to catching any last-minute bugs. Create a schedule and publish for the customer a list of which use cases will be covered each day. This will help the customer identify the proper attendees.

- Have development people available on call to assist if any technical glitches occur.

- It is vital to ask the customer to have someone in attendance at the acceptance test with sign-off authority. In some cases, this may be your best opportunity to get the customer to agree that you have met the requirements. One risk that occurs occasionally is "the project that never ends." The customer will not commit to agreeing that the project is done, but instead drags it out as long as possible to get the contractor to continually add or change functionality.

- It is also helpful to have other personnel from the project team available, especially the project manager, requirements analysts, and someone who can simply observe the reactions and general demeanor of the customer representatives.

Preparation is the key to a successful acceptance test. The end of the acceptance test should result in one of three situations: acceptance of the system, acceptance with conditions (usually conditional on any bugs discovered being corrected), or rejection of the system. Hopefully, your system will achieve one of the first two.

Outsourcing Organization's Checklist for the Acceptance Test

The customer should make the following preparations for the acceptance test:

- Be sure to bring along experts from the user community who are familiar with the functionality to be demonstrated.

- Be inquisitive about the behavior of the demonstrated functionality. If something does not seem quite right, ask questions, or exercise the functionality until you are confident it is functioning correctly.

- Don't forget to verify that any nonfunctional (supplemental) requirements have been met. This includes proof that the system can support the required number of simultaneous users, failover and reliability requirements, and so on.

Most contractors are happy to work with their customers to achieve final system sign-off. Be prepared to sign off on items that have been demonstrated successfully so that the contractor can focus on correcting any final items.

Setting End-User Expectations for Production

Users adopting a new system and incorporating it into their business is a mixed experience. Some users are excited about the chance to learn a new way of conducting their business. Perhaps, most users simply want to know what they must do differently and minimize the disruption to their jobs while learning the new system. Finally, for some users, learning a new system is an emotional event, especially if the new system is replacing a legacy system that has been in place for many years. For this last group of users, elements of fear might manifest themselves in various ways. To be successful in rolling out a new system, you need to engage these groups differently.

Identifying User Groups to Aid in Production Rollout

By the time the project has reached the Transition phase, the team will (hopefully!) have interacted with a large cross section of the people who will become the users of the new system. Most teams will have a sense of the characteristics of the various users. When planning for the rollout of a new system, I prefer to identify the users' needs according to three groups: advanced users, general users, and special-needs users.

Advanced Users

Advanced users are the first users who should be engaged when the rollout of a new system is planned. Advanced users have the following characteristics:

- They demonstrate familiarity with their jobs and their business processes.
- They typically participate heavily during the requirements elicitation process.
- They command respect and admiration from their peers in the organization. These users are recognized as leaders by the organization's management.
- They often are early adopters of new technology that helps their organization manage their business.

To aid in successful system rollout, engage this group of users first. If the project team delivers an early deployment of a release, such as the IOC, focus on getting this select group of users to exercise the release. The reasons are as follows:

- Advanced users are often very well respected in the user community. If the advanced users become proficient with the new system first, they will set an example for others in the organization. In other words, the user community as a whole will have a tendency to follow their example.
- As a corollary to the previous point, if you can "sell" the usage of the new system to these advanced users, their acceptance of the new system will have a tendency to squelch protests of those who complain simply because the system represents change in their routine.
- Advanced users can assist with training inside their organization or can help other users. They can be used for "Train the Trainer" sessions.
- Advanced users may be able to identify other users in their organization who will need extra help getting comfortable with the new system.

General Users

The general user community represents the majority of users of the new system. Usually, this group is self-sufficient, provided that they have all the essential items that are expected in a typical rollout of a production system, such as training, documentation, and Help Desk support. Make sure a contact is available to address any issues that arise.

Special-Needs Users

For this group of users, rollout of a new system provokes anxiety. Some of these users may have used the previous system for many years. The anxiety these users experience manifests itself in various ways. Be aware, and recognize users who have the following profile:

- They inexplicably miss training sessions or seem disengaged during training.
- They complain loudly about seemingly minor issues.
- They refuse to use the new system or continue using the legacy system if it is still available.

If possible, enlist the assistance of advanced users to work with special-needs users. These users may perceive you, the contractor, as part of the problem. Try not to take these complaints personally. Try to get help from these users' coworkers as well. If possible, avoid going directly to management; try to acknowledge the users' concerns. After exhausting all possible options for assisting these users, you might need to explain the situation to management. They probably are already aware of the problem.

Summary

A project's Transition phase is an opportunity to capitalize on the success of all the hard work performed during the project's earlier phases. Much interaction with the customer and user community occurs during the Transition phase—perhaps as much as or more than during the Inception and Elaboration phases. Furthermore, end users have little appreciation for the elegant solutions to the technical challenges achieved by the project team. Their focus is on the items directly affecting them. Most of the major tasks performed in the Transition phase, such as help files, tutorials, installation scripts, training, and the results of data migration, are examples of these items. In addition, remember the following points:

- Early deployment, or deployment of the IOC, is an important risk-mitigation strategy. It allows the team to discover environment-related issues affecting the product's performance that were undetectable during in-house testing.
- Be sure to prioritize all change requests received during an early deployment. The focus should be on making existing functionality as flawless as possible, rather than implementing last-minute requests for new functionality.
- Leverage relationships with knowledgeable persons in the user community to aid in the training and adoption of the new product by the rest of the user community.
- Remember that the artifacts and tasks in the Transition phase directly affect the way the user perceives the system's quality. Take special care to ensure these artifacts and tasks enhance the product's image in the users' eyes.
- Data migration is another example of a "project within the project" and should be conducted in parallel with the analysis, design, and development of a new system.

What's Next?

Transition of a newly developed system often involves transitioning the system's maintenance to a new contractor. Whether you are the contractor who developed the new system or the contractor who will maintain the new system (or both!), new activities must take place. Setting up and staffing a Help Desk is one example. The next chapter covers this and other topics.

CHAPTER 13

System Operations and Maintenance Issues

At this point in the project lifecycle, development is complete, with the possible exception of some enhancement requests or corrections, and the system is in full production use. The development team has probably been disbanded, or dramatically changed to reflect the shift to production support. From the perspective of the developers, their work is largely finished. From the perspective of the customer and user community, the system's lifecycle has just begun.

This chapter covers issues relating to maintaining and supporting software systems. Because maintenance and support are often performed by vendors other than those who developed the system, issues relating to procuring maintenance services are discussed. This chapter also discusses setting up a Help Desk, which is the first echelon of assistance when difficulties arise with a new production system.

Procuring Maintenance Services

Maintaining a system is seldom included in the same contract as the one to build the system. Often, the contractor that built the system is not the same organization as the one that maintains it. For both contractors and outsourcing organizations, it is important to clarify exactly what is meant by the term "maintenance." "Maintenance" is sometimes confused with "operations support." To help clarify the difference, the tasks and attributes associated with each are explained next. Even if your definition varies from what is stated here, it is important to verify and define this precisely so that no misunderstanding occurs between the contractor and the client.

Operations Support

Operations support is typically performed at the location (usually a data center) where the system is deployed. Most organizations have a staff dedicated to providing these services. To better understand the operations process, the goals of operations support should be identified.

Operations Support Goals

For most organizations, the goals of operations support are the following:

- Assist the business organizations that depend on the IT applications running smoothly. In other words, support the organization's business goals by keeping all IT systems functioning as they should.

- Help the organization get the most value out of its investment in technology, including both hardware and software.

- Provide a positive experience for users to help drive usage of the systems. IT systems are expensive, and return on investment is zero if the system isn't used. Most users recognize that no system is perfect. Many even tolerate a certain level of defects in the system provided that support is responsive to their needs and provides the proper answers to their questions.

These goals are straightforward. To achieve them, the organization generally forms a staff. Examples of operations support tasks are as follows:

- Performing backups and restores for system recovery or disaster preparedness
- Managing system logs
- Defining or managing user IDs and passwords
- Researching and answering typical Help Desk or usage questions
- General monitoring of system performance
- Increasing available disk space by archiving old records for long-term storage

Sometimes, operations support is referred to as "first-echelon" support. The operations support group is the first line of support users call when a problem arises. The support group probably is responsible for many systems. They may be part of the group often called a Help Desk. If you have the luxury of determining and controlling the staff for supporting a system your team has built, the following section explains key skills and attributes needed for these positions.

Staffing Operations Support and Help Desks

Help Desk and other operations support personnel have a difficult job. Like any customer support position, the only time they hear from users is when they are having a problem. In addition, users are often frustrated by the time they call for help, and this frustration is sometimes directed at the Help Desk staffers. Help Desk staffers have their own frustrations, such as users who never read manuals or follow recommended steps. Despite the challenges, working at a Help Desk can be a tremendous learning opportunity. When you're considering candidates to staff Help Desk and operations support, the following qualifications are key attributes:

- Quick learning ability. Typical Help Desk staffers support multiple systems concurrently. New systems come online frequently. Although proper training is vital for good

Help Desk support, the reality is that this is not always possible. Accordingly, the ability to learn new systems quickly and to self-teach is important.

- The ability to handle pressure. Providing correct answers often requires some research by the Help Desk staff. During peak periods, questions are directed to the Help Desk faster than their ability to find the answers. Thus, successful support staff need to perform multiple tasks concurrently and manage their time wisely.

- A good demeanor over the phone. Most Help Desks handle the majority of requests via phone or e-mail. A calm, steady, friendly voice over the phone that inspires confidence goes a long way toward soothing users' frazzled nerves.

- Initiative. Although operating a Help Desk is a reactive task, it helps to have people staffing it who take the initiative to raise and solve issues that will make the Help Desk operate more efficiently.

- A strong desire to help people solve problems. Despite all the technology involved, as with many endeavors, a Help Desk is about people and information, not technology. The best Help Desk candidates are the ones who derive great job satisfaction from helping others.

It is interesting to note that turnover is high in these positions. One reason is by the time a Help Desk staffer acquires a great deal of knowledge, he finds other opportunities where he can apply his knowledge in an environment more amenable to him. Perhaps, a more common reason is simply the burnout factor. Yet another is opportunity for career advancement. A talented Help Desk staffer is highly prized. To reduce turnover and retain those who are talented, consider rotating Help Desk personnel into other tasks for periods of time. This reduces burnout and lets the staffers apply their talents in other areas.

Equipping Help Desk Personnel

Because the Help Desk is the first (and often the only) group users interact with after deployment, a system's ultimate success and acceptance depend on the quality of the Help Desk support. As the contractor who will build the new system, you may not be able to control the staffing of the Help Desk, because a different contractor may handle it, or the customer may staff it. But you can equip the Help Desk with everything that is needed to provide responsive technical support. Consider the following points:

- When eliciting requirements for a new system, be sure to ask the operations support personnel (such as the people staffing the Help Desk) for suggestions. Help Desk staffers are in a unique position to supply useful information on the sorts of difficulties the users experience when new systems are deployed. This information can be used to make operations support of the system easier. In addition, this information may help determine the capabilities of the user population. This information can then be factored into decisions that affect the system's usability. Often, these suggestions require little in the way of additional resources as long as the requirements are identified early.

- A complete set of reference materials should be provided to Help Desk personnel. This includes user manuals, installation guides, build instructions, maintenance instructions, and any other helpful documentation. An additional document that may help is a list of error messages the system may produce and suggested ways to respond to them that are within the scope of a Help Desk operation.

- If possible, try to anticipate questions users may have. Provide a list of these questions and their possible answers in the form of a Frequently Asked Questions (FAQ) document. You may get ideas for the FAQ document from the questions that arise during acceptance testing and other hands-on demonstrations for the users prior to deployment.

- For more complex systems, hands-on training is useful to get Help Desk support started. Consider supplementing Help Desk staff with a member of the development team for a period of time after the system is initially deployed. This will facilitate knowledge transfer and enable the Help Desk personnel to become self-sufficient.

- There will be occasions when an issue reported to the Help Desk appears to be a problem requiring attention by the maintenance team. The maintenance contractor should provide guidance to the Help Desk representatives on the information they should collect before reporting a problem to the maintenance team. This will help the maintenance team replicate the problem and provide corrective action quickly.

- If you're a contractor and your organization is providing maintenance but not Help Desk support, an extra investment of time to allow the Help Desk to run efficiently will ultimately benefit your organization. Most Help Desks are staffed with the minimum number of people needed to support the user community. As a result, Help Desk staffers are under great stress to provide solutions quickly and then move on to the next problem. If a problem cannot be solved swiftly at the Help Desk level, it will quickly be escalated to the maintenance team.

Other Useful Items for Operations and Help Desk Support

If you are setting up a support organization for the first time, other useful tools can help the operations organization (including the Help Desk staffers) immensely. The majority of these tools help you manage and disseminate information. Some of these suggestions are practical only for large shops with a significant IT budget. However, consider these options when equipping any Help Desk:

- Call management systems. For Help Desks with enough call volume to have multiple staffers working simultaneously, a call management system that can automatically route calls to the next open representative is helpful. For very large organizations, they can be used to route calls to representatives who specialize in certain products or have certain skills. Trying to manage multiple phone lines manually, without a call management system, does not work for high call volumes. This means users become even more frustrated by the time they finally reach a representative.

- Web sites. Most organizations already have intranet Web sites available for employees to which pages for a support organization could be added. You could include a simple statement of the current status of the various IT systems. You also could include elaborate knowledge management systems that make it easy for users to find information they need without contacting the Help Desk directly.

- Problem tracking software. This is essential for all Help Desk operations, no matter how large or small. This is discussed further in the next section.

- License utilization software. Some companies offer license utilization software that tracks usage patterns of Commercial Off-The-Shelf (COTS) products. These tools can create graphs showing peak usage, whether anyone was denied a license due to maximum utilization, and so on. These tools can pinpoint the usage pattern of systems over time so that Help Desk staffing can be made more efficient. It also helps organizations manage their software products more efficiently so that they can achieve maximum utilization of the products before having to spend additional funds on more licenses.

Call Tracking/Problem Tracking Software

Call tracking software is the most important tool in a Help Desk's arsenal. The primary need for call tracking software is to enable the Help Desk representative to document the details of each call. During peak periods, it is difficult to remember all the various details of every call that is not immediately resolved. Hence, call tracking software is needed to effectively support multiple problem resolution efforts concurrently.

Call tracking software has another important purpose. As the call tracking database becomes populated with the details of problem solving sessions over time, it serves as a knowledge base. Help Desk personnel can search this knowledge base for previous occurrences of a problem. They can review and apply prior solutions to the problem to a new instance of the problem. This not only saves time but also accelerates the learning curve for newer Help Desk representatives. They will be able to learn solutions to problems without affecting other staff.

To facilitate use of call tracking software as a knowledge base, representatives should be certain to describe problems completely and fully, listing all the symptoms of the problem and the various solutions applied. They should strive to describe the information to the point where a review of the call log a month later, or a review by a different representative, provides enough information to understand the problem and the solution, along with the final resolution.

Another use for call tracking software is to provide historical information on call volume and trends. This can be used to anticipate future call levels and adjust staffing accordingly.

Finally, if possible, the maintenance team should have access to the call tracking system. If this is not possible, at the very least they should have the information from the logs from the reported problem that is being escalated to the maintenance team. This will facilitate replicating the problem so that the issue can be corrected quickly.

Other Best Practices for Operations Support

Hiring the right people for operations support and equipping them with the right tools to manage the job will put you on the path to success. For other best practices, consider the following:

- Try to identify peak usage periods in the user community, and adjust staffing on the Help Desk accordingly. For example, some organizations have certain times when the users must run certain reports or perform certain activities using their IT systems. Some organizations do this once a month or once a quarter. Near the end of these periods, you can expect the Help Desk to have higher-than-normal call levels. The problems reported in these calls will have a greater level of urgency, because the reports may need to be completed by a certain deadline. Make sure that sufficient staff is available during these peak periods. If not, both the Help Desk staff and users will become frustrated quickly.

- Try to view problems from the customer's perspective. Many customers are uninterested in computer systems and view them simply as a tool they must use to achieve some goal or purpose. For this reason, you need to be patient with users who may be struggling in their use of the system, even with things that are seemingly simple. Do not consider the support call complete until you are certain the client is satisfied with the response.

- Despite the best efforts of even the most talented support staff, some users will be disgruntled. Other users, perhaps through no fault of their own, will try to use the Help Desk as their own personal training tool. For these situations, have an escalation path. Someone other than the Help Desk staffers should manage users who are unhappy with the support or who continually make out-of-scope requests. The focus of the Help Desk staffer should always be on solving the specific problem reported to the Help Desk. Separating the management of these concerns preserves the Help Desk staffer's credibility.

- For issues that require several days to research and solve, contact the client periodically with an update. Do this regularly, even if you have nothing new to report or you're still waiting for something else to happen to solve the problem. Users always appreciate getting updates.

- During periods of low Help Desk activity, proactively call selected users for whom you have solved problems in the past. Ask them if the solution you provided was helpful. If this is not practical due to continual activity, have a manager perform this activity.

- One situation that happens occasionally is that the Help Desk staffer must provide support for systems of which they have a low opinion. If you're tempted to state this opinion to a Help Desk client, you should refrain from doing so. In fact, the Help Desk staff should be a proponent of all the IT systems they support. To do otherwise invites trouble. I have seen situations where a Help Desk staffer offered his true opinion to a caller. After the caller hung up, the client ran around his office stating that "Even the Help Desk thinks our IT systems are of poor quality." Don't get caught up in these situations!

Maintenance Support

Maintenance support (sometimes called second-echelon support) comes into play as a response to a specific event, as with operations support. But maintenance requires expertise and resources beyond the scope of operations support. Simply stated, the role of maintenance is to determine the cause of functionality that is failing to operate properly and then provide a solution that corrects the problem. This simple definition is technically correct, but most organizations require much more. The following tasks are typical needs of an outsourcing organization for its maintenance provider:

- Adjustments needed to software resulting from operating system upgrades
- Modifications and adjustments needed to software from a change in COTS software vendors, such as a change in databases
- Modifications and adjustments to software to take advantage of hardware improvements
- Training for new Help Desk personnel
- Assistance in relocating servers due to data center moves
- Changes in functionality to support Continuity of Operations (COOP)
- Changes or additions to functionality to support changes in business processes

I have seen all these issues arise at actual customer sites. In every case, the only source of expertise available to assist with these tasks was the maintenance team. All contractors engaging a client site for maintenance contracts should consider these items and ask whether these services may be required. If so, they should be factored into the Statement of Work and any pricing information that could be affected.

In general, fixed-price contracts for maintenance are a bad idea. They are risky to the contractor and a poor value for the client. Can you imagine an automobile dealer selling fixed-price maintenance contracts? Even with extended warranties, many things are specifically excluded. It is difficult to predict what, if anything, will go wrong with software. A Cost Plus Fixed Fee or even a Time and Materials contract is more appropriate.

When the Maintenance Contractor Is Different from the Development Contractor

When a new contractor takes over maintenance on code that was not developed by that contractor, a large amount of knowledge transfer must take place. Each of the following areas should be examined and considered when accepting responsibility for software maintenance:

- What tools did the developing contractor use to develop the code originally? Are these tools needed to maintain the code? If so, how will licenses be acquired for the tools, and who will pay for them?
- If some of the original tools must be reacquired for maintenance, find out which versions of the tools the developing contractor used. If possible, the same versions should

be used for maintenance. When the maintenance team is successful in maintaining the code, the tool versions can be upgraded if needed. If this is done too soon, and problems occur, it will be difficult to tell whether the problems are caused by the new versions of the tools or by some unrelated aspect not understood. Also find out any special configuration settings that were used or any other information that is needed to set up the tools correctly for maintenance.

- Obtain from the development contractor a complete set of design documentation, and any other documentation needed, such as build instructions. Have the maintenance team review this documentation and identify any questions they may have.

- Have the developers of the new maintenance team meet with the original development team. The goal is to answer any questions the maintenance developers have. A second goal is to allow the maintenance developers to perform a build without input from the original developers, following the documented build procedures. Any difficulties should be investigated and the build procedures corrected.

- Just as with the software build procedures, any test suites should be documented with instructions on running the test suites and properly interpreting the results. The testers on the maintenance team should try running these while the expertise from the development team is still available.

- If possible, try to arrange the periods of performance of the development contract and the maintenance contract to overlap for a period—perhaps 30 days. If that is not possible, at least arrange for the original development team to be available for consultation if the maintenance team runs into difficulty getting the software to build properly or if other questions arise.

Corrections in Software

There have been many horror stories relating to software maintenance. Many of these errors can be attributed to insufficient testing following a seemingly minor change. When a small change is made to correct a single problem, the temptation to skip thorough testing is great. For this reason, this type of change should be attempted only in emergency situations—when the disruption of a system being out of service unexpectedly overrules the risk of introducing bugs through making a quick change. For some other best practices that should be employed when performing maintenance, consider the following:

- Group changes, defects, and enhancement requests that do not constitute emergency fixes into a single release. This makes it more practical to perform thorough testing on the release before it is released.

- Never send a changed release into the field, no matter how small the change is, without changing the version number in the release. This sounds like common sense not worthy of attention, but I have seen it happen. The problem, of course, is when a defect is detected in the "new" release. Is the bug in the "old" version 5.0 or the "new" version 5.0? This causes tremendous confusion and wasted effort. Never do this.

- A robust configuration management system is vital during maintenance. It should be capable of permitting work on a maintenance release while allowing independent work on newer versions (containing new features) if needed. Refer to Chapter 6, "Establishing the Software Development Environment," for more information.

When delivering a maintenance release for deployment, remember to keep the operations group "in the loop" and informed of the expected date of delivery. Installation and deployment of a new release of software is a significant event and requires resources from the operations group. This is seldom an issue, unless the operations group was not informed of the date of delivery.

Summary

An efficient operations and maintenance group can be a powerful ally, enabling an operation to meet its business goals. The key to success is to be proactive and understand the customer environment and the application thoroughly before committing to an operations and maintenance contract. Keep in mind the following points:

- Choose the proper contract type for operations and maintenance tasks. Avoid fixed-price contracts unless you know the amount and scope of work.
- Verify that a new maintenance team understands the prospective system to be maintained.
- Retain the services of the original development team for a period of time until the maintenance team has complete confidence in their understanding of the new system.
- Provide operations personnel with the resources needed to properly support the systems deployed. This includes resources needed for contingency planning and for maintaining resources on call if needed.

What's Next?

All project teams need help from time to time. Whether it's becoming more familiar with iterative processes such as the RUP, getting up to speed on a new tool, or simply augmenting your staff, consultants are available who have a wide variety of expertise in different areas. Consultants require a significant investment in funds and typically work with the team only temporarily. How can you obtain the most from the use of a consultant? The next chapter covers this and other related issues.

CHAPTER 14

Using Consultants Effectively

Consultants are available for nearly any purpose, covering every conceivable area of expertise. If you are considering using consultants on your project, how do you choose the right consultant for your needs? Is there a difference between a consultant who charges $100 an hour and one who charges $300 an hour? How do you get the best value from the consultant you choose? This chapter discusses these topics.

The two primary types of engagement models used in consulting are staff augmentation and expert consulting. Both types, when used properly, can reap great benefits. They can round out a project team, helping the project finish on time. They also can transfer knowledge to the rest of the staff that can pay benefits for the next several projects.

Staff Augmentation

Staff augmentation is straightforward. Your project team may be fully staffed except for a specific position or set of positions. For whatever reason, your company cannot staff the position or prefers not to. The solution is to seek out a firm that provides qualified individuals to augment your staff. You identify the requirements and skills needed for the position, negotiate a rate, and conduct interviews. The best candidate then joins the project.

Usually, staff augmentation is used to fill full-time positions. The person (or persons) joins the project team and functions just as the other team members, except her paycheck comes from a different company. Her daily tasks are determined and reviewed by the same managers as those for the rest of the team. She works in the same location as the rest of the team and is considered a peer by the other team members.

The management of the company providing the resource stays on the periphery of the engagement. The consultant may provide periodic status reports to her company's management.

The staff augmentation firm touches base with the project manager (in other words, the client) to verify that the consultant is providing satisfactory results.

Using staff augmentation in this manner provides the following benefits:

- The client can seek consultants who already have the skills needed for the position, rather than expending time and resources training existing staff.

- If the consultant does not perform well, it is much easier to try another consultant than to fire an employee of the company.

- For specialized skills, hiring a new employee may not make sense. The specific skills may not be applicable to other projects at the company, so after the project is completed, no other projects are available for the employee to leverage her talents. Using a consultant solves this problem.

- A consultant can transfer knowledge to other members of the team, thus helping employees of the company acquire new skills.

- Introducing new talent on a project team (particularly if the consultant is enthusiastic and energetic and has special skills) can motivate the rest of the project team.

There are certain cautions to consider when using other firms to augment your staff:

- Staff augmentation is not contractually the same as a subcontracting arrangement. The original project team is still completely responsible for performance of the project contract. In other words, if the consultant fails to perform and causes the team to miss deliveries, the company owning the project team is responsible.

- In addition to technical qualifications, make sure that the consultant subscribes to similar philosophies and opinions regarding the methodologies and environment in use on the project. In other words, if the project development environment is run on a Windows platform, make sure the consultant is happy with this arrangement, in addition to being technically qualified. For example, you do not want a UNIX aficionado working on a team of Windows enthusiasts, even if the consultant can use Windows effectively, because this can result in tension on the team. However, this does not apply to expert consultants (as opposed to staff augmentation consultants). Expert consultants are used when it may be desirable to push a team outside its comfort zone. For staff augmentation, you want the consultant to blend in with the rest of the team.

- Monitor a new consultant closely. Although it's rare, consultants sometimes push their own agenda within the project team, attempting to sell products and more services to the point of disrupting the project team. Certainly, the consultant should promote her own company's services if a need is clearly identified, but the focus should always be on the tasks assigned. In rare cases, I have seen a consultant recruit members of the project team to work for the consultant's company! Such consultants should be promptly escorted to the exit.

- Monitor the members of your project team who work closely with the consultant, and watch the quality of their interaction. If team members are actively interacting with the consultant, this is a good sign. If there are indications that the team members are not getting along, you should investigate. In the event of personality conflicts, you need to decide whether the situation can be peacefully resolved. If not, the team could be restructured to separate the conflicting personalities, but in general, situations that cannot be resolved mean that the consultant needs to leave. Try another consultant.

- Give consultants in staff augmentation mode (meaning that they are working full-time on your project) the same amenities as the rest of the project team. In other words, if each team member has his own cubicle, provide one for the consultant. The same goes for supplies and equipment. The purpose is to create an environment that encourages team building. In other words, each member of the team should be treated the same, regardless of who signs his paycheck.

- Be careful not to use too many consultants on the same project team. When there are more consultants than actual employees, the team dynamics may suffer. Consultants have their own agenda. They may not share the same sense of urgency in making the project successful. When circumstances force you to use a large number of consultants, the project manager should be particularly vigilant for signs of lack of urgency on the team. Provide very clear goals, and establish a sense of mission for the team. Another option is to set up a subcontracting arrangement and allow the subcontractors to choose and control their own team.

Staff augmentation is not always the best solution to supplement your team's talents. Perhaps, you have a specific problem to solve that requires highly specialized skills to come up with a specific solution. After the problem is solved, the team can apply the solution to accomplish the project's goals. An expert consultant (sometimes called a subject matter expert) may be appropriate to solve this problem.

Expert Consultants

Expert consultants are available to solve every conceivable type of problem. These consultant engagements tend to be for a shorter period of time than with a staff augmentation model. Because expert consultants have highly specialized (and often high-demand) skills, and the engagements tend to be for a shorter term, expert consultants are more expensive than consultants in a staff augmentation model.

Expert consultants come from two sources. Some consulting firms offer expert consultants in various areas because this is their primary line of business. Some vendors may also offer expert consultants. These consultants specialize in the tools and technologies offered by that vendor. Both of these are discussed in detail next.

Expert Consultants from Vendors

Depending on the vendor's business model, its consultants may command a premium. These vendors do not want to be in the consulting business. They offer consulting services strictly to promote use of the tools and technologies they offer. Another contributing factor to the higher rates from the vendor is the perception that the vendor is the best (and perhaps the only) source of expertise. This is not always the case. Many vendors have partnership arrangements with companies that offer the same consulting services. If cost is a limiting factor, consider using a partner company as an alternative source. It's not uncommon for these partner companies to have former employees of the vendor. This allows you to purchase the same expertise at a significantly lower rate.

Is there a risk in using a vendor's partner at a lower rate? One concern is if the tools or technologies from the vendor are new or unproven or are being used in an unusual way. The vendor's consultants will have more extensive resources to call on if problems occur. Otherwise, a partner's consultants provide a better value. Another possible reason to use a vendor's consultants is if your project (or other projects in your company) includes plans for future purchases from that vendor. In this situation, the vendor will bend over backward to ensure that the current engagement is as successful as it can be. Sometimes, the vendor will compensate partner companies for their involvement in promoting future sales as well. Be honest with your vendor. If you don't anticipate future sales, say so.

Getting the Best Value from a Vendor Consultant

Given the high cost of vendor consultants, it is important to make their time as productive as possible. To assist in this endeavor, consider the following:

- Keep the task well defined, with a clear entry and exit point. Make it clear what the objective is, and provide a written statement of the objective before the scheduled engagement.

- Work with the consultant to map out a schedule of events and tasks.

- Be prepared and ready for the consultant. Ask the consultant prior to the engagement what needs to be in place for the engagement to be a success. If the consultant will be conducting knowledge transfer sessions with your staff, ask if there is anything your staff can do to prepare ahead of time (such as receiving additional training and reading documentation).

- Make sure the consultant has access to any needed resources. For example, if the consultant will be installing software, alert a system administrator that you may need her services. That way, if the consultant runs into problems with a server, the system administrator can immediately work on the problem. If the consultant has idle time because of an environment problem, she will still charge for that time. Furthermore, if the consultant has to troubleshoot problems other than the intended ones, she might be working outside her area of expertise. This is inefficient and a poor use of the consultant's time.

- At the conclusion of the engagement, have the consultant deliver a write-up detailing her activities, any conclusions and recommendations for the next steps, and the current status of the work performed. This is important, because it represents a formal conclusion to the consultant's work. This is the last opportunity to ask questions and verify understanding.

As an example, on one project, a certain Commercial Off-The-Shelf (COTS) tool was chosen to produce reports based on information stored in an Oracle database. After the tool was chosen, it had to be installed and configured. No one on the project team had expertise with the tool. Training was scheduled, but it was at a late date. The project schedule indicated that the team would need to start working with the COTS package immediately after training. This left no time for the project team to install and configure the product.

A consultant from the vendor was retained to provide these installation and configuration services. Over a four-day period, the consultant installed and configured the software with a member of the project team "shoulder surfing." The project team member took notes and asked questions during the engagement. A problem was discovered with some settings on the server, which a system administrator quickly corrected.

At the conclusion of the engagement, the consultant created a summary write-up of the installation, all the settings determined at installation, and other pertinent facts. The project team members took this write-up to the training class. As a result, the project team was ready to use the product immediately after training, and they were highly successful.

Another example using an expert consultant involved technology rather than a specific vendor product. In this example, the project had a requirement that the user interface must be Section 508-compliant. Section 508 involves designing the user interface so that it can be used more easily by the vision-impaired. In addition, this application had to present a tremendous amount of information and allow users to act on it. Finally, the users of this application were minimally fluent with modern IT systems.

The project team was struggling with two issues. First, no one had experience with designing Section 508-compliant user interfaces. Second, the team had built prototype user interface screens. The problem was that the amount of information on the screen made the user interface complex. The prototype was presented to users, and the reaction was mixed. The team was having difficulty figuring out how to architect the user interface in a way that would make it easy and intuitive. The solution to both of these problems was found by retaining an expert consultant. A consultant was found who had experience with designing Web sites. The consultant had also built many Section 508-compliant user interfaces. What distinguished this consultant from many others was his extensive art and graphic-design background. It was a perfect fit.

During initial meetings with the consultant, the project team demonstrated the user interface prototype. The problem given to the consultant was threefold. First, we wanted to build a new user interface based on the prototype that would be Section 508-compliant. Second, we wanted the consultant to use his graphic-design background to design a user interface that was aesthetically pleasing and that would be easy for novice users. Finally, we wanted the consultant to deliver his work in the form of screen templates that could easily be used by the project team. The result was a user interface design that drew raves from the user community and that met the requirements for Section 508. The consultant documented how to use the templates and met with the team to review the document's contents.

Both of these examples were successful because each had a clear entry point and clear objectives to be accomplished. Also, the work performed by the consultant in each example was directly related and constrained to his primary area of expertise. In the second example, although the consultant was asked to indulge himself creatively, the prototype he received as input was helpful to illustrate the system's general concept and to provide focus for his efforts.

Expert Process Consultants from Consulting Firms

Some consulting engagements are less focused than in the preceding examples. A consultant can be an excellent resource for helping a project team shift to a new paradigm. Years ago, the new paradigm was object-oriented analysis, design, and programming. Today, a common goal of project teams is to move toward modern processes such as iterative and Agile development. The transition from one process to another is a major one, and most organizations struggle with it. Even with training, the circumstances on each project differ enough that a training class is insufficient. You need an experienced practitioner to guide the organization. These engagements tend to be fairly long-term (perhaps for the project's duration), and the consultants work closely alongside the rest of the team.

Choosing a Project Suitable for Working with a Process Consultant

Before you decide whether to work with a process consultant, you must choose a suitable project. The following characteristics are important when you select a project:

- The project should not be in the critical path of other important projects or events. Most companies choose an internal project for this purpose. By choosing an internal project, the company has complete control over schedule, cost, and staffing. Despite the project's noncritical nature, it should still be technically challenging and produce something of importance.

- Staff the project only with people who are interested in and motivated to learn a new process. They should expect some uncertainty on the project and should be willing to work with a consultant.

- The project must be one in which management is comfortable with an outside consultant being involved in every aspect of the project. To properly advise the project, the consultant needs to understand the project requirements, help develop the schedule, and understand the qualifications and capabilities of the people staffing the project. The consultant will be working closely with the project manager.

- The project should have flexible deadlines.

- The company's management (as well as the project's managers) should be willing to commit the time and resources required to achieve the project's goals. Changing a process is a difficult undertaking that involves cultural change and learning new ways of accomplishing a project's goals. Management must also have an interest in the outcome and be committed to the goals. I have seen too many of these efforts fail because of this one item. It is more than simply learning a new skill. It is a change in the organization's culture.

First Steps of a Process Consultant

Suppose your company has decided to change from traditional Waterfall lifecycle development to a modern methodology such as iterative or Agile. Before the project begins, the consultant must perform a significant amount of background work. The consultant must conduct an organizational assessment. This consists of the following:

- A review of the current process used on software development projects (if there is one). What methodologies, technologies, tools, and techniques are used on the project?
- A review of the track record on previous projects. What have the successes been? What have the failures been? What is the clients' satisfaction level?
- An analysis of any failures that have occurred. This takes some time to prepare, because the consultant must interview a number of people to understand the problems. It may be difficult, because there may be disagreement regarding the cause of the failure.
- An analysis of the skills of the people staffing the projects. It is important that the consultant be discreet during this activity. You do not want project staff believing that the consultant's purpose is to eliminate staff members. Even if a staff member's skills are insufficient for the role he plays on the team, his skills could be upgraded, or there may be other new roles for him on the project team.
- The consultant must develop an understanding of the organization's business goals and how the ability to develop software affects the accomplishment of these goals.
- The organization might want to focus on particular areas first. For example, it might want to improve its practices in one of the disciplines used in software development— configuration management, requirements management, change management, or testing. In fact, some consultant engagements, at the client's request, are limited in scope to a specific problem in one or more disciplines.
- Any other issues, at the request of the client, should be prioritized and investigated.

Second Steps

The consultant should prepare an implementation plan for the organization and submit it to the organization's management for approval and comment. The implementation plan is the instrument that explains what is to be accomplished, by whom, and when. It is essentially a project plan defining the work the consultant will perform in conjunction with the team. Each consultant's implementation plan varies depending on the situation. The consultant probably has a template that will be used for the implementation plan. At a minimum, the implementation plan should contain the information described in the following sections.

Background

This section explains the work performed during the organizational assessment. If a separate assessment document was prepared, it can be referenced from this section rather than repeating the information. This section should describe what was done to assess the organization. It should answer the following specific questions:

- What was the assessment's primary purpose? Did it have a specific focus?

- How was the information for the assessment acquired? Were specific artifacts reviewed? If so, list them.

- Who was interviewed for the assessment, and how were they chosen? What are the roles of the people interviewed?

- Were any previous projects reviewed for the assessment? If so, which projects were examined, and why were they chosen?

- Explain the organization's goals. In other words, why has the consultant been asked to work with the organization?

Findings

This section describes the results of the assessment effort. The information in this section should identify any gaps in the existing business processes. Questions answered here include items such as the following: Are any activities missing or insufficient? What areas need improvement? How do these findings relate to the goals listed by the organization? Also, what processes are working correctly? In other words, what should not be changed? Most assessments seem to omit this information. Even the most dysfunctional organizations have something positive that should not change. This needs to be mentioned so that these items will be preserved. Also, given that the primary purpose of the assessment is to identify areas that need improvement or correction, the organization should be reassured to know that it is performing some activities correctly.

Recommendations

This section should list the recommendations the consultant has for the organization. It takes into account the findings and also the organization's stated goals as described in the background section of the implementation plan. This section should discuss the following information:

- Recommendations on various solutions to close the gaps discovered in the Findings section. This should be a prioritized list, beginning with the most important items. Under ideal circumstances, it would be best if every recommendation could be followed. The reality in most situations is that time and resources are limited. Therefore, it is important to focus on the most important changes first and follow up with the lower-priority changes as time and resources permit. An explanation indicating why the priorities are in the order given is important as well so that the organization can weigh the possible consequences of reordering the list or skipping the higher-priority items.

- A complete set of recommended tasks, including process changes, staffing adjustments, training, and acquisition (such as purchasing a configuration management or requirements management tool). Each recommended task should be tied back to the gaps identified and explain how the task will help close the gap. If training is recommended, what specific classes are recommended? Is a particular vendor's class recommended? How much does the training cost, and who from the project team should attend?

- Sequencing. Should the tasks be conducted in a particular order? Depending on the complexity of the tasks, it may not be possible or reasonable to attempt every task at once. A phased, or iterative, approach may be indicated.

- A list of the risks involved through implementing the tasks. What items should be in place before the tasks are undertaken? What could go wrong, and how can the risks be mitigated?

- Unrealistic goals. Has the organization stated goals (listed in the Background section) that are unreasonable or unattainable given the current set of circumstances? What must change first so that these goals are attainable?

- Missing goals. Did the organization fail to list any goals that should be considered? What should the priority of these new goals be, and why should they be considered in addition to the other listed goals?

- Goal conflicts. Did the organization list any conflicting goals? If so, why are the goals conflicting? Which goals should take precedence?

- Cost. What is the anticipated cost of implementing the recommendations? How long will it take to implement them? Are additional resources (besides the consultant) needed?

Presenting the Findings and Recommendations

The organization should expect a presentation by the consultant after management has had a chance to review the implementation plan. The presentation lets the organization ask questions to better understand the assessment and the implementation plan. Members of the organization should carefully review the documents supplied by the consultant and consider each of the recommendations made. Any questions should be formulated and asked during the presentation. To put it another way, the client needs to prepare for this presentation. This is an opportunity to correct any misinformation and to shape the implementation plan to better fit the organization's needs.

Third Step

After the organization has had a chance to attend the presentation and ask questions of the consultant, it must decide which recommendations, if any, to implement. This can be communicated to the consultant through a follow-up meeting. In addition, cost factors are often discussed at the meeting as well. Finally, a start date for the engagement should be discussed.

Fourth Step

After the consultant has been told which recommendations have been accepted and a requested start date for the services to begin has been determined, the consultant prepares a detailed schedule for the tasks to be conducted. This includes a list of the staff members who will be involved in the various activities. A list of assumptions and an updated risk list, along with the risk mitigation plan, should also be included. This package is submitted to the customer for approval. Then, it is time for the consultant and the project staff members to roll up their sleeves and begin work.

Working with the Consultant

Several artifacts have been generated: an assessment document, an implementation plan, a risk list and mitigation plan, and a schedule. On the start date, the project team should meet. The project manager should lead the meeting, with the consultant in attendance. Those project team members who have not met the consultant can be introduced. The implementation plan should be presented to the team. The consultant should explain the plan and go over the schedule. The team will probably have questions, which can be answered in this session.

With the preliminary introductions and orientations out of the way, it is time to begin the tasks. The following are suggestions for getting the most benefit from working with the consultant:

- The project team should review the list of risks and assumptions shown in the implementation plan. The project team should ensure that any dependencies and contingencies have been satisfied. This includes any training the consultant has recommended before work commences, any recommended software procured, and so on.

- The project team should review the schedule. Each member of the team should examine the schedule for any activities assigned to him and prepare to be ready to conduct those activities. In other words, don't wait for the consultant to tell you what to do. Take the initiative and prepare ahead of time. For example, if the next activity involves working with the consultant to identify candidate use cases for the project, start familiarizing yourself with any requirements and stakeholder requests you already have.

- The project manager should instill a sense of urgency in the project personnel. Even though this project may be an internal project, it is still important to set goals and deadlines just as you would for any project.

- Try to anticipate things that may go wrong, and have an action plan ready to solve problems that arise. If an activity involves installing and configuring software, have a system administrator available on standby in case a problem occurs with the system or environment.

- Be sure to document any important experiences or lessons learned from the consulting engagement. This information can then be reviewed later or placed in the project's history file. (This is discussed further in Chapter 15, "The Project Postmortem.") On many projects, schedules are hectic; if you don't document this information, the key lessons learned may be forgotten. Some consultants provide their own summary. However, you should still take notes to provide your own summary.

Consultant Pricing

Prices vary widely for consultants, so its pays to shop around. It's important to find one with the right skills and qualifications. In general, the highest-priced consultants come from vendors. Most offer consulting services primarily to enable further sales of their products. Unless there is a compelling reason to work directly with a vendor's consultants, you may find a better value elsewhere.

It is important to ask for and check references when using consultants. Also, find colleagues who have used the consultant, and ask about their experience. Ask the consultant about her prior consulting experience. Ideally, you want a consultant who has worked in situations similar to yours. Be sure to meet with the consultant who will be working on your project before you sign the contract. Introduce the person to key members of your project team. Good chemistry between team members and a consultant is important, especially for high-level process consulting.

Summary

Retaining a consultant can be a positive experience that fills in the gaps on a project team. Consultants can provide the changing agent needed to transition your organization to a new methodology or way of doing business. Keep in mind the following points from this chapter:

- A consultant's price does not necessarily indicate quality. It is far more important that a prospective consultant have experience with engagements and tasks or goals similar to the ones proposed on your project.
- The relationship between the project team and the consultant is as important as the consultant's qualifications. This is even more important when the consultant is engaged as an expert process consultant. If key individuals on the team do not work well with the consultant, they will be less open to learning from that person. This can be a showstopper for a successful engagement.
- Always be prepared for consultant visits. Review the project schedule and verify that any prerequisite tasks needed before a consultant visit are completed before the consultant

arrives. Otherwise, the consultant's time (and your project money) is wasted in unproductive pursuits by the consultant.

- If you have consultants engaged in a staff augmentation model, try to give them the same resources and furnishings you would provide to any other team member. The key is to allow the consultant to become part of the team and to act as any other team member. Avoid providing substandard equipment and furnishings "because the consultant is not an employee."

What's Next?

Team members learn many lessons during a project. Whether it's information about applying a certain technology or method, or simply ways to interact effectively with a certain customer, these lessons learned can be effectively applied to other projects. For this to happen, these lessons learned must be captured and instilled in the company's corporate memory. The next chapter discusses these and other activities that should be conducted as part of a project's postmortem.

CHAPTER 15

The Project Postmortem

For an organization to improve its ability to develop software, it should take the time to reflect on a project's successes and failures. Even failed projects have some successes, and projects considered successful often have some failures. The purpose of a project postmortem is to collect the lessons learned, instill them in the organization's memory, and apply them to the next set of projects. This chapter discusses the best practices for this process.

Defining the Project Postmortem

A project postmortem is the process of reviewing the project's history to understand how each event contributed to the success or resulted in challenges for the project's outcome. In other words, it is the process of ascertaining the lessons learned from the project. Hopefully, your project postmortem will be a bit more civil than the one in the Dilbert cartoon shown in Figure 15-1!

Figure 15-1   Dilbert's project postmortem

DILBERT: © Scott Adams/Dist. by United Feature Syndicate, Inc. Reprinted with permission.

The following sections expand on the purpose of the project postmortem.

Sources of Information for Lessons Learned

As software projects progress, many decisions are made and activities conducted that use the information available at the time. These decisions and activities are conducted in the project's best interests. Given the context of time and the project's progression, you can determine, in retrospect, whether the decisions made were the right ones. Where does this information come from? Consider the following sources:

- The project risk list. The Rational Unified Process emphasizes the importance of risk management. If the project actively managed its risks, there should be a list of risks, along with the information gathered to explain the risks. A risk mitigation plan also should be available.

- The data obtained through the execution of the various disciplines employed on the project. A review of the Requirements Management, Configuration and Change Management, Testing, Project Management, and so on can help identify lessons learned for subsequent projects. If your project uses automated tools for these disciplines, you may be able to capture metrics during and after the project to spot trends and trouble spots. You'll read more about this later in the chapter.

- Analysis of the role of consultants. Were any consultants used on the project? Were the results satisfactory?

- Interviews and discussions with team members. Speak to members of the project team after their role on the team has concluded. Candid discussions with team members after the stress of the project is over can yield some useful insight.

- The proposal. Review the proposal that was developed when the team was bidding on the project. What assumptions were made in the original proposal? Which assumptions held true, and which ones did not? Should any assumptions have been added? Were any clues overlooked that could have foretold the challenges that were encountered?

- Original estimates. Review the estimates produced for the proposal for bidding on the project. How close did the estimates come to the actual amounts?

Much of the data useful to the study of a project after its conclusion can be collected during the project. A suggested practice is to publish selected data in a public area, such as near printers or break rooms. This helps keep project personnel informed of the project's status.

Note that the primary purpose of the project postmortem is to help the organization make subsequent projects more successful. Much of the information described here may come too late to help you effectively manage the current project. Instead, use the lessons learned from each iteration to guide the current project from iteration to iteration.

Why Bother with a Project Postmortem?

As just discussed, you can draw upon many sources of useful information from completed projects. Taking the time to distill the lessons learned from each project experience is worthwhile. Examining past performance, extracting lessons learned, and incorporating them back into the processes the organization uses are basic tenets of continuous improvement. Yet, many organizations do not take the time to do this. As work on a project winds down, the participants are eager to move to the next project. As a result, the people with the knowledge needed to record the project's experiences may no longer be available. At best, the information may be passed on, but only by word of mouth. Documenting this information is a better way to distribute these best practices uniformly across the organization. Accordingly, an organization's management must encourage this activity if they want the organization to improve. Why bother? Consider the following motivations:

- Project staff members come and go, but the organization's capabilities and understanding should be cumulative. Another way of putting this is that each member of a project team learns how to conduct (or how not to conduct) a project. A fact of life in any business is that these team members eventually move on to other activities. They change positions, get promoted, or join other companies. You do not want valuable information on lessons learned to walk out the door or, worse yet, walk through your competitors' doors. Instead, the information should be preserved and made available for future team members to review and understand.

- Project teams do not remain intact from project to project. As each new project begins, new people will be on the project who were not involved in previous projects. Without access to the lessons learned, they may repeat the same mistakes made in earlier projects.

- As the software services market evolves, organizations will continue to be squeezed to produce higher-quality software at a lower cost. Examining previous projects is one important aspect of a continuous-improvement program to enable the organization to remain competitive.

- If the contracting organization can retain artifacts created on a project, they can be harvested and cleansed for use on future projects. This way, future project teams do not have to start from scratch.

- Applying lessons learned to the software project estimation process used during proposal development provides a couple benefits. First, it helps the organization avoid projects that are destined to be unprofitable. Second, by honing the estimation process to be both precise and accurate, the organization can price a bid more aggressively. When the organization has confidence in its estimation and costing abilities, it has less need for a "padding factor" to add to the cost if it has underestimated the work. This allows the organization to be more competitive.

This last item, concerning the software estimation process, may seem to contradict earlier statements in this book. Given the creative and uncertain nature of software projects, it is still not possible to accurately estimate the cost and time needed to complete a software project in the beginning stages. Yet, as the development organization becomes more fluent and comfortable with an iterative development process, it will recognize how the estimation process becomes easier and more accurate after some iterations are completed. The most difficult aspect is explaining to and convincing the client why it is not possible to give a complete, accurate, and precise estimate before the work begins. In the past, the client has probably used contractors who provided these estimates up front. As a result, clients are not easily convinced that this cannot be done reliably. Clients often explain that they must have this information to plan their expenditures in advance. This is a valid issue. This is where the concept of staged contracts is useful (as explained in Chapter 3, "Getting Started: Request for Proposals (RFPs), Proposals, and Contracts"). Figure 15-2 illustrates this. Most early estimates are unreliable and unrealistic. This is partly because the estimates are produced without a good understanding of the system to be built. It's also partly because of wishful thinking, competitive pressure, and the human tendency to overestimate the ability to build a complex product from scratch. It is far better to estimate during or near the conclusion of the Elaboration phase. By the end of the Elaboration phase, information useful to the estimation process can assist with developing the estimate, yet competitive pressure still exists to balance the estimation effort. The amounts shown in Figure 15-2 are not meant to be exact. In other words, estimating the remaining effort at the end of Elaboration doesn't guarantee an accuracy of plus or minus 30%, as the figure implies. You may be able to do considerably better (or worse, depending on your estimation skills!). It is helpful to create a chart similar to Figure 15-2 and populate it with the results of periodic estimates taken during each project's duration. This will help you understand and refine the team's ability to estimate.

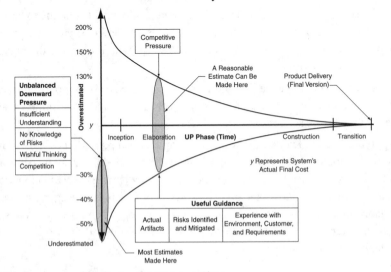

Figure 15-2   Accuracy of project estimates over time

Derived from *Agile & Iterative Development: A Manager's Guide.* Used with permission.

Instilling Lessons Learned into the Organization's Memory

When a project ends, participants are usually in a hurry to get to their next project or opportunity. That's why it is vital to capture as much information as possible before the participants scatter.

It is not necessary to create elaborate documents inches thick to be placed on the corporate bookshelf (which few people take the time to read). Instead, it is quite sufficient to create a PowerPoint-style presentation, or a brief five- or six-page document describing the key information needed. This presentation should contain the following information:

- Project identification—the project's name, dates it was conducted, and names of the participants. List the updated contact information for the participants if it is known.

- A description of the project, its purpose, and the client.

- A description of the end-user community in terms of size and general attributes.

- A description of the program size in terms of the number of project team members, the project's duration, funding, and so on.

- A list of the program's key risks and what was done to mitigate them. Was the mitigation successful? What risks were unanticipated, how did they affect the project, and what was done about them?

- A description of the technologies used on the project in terms of programming languages, methodologies, and techniques. What was successful? What were the pitfalls, and how were the problems and challenges met?

- A description of how the customer relationship evolved throughout the project. What was the customer's perception of the project organization at the conclusion of the project?

- A description of the budget and schedule. What were the project's original budget and time duration estimates? What were the final budget and time figures?

- A readily accessible copy of the documentation. If possible, save the artifacts from the project in a central location on a LAN. Create hyperlinks to the artifacts from the project. (This may not always be possible if the customer does not consent or if regulations prohibit it.) This can be a great help for future projects. The artifacts can be used as examples to follow or can be improved for the next project.

Project Management Forums

Another useful idea for contracting organizations is a messaging board that can be accessed over a company intranet. If managed properly, it can be helpful for obtaining quick "second opinions" or answers to questions. Another useful aspect is the ability to place a simple query such as "I am experiencing situation X on project Y. How should I handle this situation?" Here are some suggestions for operating a project management forum:

- It should have several categories of topics. For example, technical topics might include things such as development, programming language, platform, software process, Configuration Management, and Requirements Management.

- The forum should be kept strictly as a problem-solving dialog. There should be no prose-lytizing, unhelpful criticism, blaming, or complaining. Instead, the tone for answering problems should take this form: "We experienced that problem on Project N. Here's what we did to solve it." Another type of response might be, "If the audience is particularly large, a moderator may be needed to monitor the group, to keep the dialog on target."

- Posts should be kept online as long as practical. When this is done in conjunction with a good search engine, the message board becomes a storehouse of searchable information that can be useful for future projects.

The point is to have a forum where company team members can feel comfortable discussing ideas and can collaborate on solutions to problems without fear of ridicule or unfair criticism.

Examples of Trends from the Configuration Management Discipline

With iterative development, the features to be implemented for a given iteration are determined at the beginning of the iteration. The implementation of these features and requirements takes place during the iteration. Toward the conclusion of the iteration, these new features are integrated with the previously developed code. At the end of the iteration, a stable, executable release is created that is ready for thorough testing. Some configuration management tools tell you how many lines were inserted, deleted, or changed since a prior baseline. If you plot these numbers during the course of an iteration, you should expect to see a trend, as shown in Figure 15-3, where you can see that the number of lines inserted (in other words, new lines of code entered) ramps up quickly at the beginning of the iteration. The number of changed lines follows a similar trend, although the actual number of changed lines probably lags inserted lines (especially early in the project's life cycle). The key point in Figure 15-3 is that trends should ramp down quickly before the end of the iteration as code is integrated with the rest of the system and checked in. The exact shape of the curves may differ from project to project, and even from iteration to iteration within the same project. But a common theme is that code changes should trend down toward the end.

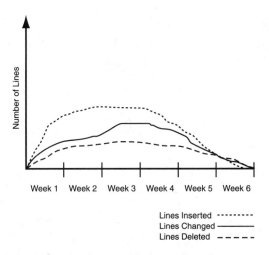

Lines Inserted ·········
Lines Changed ─────────
Lines Deleted ─ ─ ─ ─ ─

Figure 15-3 A normal trend of code changes during an iteration

Be vigilant for situations such as the one illustrated in Figure 15-4 where the code change trends start normally but do not trend down at the end. A release produced at the end of an iteration with code change trends such as shown in Figure 15-4 is likely to experience problems during testing. The code never stabilized in this iteration. This is a somewhat common situation that occurs in teams who are unaccustomed to iterative development. In this scenario, there is a strong temptation to extend the iteration's end date. You should strongly resist this urge. Instead, you should quickly shorten the list of features or requirements planned for implementation during this iteration. With practice, the team will learn to recognize in the second half of the iteration if it will be able to complete the planned work by the end of the iteration. As soon as the team realizes it cannot get everything done, enough work should be removed from the iteration to enable the trends to resemble Figure 15-3.

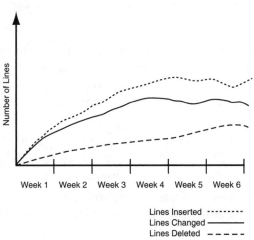

Lines Inserted ·········
Lines Changed ─────────
Lines Deleted ─ ─ ─ ─ ─

Figure 15-4 An example of code change trends that did not stabilize

Interestingly, the trend of code changes over a project's entire life cycle should tend to resemble the trend within an individual iteration. Figure 15-5 shows an example of the code change trends over the life cycle of a hypothetical project.

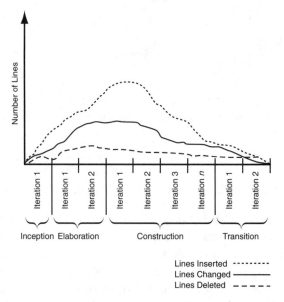

Figure 15-5   Code change trends over the entire project life cycle

Defect Trends on Iterative Projects

One of the advantages of iterative development is that independent testing can begin after the first iteration is completed, typically in the Elaboration phase. (Note that the developers can perform some testing even sooner. By "testing," I mean independent testing performed by test engineers.)

I prefer using a simple, three-level rating for defect priorities:

- Priority 1: Serious, showstopping defects that either make the system unusable or prevent a key part of its functionality from performing as it should. A defect in this category needs to be corrected as soon as possible, before the system is released to users. If a priority 1 defect is discovered after release, an emergency release should be made, correcting the defect.

- Priority 2: Defects that are a major inconvenience but that have workarounds. The system can still accomplish its primary functions, although the problem caused by the defect is annoying and, in some cases, is disruptive or causes extra work for users.

- Priority 3: Minor defects, such as spelling errors, inconsistencies in the user interface, formatting errors, or minor problems that do not inhibit use of the system.

Certainly, it is ideal to fix all defects prior to release. But if this is not possible, focus on the highest-priority defects first. As a matter of principle, I prefer never to release software with a known priority 1 defect. If you must release software with known defects, provide the users with release notes. Also follow up with discussions or verbal contact with key customer and user representatives to discuss the defects (as well as any information that helps avoid or work around the defect). Release notes are seldom read, so this verbal follow-up is extremely important. Many users can tolerate some defects if they are notified about them in advance and know that corrections are forthcoming.

Figure 15-6 shows typical defect trends over a project's life cycle. As the software is tested, defects are discovered and logged in a defect-tracking system. During Elaboration and the earlier Construction iterations, the focus is on establishing and proving the system's architecture, eliciting the proper features to build, and then building the system's main functionality. As the highest-priority risks (such as determining a viable architecture) are retired, attention can begin to turn to working on the defects detected. As a result, the number of open defects reaches a peak during Construction but tapers off rapidly in the later Construction iterations and Transition.

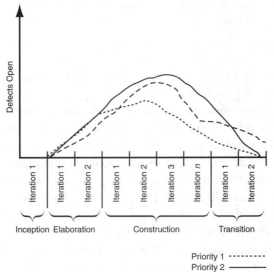

Figure 15-6   Defect trends over a project's life cycle

Trends in the Requirements Management Discipline

The requirements management discipline takes on even more importance on a project employing iterative development, such as projects that use the Rational Unified Process. On iterative development projects, requirements are not static, and they are not all collected up front. As a result, requirements must be carefully tracked. One metric I have used in the past is to plot the number of requirements successfully implemented and tested on a project. An example is shown in Figure 15-7. I like to print graphs like these on a plotter and post them in public areas in the project facility, such as near printers or break/conference rooms.

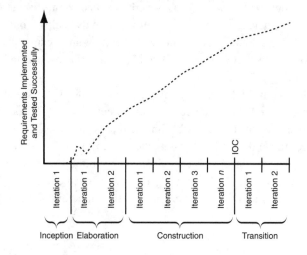

Figure 15-7   Graph of implemented functionality over time

Tracking requirements in this fashion serves three purposes. First, it gives the team a sense of accomplishment. Although developers focus on technology and building things, most want to know that their efforts are accomplishing something useful and are helping further the project's goals. Second, such a graph can be included in presentations to customers. (However, not all customers are interested in demonstrations, particularly finance and contracts personnel.) Graphs such as these provide another sense of getting closer to the project goals. Finally, you can study the graph to ascertain and provide data on the time and resources required to produce something tangible on a project. This can help with estimates for future projects and proposals.

Finally, note the "glitch" in the first iteration in this project's Elaboration phase. It is not uncommon to have some occasional "backward" progress early in the project. This is not a reason to panic, provided that it occurs for the right reasons. Figure 15-7 represents an actual project. On this project, a candidate architecture was chosen, and some key requirements were implemented to test the architecture. Problems were encountered during the testing of these requirements. This led to a decision to partially change the architecture and reimplement the requirements to test it. This second attempt was successful.

This is an example of "healthy" failure. It was discovered early in the project, through a deliberate effort to implement a high-risk portion of the system. If this situation occurred many times, or occurred much later in the project's life cycle, it would be cause for concern and would warrant investigation to take corrective action.

Another interesting item of data to collect is the amount of time between when a requirement is identified and when a tested, correct implementation of that requirement appears. Again, individual data items are not terribly useful, but together they are illustrative.

Collecting the Project Data

If the data described in the preceding sections is collected periodically during the project, it becomes much less of a chore to collect it at the end of the project. I recommend that someone on the project be assigned to collect and display this kind of data during the project. The project manager is a good candidate, but it can be anyone, provided that he is motivated to handle the task.

Some commercial tools can collect and manage this data. Certainly, the cheapest and most widely available tool is a simple Excel spreadsheet. Other options include tools such as IBM Rational's ProjectConsole, which can extract data from a variety of tools and produce charts, graphs, and statistics in an automated fashion. Although it takes significant up-front work to set up, configure, and customize, the data is automatically collected and displayed without intervention. The data is produced as a normal side effect of the project team using the tools they normally use in the course of their project work.

(Mis)Using Metrics Data

The best use of data such as that described in these sections is simply to provide insight into what is happening (or what happened) on a project. Using this data for future project cost and schedule prediction can be tricky and misleading. Be careful of hidden assumptions that the data represents. If you average the number of requirements over the amount of time and number of resources consumed, the result is a number that is applicable only to that specific project. Future projects will involve different customers, different project personnel, newer or different technologies, and a different environment, as well as a different application to be developed. Also, the amount of time needed to implement and test individual requirements varies by orders of magnitude. (It's like asking Boeing how many pounds of airplane were built in a given day!) Individually, the data has little meaning. However, taken in aggregate, the data is more meaningful.

When you use historical data such as this for project estimation, the data should be used as a starting point only. Then, you can make adjustments to account for all the aspects that will be different on the new project (and many things will be different!).

Exercise caution when using charts and metrics to justify making decisions or adjustments on a project. I am reminded of something a physician friend once told me: "Treat the patient, not the X-ray." Don't make changes on a project solely because a trend or metric doesn't indicate what you anticipated. In other words, the data shows you something is happening. You must investigate further to decide how to properly react to the data or whether to take action at all.

Summary

After spending many grueling months (or even years) on a project, reviewing early artifacts such as the original proposal, cost estimates, and analyses can help you identify the lessons learned on any project. The whole point is to answer the question "Based on what we know now, what would we have done differently had we known then what we know now?" You also should ask, "What did we learn from this project that we can apply to our next project to make it even better?" Taking the time to ascertain this information is useful to honing your organization's project knowledge and wisdom. Remember that the people in any organization come and go. The knowledge retained can reap benefits for future project team members. Also remember the following points:

- Decide early in a project's life cycle what metrics are useful. Fewer, concise, consistent, and clear metrics are better than loads of metrics few people have time to produce or analyze.

- Never hand responsibility for producing metrics to someone who is not motivated to perform that activity. If necessary, the project manager can produce the metrics. Don't assign the responsibility to developers unless they are interested and want to do it.

- Incorporate the production of metrics into a project's normal business routine. Producing the metrics while the project is under way yields a set of information that is of better quality than if they were produced haphazardly after the project.

- Post in public areas the more interesting metrics and graphs that reflect the team's accomplishments, where they can be easily seen and reviewed by team members and visitors.

- Never publish metrics that single out an individual's performance, whether good or bad. The purpose of metrics is to help the team recognize its accomplishments as a team and to communicate those accomplishments to others. If progress is hampered by a single individual or group of individuals, handle this discreetly.

- Be wary of using metrics from previous projects without a thorough understanding of the conditions on the project that produced them. Always adjust prior metrics to project the expectations for a new project.

- Try to create materials summarizing lessons learned on a project during the Transition phase or at least while the participants are still available and while the information is still fresh.

Common Mistakes Utilizing RUP

I have received many comments from practitioners who read about the RUP and become excited at the prospect of implementing it on their own projects. Indeed, it seems like applied common sense. Yet situations seem to occur that derail many people attempting RUP, especially for the first time.

Applying the RUP is not always intuitively obvious—certainly it's less so than traditional Waterfall processes. Most of the difficulties organizations experience with implementing the RUP center on the correct use of iterative development. Many organizations struggle with this. By examining some of the mistakes organizations make when applying the RUP, you can take steps to avoid them. Although it is not possible to cover every conceivable way things can go wrong, this appendix explores the more common ones. The scenarios covered in this appendix are situations I have encountered working as a consultant.

Mistake 1: Iterations of Inappropriate Length

The appropriate time length of iterations depends largely on the size of the team involved. A small team of 3 to 4 people might have iterations two to three weeks long. An appropriate length for a medium-size team of 5 to 20 people would be anywhere from three weeks up to six or seven weeks. Teams much larger than 20 may have iterations several months long. These are only rough guidelines. In general, shorter iterations are better. But the larger the project and the more contractors and the amount of ceremony involved, the iteration lengths need to be longer.

I have seen projects with relatively small teams define iterations several months long. This is a mistake. The advantages of iterative development cannot be realized in these situations; these projects tend to resemble and experience the disadvantages of Waterfall projects.

The key is to define iterations that are long enough to get something meaningful completed given the group's size, but short enough to maintain a sense of urgency. Another reason for keeping iterations short is the importance of exercising all the activities involved in the project. In other words, integration, testing, demonstrations, incorporating feedback, and replanning, among others, should be performed frequently. This allows risks to be identified and addressed and needed course corrections identified and implemented quickly. Also, iterations should be of equal length. This allows teams to fall into a natural rhythm.

Mistake 2: Iterations with No Clear Goal

I have seen several instances where project managers simply take the total amount of time available for development and schedule the work across the entire period of time. They divide the schedule into equal segments of time and name them Iteration 1, Iteration 2, Iteration 3, and so on. This completely misses the point of iterative development. The content of the iterations should be determined partly by the phase of the RUP lifecycle (Inception, Elaboration, Construction, and Transition) and by the highest risks appropriate for the current lifecycle phase. For example, consider the following:

- **Inception phase:** The iterations in the Inception phase should cover the following:
  - Is this project possible? Is it technically feasible? What business need motivates this project's execution?
  - Do we understand conceptually what the stakeholders want? Have we identified all the stakeholders?
  - Identify candidate architectures to accomplish the system's goals.
  - Identify requirements that are of particularly high risk.
- **Elaboration phase:** Iterations in the Elaboration phase should focus on the following:
  - Which of the identified architectures is the best choice for the system?
  - Elicit and define the system's requirements.
  - Implement functional requirements that fully exercise the chosen architecture. This requires a small portion (about 20%) of the system's functional requirements to be implemented.
  - Implement any units of code that must be in place before the bulk of development is performed (such as common code and libraries).
  - Implement any other requirements that are particularly high-risk.
  - Demonstrate releases to stakeholders, and elicit and incorporate feedback received into the subsequent iterations.

- **Construction phase:** By the time you reach the Construction phase, you should have eliminated or mitigated all the high-risk items on the project risk list. By this point, the developers are mostly "heads down," developing and creating periodic releases at the end of each iteration. Here are some suggestions for determining the content of iterations at this point:
  - First, focus on scheduling requirements for iterations that developers are not completely certain how to implement. In other words, schedule the most-difficult-to-implement requirements in the earlier iterations.
  - Also in the earlier Construction iterations, schedule requirements in which stakeholders seem to have particular interest. These are the features that the stakeholders will want to see first. They are also the most likely features to elicit change requests from stakeholders, because the implementation of these will be scrutinized the most.
  - Continue with demonstrations to stakeholders, and elicit and incorporate feedback.
- **Transition phase:** By this point, the product is functional. The focus in the Transition phase should be on any adjustments required for the product to function well in its production environment. The system must be installed in its operational environment so that the users can exercise the system to ensure that it is fit for production. Defect reports may be received at this point. These should be prioritized and corrected in the Transition phase before the project is concluded.

Mistake 3: Choosing the Wrong Project for Your First Experience with the RUP

Although the RUP is truly an excellent process, it is a major transition for a project team to undertake, particularly for teams used to Waterfall-oriented methods. The project selected for a team's first use of the RUP is of key importance. Most practitioners who are experienced with the RUP recommend that you select a noncritical project first; however, in today's business world, few projects can be described as noncritical. If you're a contractor whose primary business is developing outsourced projects, I recommend that you identify an internal project, along with a core team, for a first-time RUP implementation. The project should be one in which failure or schedule delays will not harm the company's reputation. On the other hand, it still needs to be a project with enough significance to provide a sense of accomplishment for the team involved. Finally, the team members for such a project should be those who are interested in and motivated to try something new. The team will face enough challenges without having to deal with team members who are not motivated.

It is also important to note that the project team is not the only group affected by the move to the RUP. Switching to the RUP involves a cultural change for the customer and stakeholders as well. In particular, the customer and stakeholders must embrace the notion of working with project team members for requirements elicitation. They must be willing to participate in reviews and assessments of iterations and to have "hands-on" time with the product before it is complete. In addition, they must embrace the notion of adaptive planning versus predictive models commonly used in Waterfall-based projects. Finally, the customer must understand that firm, fixed costs, schedules, and functionality cannot be realistically determined before the project begins. They must be willing to trade off completeness and schedule. Iterative projects provide the flexibility to deliver to a fixed date, but some functionality may need to be deferred. If a multitiered contract model is employed (as described in Chapter 3, "Getting Started: Request for Proposals (RFPs), Proposals, and Contracts"), the customer must be willing to delay firm commitments for cost and schedule until near or at the end of the Elaboration phase.

Mistake 4: Failing to Integrate Change Requests into Iterations

One potential complication can occur with iterative development. Because you can create early releases and allow stakeholders to see them, you will receive change requests (both requests for changes to requirements and defect reports) much earlier in the lifecycle. You need to review these very carefully. In the earlier phases, such as Elaboration, only change requests that affect architecture or have a major impact on the project's direction should be implemented immediately. Other change requests should be considered lower-priority until the Construction iterations.

In general, requests for changes to requirements should be viewed as an opportunity to refine the product to better meet customer needs. But this must be balanced with the existing requirements, plus constraints on costs and schedule. It is a good idea, when receiving requests for new requirements, to have the customer prioritize them in the context of requirements already received. In other words, are the new requirements more important than the existing requirements? Can some existing requirements be eliminated to accommodate the new requirements in the schedule? Discussing these considerations with the customer helps keep requirements from growing to the point where the cost and schedule grow beyond what the customer is willing to commit to.

Also, the requirements and scope of each iteration are fixed at the beginning of an iteration and remain so for its duration. Change requests received should be evaluated along with the results at the end of the iteration and should be incorporated into planning for subsequent iterations.

Mistake 5: Failing to Tailor the RUP Appropriately

I have seen some project teams learn about the RUP, decide to adopt it, and enthusiastically jump right in, determined to implement the RUP "by the book." However, the RUP should not be used "in its entirety." In other words, the RUP should be tailored. Some of the artifacts and activities suggested by the RUP may not be appropriate for all situations. Also, some teams may have adopted other artifacts that have worked well for them in the past. There is no reason that these cannot be continued in a RUP-based process. The RUP was intended by its designers to be a suite of processes and artifacts to choose from. The RUP should not be utilized blindly, without eliminating unnecessary artifacts or activities. Most projects should be documented to include their tailoring decisions in a document called the Development Case.

Mistake 6: Failing to Test Properly During the Iteration

It is important to remember that prior to reaching the end of an iteration, you must test the contents developed during that iteration and find and correct the key defects. In addition, you should conduct regression tests on previously implemented functionality and correct the results by the end of the iteration. This means that the project manager must be sure to allow enough time within the iteration for these activities to occur. Do not attempt to force so much functionality into the iteration that testing cannot be properly conducted and the defects corrected.

Mistake 7: Assuming You Can Implement the RUP Perfectly the First Time

Transitioning to a new process such as the RUP takes time and practice. It is a challenge that requires a cultural change for both the project team and the customer. If you can, it is best to avoid making this transition at the same time (and on the same project) as your customer and stakeholders (hence the suggestion to use an internal project for your first attempt at the RUP).

If you are a project manager embarking upon your first RUP project, note that some of the cultural changes involve your company's management. It is imperative that projects receive management support and commitment toward making this change. This includes allowing the team to make mistakes along the way, learn from them, and regroup. Without management commitment, the shift to the RUP will wither at the first sign of trouble. Don't forget to consider using an experienced consultant to help you with necessary cultural changes. This assistance can be invaluable.

Implementing a Two-Stage Procurement Process

As a manager in an outsourcing organization, you have chosen a small software project in which to break the acquisition process into two phases. The first phase (system specification) covers the Inception and Elaboration phases. The second phase (system realization) covers the Construction and Transition phases. This appendix gives you some guidance on how the first phase (system specification) should be conducted and what artifacts should be produced for the Request for Proposal (RFP) for the second phase.

Cultural Changes Needed

Most users know that custom software development is expensive and time-consuming. In many cases, they also have become conditioned to the fact that most software projects are late and over budget. We stated earlier in this book that a reasonable, firm estimate of a software project cannot (and should not) be made until the end of the Elaboration phase, where perhaps 20% of the system has been implemented. How can you convince them to supply funding for the first phase of a project when you will not make a firm commitment to the entire cost until the end of the first phase? On top of this, you then proceed to tell them it will require a commitment of resources from user community participation (and other stakeholders) to get to the point where you *will* be able to commit to a cost figure.

Unfortunately, I know of no magic way to easily overcome users' understandable angst. Education is the only way. I suggest preparing a briefing for the leaders of the user community, and other stakeholders as needed. The people giving the briefing should be members of the procuring organization. Contractors tend to have less credibility giving this briefing. If possible, start this educational process outside the context of starting a new project. The briefing should do the following:

- Stress the advantages of iterative development and the importance of building a small portion of the project to identify the risks.

- Explain that the participation of stakeholders provides numerous advantages. In particular, their involvement helps the contractor better understand their needs and helps demonstrate progress along the way. The stakeholders can help the contractor craft the product to better meet their needs.

- Most importantly, this two-step process is for the purpose of risk mitigation. If at any time the stakeholders are dissatisfied with the progress shown, they can redirect the activities and alter the project's course to be more in tune with their needs.

Perhaps, the single best answer to give the users is that they will have more control over the project. The first phase is relatively inexpensive compared to the cost of the second phase. If the stakeholders are unconvinced that the project is viable, or that it will meet their needs at the end of the first phase, they can terminate the project, alter it, or recompete it to a new contractor. They can do this *before* the bulk of their funds have been spent. This is a good message to give to the user community, because it puts them in control.

Finally, if the user community is receptive to the opinions of outside experts and consultants, consider bringing an expert well known in the community to discuss the advantages of iterative development and procurement methods with the user community.

Contract Types

What type of contract should be used for the system specification phase? Should it be Firm Fixed Price (FFP), Cost Plus Fixed Fee (CPFF), or Time and Materials (T&M)? This really depends on the stakeholder environment and the complexity of the application to be developed. FFP contracts can be utilized successfully for the first phase for projects with the following characteristics:

- The stakeholders are easily identified, colocated, and accessible to the project team.

- The project's scope is well known.

- The organization's business process is well known and stable, and stakeholders are in general agreement on their business process.

- The technologies anticipated for use on the project are well known and stable.

These projects are quite straightforward. At the other extreme, some system specification contracts are better served with CPFF or T&M contracts. The conditions making these contract types more suitable are mostly the opposite of the conditions for FFP system specification contracts. I will elaborate a bit on each condition:

- The stakeholders are not easily identified, are geographically distributed, or are inaccessible to the project team. Software systems in which users are scattered over a wide area present additional challenges. Some of these challenges are obvious, such as the travel and overhead required to work with the stakeholders. Others are less obvious. I have worked on several small projects (two or three developers on a one-year project) in which the stakeholders were scattered over more than 50 cities across the U.S. The outsourcing organization at the headquarters location believed that the system's stakeholder needs were identical regardless of the users' locations, since all stakeholders worked in the same logical organization, performing the same job. It was discovered that significant variations in the business process at each location were unknown to the headquarters location, where the system was being developed.

- The project's scope is not well known. If the outsourcing organization is unclear what functionality is to be developed or automated, this means that the analysis work required is unclear as well. Accordingly, T&M or CPFF contracts are more appropriate.

- The outsourcing organization's business process is not well understood or is unstable, or the stakeholders do not agree on their business process. It is not uncommon for stakeholders to disagree on certain details of a business process. But widespread disagreement indicates that a significant amount of work may be needed, or perhaps the business process needs to be changed. This means that the contractor must tread into sensitive territory, where it may not be possible to fully anticipate the amount of time and number of resources needed to address the issues. These efforts should not use FFP contracts.

- At first glance, the technologies to be utilized on a project may appear to be more of a Construction phase issue. But remember the goals of the Inception and Elaboration phases. If the technologies involved affect the architecture of a product to be built, they will be addressed directly in the Elaboration phase and, therefore, are covered by the contract's system specification phase. It may be necessary to conduct trade studies and possibly build prototypes to explore the technologies further to better identify the risks. Unless it is possible to determine up front exactly what additional activities are needed to fully identify the risks, CPFF or T&M contracts are more appropriate.

Who Bids on the Second Phase?

On some government projects, contractors who win and perform work on the first phase are not permitted to bid on the second phase. This is done so that the contractors bidding on the second phase all start from the same knowledge base. But if the right artifacts are built during the first phase and are made available to potential bidders for the second phase, this negates most of the competitive disadvantage. I believe contractors who perform the first phase well should be permitted to bid on the second phase. This gives them additional incentive to perform. If you allow this, you must also consider what to do if the bid from the first-phase contractor is significantly different (higher or lower) from those of the other bidders. Does that contractor know about risks in the artifacts that are not available to the other contractors? Does that contractor possess knowledge of risks that is unavailable to the other bidders? Be prepared to consider these scenarios.

What Artifacts Should Be Produced and Made Available During the First Phase?

This section identifies and discusses the artifacts that should be produced during the system specification contract. These artifacts should be made available to contractors bidding on the system realization contract.

Glossary

Every project brings a plethora of terms and phrases. A project glossary defining these terms should be produced and made available to bidders for the system realization phase. This will greatly aid contractors in the frenzy of activity that occurs during the proposal generation process.

Vision Statement

The Vision Statement (sometimes called a Concept of Operations [CONOPS]) is vital. It should be written from the perspective of the project stakeholders. The reason for supplying this with the RFP for the second phase is to quickly communicate the project's motivation to prospective bidders. This helps set the context for the project. The vision statement is discussed further in Chapter 7, "Inception: Kicking Off the Project."

Software Architecture Document

The Software Architecture Document is another vital set of information. It describes the architectural decisions that were made during the Elaboration phase. It should also describe how the architecture meets the system's supplementary requirements covering response time, throughput, reliability, scalability, and so on. This helps the bidders understand the system's complexities.

Set of Business and System Use Cases

This information helps the bidders understand the complexity of interactions (as well as the number of interactions) actors can have with the system. The actors should be clearly identified, especially those who have an interface to other (external) systems. If possible, an estimation of the completeness of the use cases should be given. (Usually requirements are not 100% complete by the end of the Elaboration phase.)

UML Models

Models illustrating the system's analysis and design should be provided.

Set of Supplementary Requirements

The supplementary requirements describe the nonfunctional requirements to which the system must conform. Supplementary requirements describe areas such as scalability, reliability, response time, and the number of users the system must support. These requirements can be significant cost drivers. Usually, the supplementary requirements are 100% complete by the end of the Elaboration phase. If they aren't, an estimate of their completeness should be given.

Executables Produced by Iterations

Since the Elaboration phase produces some early releases of the system, potential bidders should be given these releases. Accompanying these releases should be the list of requirements that the releases satisfy, and a list of risks that the iteration was designed to address. The source code should be provided or be available for inspection. Build instructions to perform a build of the releases should be included.

List of Risks and Risk History

An important aspect of the Elaboration phase is to directly address project risks. A risk history, containing risks identified in the Inception and Elaboration phases, should be provided. The history should include which risks have been successfully retired and how they were retired. If risks remain, they should be identified, and a suggested course of action to address the risk provided.

Other Information

The contractor supporting the system specification phase will have other information that can assist those bidding on the second phase. For example, what software tools will be used to build the executable releases? The tools (and their version numbers) should be identified. Also, the contractor may have a sense of the size of team that will be needed to develop the system in the customer's time frame. If possible, the initial contractor should be made available for a period of time (perhaps 2 months) for questions after the second phase is awarded to the new contractor.

Summary

A bid for the Construction and Transition phases is much more likely to be accurate and successful if the information described in this appendix is used as input. It is not possible (except through luck) to produce a single bid for an entire project of significant complexity at the beginning. Outsourcing organizations using this two-stage process will experience higher levels of success and will better use limited funds for procuring software systems.

GLOSSARY

acquisition

The process of procuring a software system through a contract with an outside services provider (contractor).

actor

An entity outside a system's boundaries that interacts with the system. An actor may be a user performing a certain role, or it could be another system, or even hardware.

ACWP

Actual Cost of Work Performed. A term associated with the use of Earned Value techniques for evaluating progress on a project. Actual Cost of Work Performed is a calculation of the funds expended to complete a portion of work.

adaptive planning

A method of planning and conducting a project in which detailed planning takes place only for activities planned for the immediate future. Planning for the longer term is at a high level at most (in other words, not detailed). As the short-term plan is executed, the knowledge gained and changes from the environment (especially stakeholders) are factored together to create the next short-term plan. This includes artifacts such as the schedule and list of requirements.

Agile

A set of values and principles for software development that use lean production techniques to deliver value to stakeholders quickly and frequently.

API

Application programming interface. A set of definitions (typically in a programming language) that define how a software artifact can be used.

architect

A role defined by RUP for the person responsible for a system's architecture.

architecture

The identification of major components in a system and how they are organized, including the interfaces for each component, as well as the relationships between the components.

artifact

A work product created by executing an activity or process.

BAFO

Best and Final Offer. Usually used in the context of an outsourcing organization to ask a prospective bidder to refine an earlier bid or proposal with more aggressive pricing.

baseline

A set of versions of artifacts that collectively represent some milestone in development. Typically, in a configuration management tool, baselines are read-only and cannot be changed, although they can be copied.

BCWP

Budgeted Cost of Work Performed. A term associated with the use of Earned Value techniques for evaluating progress on a project. It is a calculation based on the original anticipated cost of work performed for a period of time, multiplied by the percentage completed. Also called Earned Value.

BCWS

Budgeted Cost of Work Scheduled. A term associated with the use of Earned Value techniques for evaluating progress on a project. It is the anticipated cost of performing an activity during a specific period of time.

Business Use Case

A description of how an actor uses a business process to accomplish a goal of value.

ceremony

The degree of formality involved when conducting activities on a project.

CMMI

Capability Maturity Model Integration. A set of best practices that address product development and maintenance. CMMI emphasizes both systems and software engineering and the integration necessary to build and maintain a product.

collaboration

Two or more entities (people or software components, depending on the context) working together to achieve a common goal.

component

A unit of functionality that performs a clear task and has a well-defined interface.

configuration management

The process of controlling and tracking changes to artifacts for the purpose of providing an orderly environment for accomplishing project goals. Configuration Management processes provide ways for project staff to identify sets of artifact versions that collectively represent a certain state or milestone.

CONOPS

Concept of operations. *See* Vision Statement.

Construction phase

The third of four phases in the Rational Unified Process. Typically the longest phase in the Rational Unified Process, used to implement the majority of system functionality.

Contract Work Order (CWO)

A short-term contractual mechanism that specifies deliverables to be accomplished in a set period of time, under the control of an "umbrella" head contract.

contracting officer

A role within an outsourcing organization that has the authority to commit funds on behalf of the outsourcing organization for the purpose of acquiring a software system from an outside contractor.

contractor

An organization that performs software development under contract to an outsourcing organization.

Cost Plus Fixed Fee (CPFF)

A type of contract in which the contractor's profit is a fixed amount, determined in the beginning. The number of hours required to complete the work is not fixed. This tends to divide some of the risk between the outsourcing organization and the contractor. Regardless of the amount of work required, the contractor makes a fixed profit. Accordingly, the percentage of profit goes down as the number of hours required to complete the work increases, giving the contractor incentive to complete the work within a reasonable amount of the original estimate.

COTS

Commercial Off-The-Shelf. A product available for purchase that is ready to use. Usually used in conjunction with software.

customer

One of the principal stakeholders in a business arrangement between an outsourcing organization and a contractor. The customer may or may not be the actual end user of the system.

deployment

The process of transitioning a system from its development to fully operational status in the customer environment.

discipline

A collection of activities related to a major area of concern on a project. Examples of disciplines in the RUP are Project Management, Requirements, Business Modeling, Analysis and Design, Implementation, Test, Deployment, Configuration and Change Management, and the Environment.

domain

A specific problem category that is characterized by a body of knowledge, activities, and behaviors.

down select

The process used by an outsourcing organization to narrow down the number of proposals to a shorter list of proposals considered the most attractive by the organization.

Earned Value

The value of work accomplished on a project for a specific period of time. It is calculated based on the original anticipated cost of the work performed for a period of time multiplied by the percentage complete. Also referred to as the Budgeted Cost of Work Performed (BCWP).

Elaboration phase

The second of four phases in the Rational Unified Process. This phase is characterized by efforts to establish a proven architecture by implementing the system's key use cases, together with establishing a high-level plan for implementing the system.

Extreme Programming

An Agile process characterized by an emphasis on developing tests first (test-driven development) and very short (1- to 3-week) iterations. Also called XP.

feature

A high-level requirement typically requested by a user or other system stakeholder.

Firm Fixed Price (FFP)

A type of contract in which the cost of the contract is fixed and determined before work starts. The financial risk burden is on the contractor, because the price is fixed regardless of whether the work can be completed in the time estimated. These types of contracts should be used where the scope of the work is well-defined and unlikely to change.

functional requirement

A requirement that describes how a system behaves, often involving interaction with actors. In the RUP, these are usually described by use cases.

glossary

An artifact in the RUP that defines the vocabulary and other important terms that are part of a project and the problem domain.

head contract

A long-term, "umbrella" contract that defines the basic terms and conditions to set the stage for a series of short-term Contract Work Orders (CWOs) to be issued.

Inception phase
The first of four phases in the Rational Unified Process, characterized by the establishment of a business case for developing the system and a vision for the product to be built.

iterative lifecycle model
A process for developing a software system in which small increments of a system are built, building more functionality over time.

lifecycle model
The methods or processes used to develop a software system.

offshoring
A subset of outsourcing in which the contractor is located in a country overseas from the outsourcing organization.

outsourcing
The practice of hiring contractors to develop a software system instead of using people internally (within the same company) to develop a system.

outsourcing organization
The company that pays contractors to perform software development services.

PMI
Project Management Institute. An organization advocating project management as a profession. PMI sets industry standards, conducts research, and provides education and certification designed to strengthen and advance the profession.

PMO
Project Management Office. Typically refers to the group of managers who run a project.

postmortem
The process of reviewing the activities and events during project execution to determine the lessons learned for the purpose of improving an organization's ability to conduct software development projects.

predictive planning
A method of planning and conducting a project in which detailed plans for the project's duration are developed. Progress on the project is measured by comparing the completion of items to the originally planned schedule.

prime contractor
When multiple contractors are used on a software project, the prime contractor is the "main" contractor that has the principal relationship with the outsourcing organization.

procurement
The process of acquiring services in connection with developing a software system.

product acceptance plan
A document developed collaboratively with the project stakeholders (especially the contract representative) that lists the evaluation criteria that constitute acceptance of the system by the stakeholders.

proposal
A detailed offer from a contractor in response to a Request for Proposal (RFP) to build a software system for an outsourcing organization.

prototype
An early release of software, usually a small subset of a system's functionality, built for the purpose of a proof of concept or to address a specific risk.

Rational Unified Process (RUP)

A framework for developing software projects. Also, an instance of the Unified Process.

release

A baselined set of project artifacts, usually produced at the end of an iteration or to meet a specific lifecycle objective or milestone.

requirement

A condition, behavior, or capability that a system must conform to or provide.

Requirements Analysis

An activity conducted in an attempt to understand a system's requirements from the perspective of the system's stakeholders.

Requirements Management

The process of eliciting, organizing, categorizing, and documenting a system's requirements.

RFP

Request for Proposal. A document issued by an outsourcing organization to elicit an offer from contractors to build a system for the outsourcing organization.

RFS

Request for Solution. Synonymous with Request for Proposal (RFP).

risk

A condition that can potentially affect, prevent, or limit a project's success.

role

A set of behaviors and responsibilities associated with a person (or persons) operating in a specific context or domain.

RUP

See Rational Unified Process.

scenario

An instance of a use case, or a thread of execution within a use case.

scope

A description of the breadth of a system's behavior, specifying the boundaries of the problem domain or system.

scrum

An Agile process characterized by certain key practices and attributes, such as daily meetings, self-organizing teams, and iterations associated with calendar months.

Service-Oriented Architecture (SOA)

An architectural concept that defines shared, common services available over a network. This consolidates services needed to build systems in a given environment and eliminates multiple implementations of common services in each software system.

software development process

The methods and practices used by an organization to conduct software development.

stakeholder

An individual with a vested interest in a software system and in the successful outcome of a software project.

Statement of Work (SOW)

A document written by an outsourcing organization. Specifies the activities and tasks to be performed by a contractor under the terms of a contract.

subcontract

A contract between a prime contractor and another contractor, with each performing a set of activities to develop a system for a particular outsourcing organization.

supplementary requirement

A requirement that is not functional in nature, but instead specifies certain conditions or standards to which a system must conform.

supplementary specification

A document that contains all the nonfunctional requirements and any requirements not contained in the system use cases.

system

A group of components that work together to form a comprehensive collection of services of value to a user.

System Realization Contract

The second contract used in a two-step contract model. Follows the System Specification Contract. The System Realization Contract directs a contractor to implement the system described by the artifacts created for the System Specification Contract.

System Specification Contract

The first contract used in a two-step contract model. The System Specification Contract directs a contractor to perform activities roughly equivalent to a project's Inception and Elaboration phases. The System Specification Contract precedes the System Realization Contract.

Time and Materials (T&M)

A type of contract in which the contractor is paid by the hour and is reimbursed for any other costs (such as travel). This type of contract places the financial risk on the outsourcing organization, because the contractor bills for as many hours as necessary to complete the work.

toolsmith

A role on a project. A technical person (often a developer) who has experience with and interest in setting up and customizing the tools used to establish the software development environment.

traceability

A relationship that is established between two or more entities in a software system.

Transition phase

The fourth and final phase of the Rational Unified Process. In this phase, a system begins the process of moving from implementation to being deployed to fully operational status.

Unified Modeling Language (UML)

A graphical language for visualizing, specifying, constructing, and documenting a software system's artifacts.

unified process

A process framework that is risk-driven and iterative in nature for developing software systems.

use case

An artifact (usually a document) that describes how an actor can use a system to achieve something of value to the actor. A use case describes the interaction between an actor and a software system.

user interface prototype

A mock-up of the portion of a system stakeholders use to interact with the system. User interface prototypes are often used in conjunction with use cases to elicit and understand a software system's functional requirements.

Vision Statement
A document that describes how stakeholders believe a system can solve a problem or provide something of value. Sometimes called a concept of operations (CONOPS) document.

Waterfall process
A method of conducting a project in which each major activity is conducted in its entirety before you move on to the next activity or phase.

Work Breakdown Structure (WBS)
A document or other artifact (possibly entered into a tool) that breaks the project into individual units of work, or tasks, for which cost, milestones, and activities can be allocated and tracked.

XP
See Extreme Programming.

This bibliography lists books and articles I have found particularly helpful. A couple of these are dated, but they helped influence my thinking just as the Rational Unified Process was getting started. They are excellent references if you want to explore certain topics further.

The Rational Unified Process

Ambler, Scott W., 2000. *The Unified Process Elaboration Phase: Best Practices in Implementing the UP.* Lawrence, KS: CMP Books.

Ambler, Scott W., 2002. *The Unified Process Transition and Production Phases: Best Practices in Implementing the UP.* Lawrence, KS: CMP Books.

Ambler, Scott W. and Larry L. Constantine, 2000. *The Unified Process Inception Phase: Best Practices in Implementing the UP.* Lawrence, KS: CMP Books.

Bergstrom, Stefan and Lotta Raberg, 2004. *Adopting the Rational Unified Process: Success with the RUP.* Boston, MA: Addison-Wesley.

Eeles, Peter, Kelli Houston, and Wojtek Kozaczynski, 2003. *Building J2EE Applications with the Rational Unified Process.* Boston, MA: Pearson Education.

Jacobson, Ivar, Grady Booch, and James Rumbaugh, 1999. *The Unified Software Development Process.* Boston, MA: Addison-Wesley.

Kroll, Per and Philippe Kruchten, 2003. *The Rational Unified Process Made Easy: A Practitioner's Guide to the RUP.* Boston, MA: Pearson Education.

Kroll, Per and Walker Royce, 2005. "Key Principles for Business-Driven Development." *The Rational Edge*, October 2005 issue, IBM.

Kruchten, Philippe, 2004. *The Rational Unified Process: An Introduction*, Third Edition. Boston, MA: Pearson Education.

Pollice, Gary, Liz Augustine, Chris Lowe, and Jas Madhur, 2004. *Software Development for Small Teams: A RUP-Centric Approach.* Boston, MA: Addison-Wesley.

Rational Software, 2003. "The Rational Unified Process 2003.06.15."

Wideman, R. Max, 2002. "Progressive Acquisition and the RUP Part I: Defining the Problem and Common Terminology." *The Rational Edge*, December 2002 issue, IBM.

Wideman, R. Max, 2003. "Progressive Acquisition and the RUP Part II: Contracts that Work." *The Rational Edge*, January 2003 issue, IBM.

Wideman, R. Max, 2003. "Progressive Acquisition and the RUP Part III: Contracting Basics." *The Rational Edge*, February 2003 issue, IBM.

Wideman, R. Max, 2003. "Progressive Acquisition and the RUP Part IV: Choosing a Form and Type of Contract." *The Rational Edge*, March 2003 issue, IBM.

Wideman, R. Max, 2003. "Progressive Acquisition and the RUP Part V: Contracting Activities." *The Rational Edge*, April 2003 issue, IBM.

Requirements Management and Use Cases

Armour, Frank and Granville Miller, 2001. *Advanced Use Case Modeling Software Systems.* Boston, MA: Addison-Wesley.

Bittner, Kurt and Ian Spence, 2003. *Use Case Modeling.* Boston, MA: Addison-Wesley.

Cockburn, Alistair, 2001. *Writing Effective Use Cases.* Boston, MA: Addison-Wesley.

Jacobson, Ivar, Magnus Christerson, Patrik Jonsson, and Gunnar Overgaard, 1992. *Object-Oriented Software Engineering: A Use Case Driven Approach.* Reading, MA: ACM Press.

Leffingwell, Dean and Don Widrig, 2000. *Managing Software Requirements: A Unified Approach.* Reading, MA: Addison Wesley Longman.

Rosenberg, Doug and Kendall Scott, 1999. *Use Case Driven Modeling with UML: A Practical Approach.* Boston, MA: Addison-Wesley.

Rosenberg, Doug and Kendall Scott, 2001. *Applying Use Case Driven Object Modeling with UML: An Annotated E-Commerce Example.* Boston, MA: Addison-Wesley.

Schneider, Geri and Jason P. Winters, 2001. *Applying Use Cases: A Practical Guide*, Second Edition. Boston, MA: Addison-Wesley.

Object-Oriented Technologies and UML

Booch, Grady, 1994. *Object-Oriented Analysis and Design with Applications*, Second Edition. Redwood City, CA: Benjamin/Cummings Publishing Company.

Fowler, Martin with Kendall Scott, 1997. *UML Distilled: Applying the Standard Object Modeling Language.* Reading, MA: Addison Wesley Longman.

Jacobson, Ivar, Maria Ericsson, and Agneta Jacobson, 1995. *The Object Advantage: Business Process Reengineering with Object Technology.* Reading, MA: ACM Press.

Rumbaugh, James, 1996. *OMT Insights*. New York, NY: SIGS Books.

Rumbaugh, James, Ivar Jacobson, and Grady Booch, 2005. *The Unified Modeling Language Reference Manual*, Second Edition. Boston, MA: Pearson Education.

The Agile Process

Cockburn, Alistair, 2002. *Agile Software Development*. Boston, MA: Pearson Education.

Highsmith, Jim, 2004. *Agile Project Management: Creating Innovative Products*. Boston, MA: Pearson Education.

Larman, Craig, 2004. *Agile & Iterative Development: A Manager's Guide*. Boston, MA: Pearson Education.

Martin, Robert C., 2003. *Agile Software Development: Principles, Patterns, and Practices*. Upper Saddle River, NJ: Pearson Education.

Schwaber, Ken, 2004. *Agile Project Management with Scrum*. Redmond, WA: Microsoft Press.

Project Management

Booch, Grady, 1996. *Object Solutions: Managing the Object-Oriented Project*. Reading, MA: Addison-Wesley.

Cantor, Murray R., 1998. *Object-Oriented Project Management with UML*. New York, NY: John Wiley & Sons.

Cantor, Murray, 2002. *Software Leadership: A Guide to Successful Software Development*. Boston, MA: Addison-Wesley.

Fleming, Quentin W., and Joel M. Koppelman, 2000. *Earned Value Project Management*, Second Edition. Newtown Square, PA: Project Management Institute.

Frame, J. Davidson, 2002. *The New Project Management: Tools for an Age of Rapid Change, Complexity, and Other Business Realities*, Second Edition. San Francisco, CA: John Wiley & Sons.

Jalote, Pankaj, 2002. *Software Project Management in Practice*. Boston, MA: Pearson Education.

Kerzner, Harold, PhD, 2003. *Project Management: A Systems Approach to Planning, Scheduling, and Controlling*, Eighth Edition. Hoboken, NJ: John Wiley & Sons.

McConnell, Steve, 1998. *Software Project Survival Guide: How to Be Sure Your First Important Project Isn't Your Last*. Redmond, WA: Microsoft Press.

Royce, Walker, 1998. *Software Project Management: A Unified Framework*. Reading, MA: Addison Wesley Longman.

Whitehead, Richard, 2001. *Leading a Software Development Team: A Developer's Guide to Successfully Leading People & Projects*. London, UK: Pearson Education.

Outsourcing

Carmel, Erran, 1999. *Global Software Teams: Collaborating Across Borders and Time Zones.* Upper Saddle River, NJ: Prentice Hall.

Duarte, Deborah L. and Nancy Tennant Snyder, 2001. *Mastering Virtual Teams: Strategies, Tools, and Techniques That Succeed,* Second Edition. San Francisco, CA: Jossey-Bass.

Gartner, Inc., 2004. "Forecast for IT Outsourcing Segments Shows Strong Growth."

Karolak, Dale Walter, 1998. *Global Software Development: Managing Virtual Teams and Environments.* Piscataway, NJ: Institute of Electrical and Electronics Engineers.

Sahay, Sundeep, Brian Nicholson, and S. Krishna, 2003. *Global IT Outsourcing: Software Development Across Borders.* New York, NY: Cambridge University Press.

Sathyanarayan, M. M., 2003. *Offshore Development: Proven Strategies and Tactics for Success.* Cupertino, CA: GlobalDev Publishing.

Yourdon, Edward, 2005. *Outsource: Competing in the Global Productivity Race.* Upper Saddle River, NJ: Pearson Education.

Miscellaneous

Buckley, Christian D. and Darren W. Pulsipher, 2005. *The Art of ClearCase Deployment: The Secrets to Successful Implementation.* Boston, MA: Pearson Education.

Chrissis, Mary Beth, Mike Konrad, and Sandy Shrum, 2003. *CMMI: Guidelines for Process Integration and Product Improvement.* Boston, MA: Pearson Education.

Glass, Robert L., 2003. *Facts and Fallacies of Software Engineering.* Boston, MA: Pearson Education.

Hohmann, Luke, 1997. *Journey of the Software Professional: A Sociology of Software Development.* Upper Saddle River, NJ: Prentice Hall.

Wilkens, Tammo T., 1999. "Earned Value, Clear and Simple." Primavera Systems.

Yourdon, Edward, 1997. *Death March: The Complete Software Developer's Guide to Surviving "Mission Impossible" Projects.* Upper Saddle River, NJ: Prentice-Hall.

Index

A

abstraction, elevating level of, 32-34
acceptance testing
contractor's checklist, 208-209
   outsourcing organization's checklist, 209
acquisition, 43
   fixed-price projects, 55-56
   government procurement process
      advantages of, 47
      Best and Final Offer (BAFO), 46
      contract award, 47
      contractor answers, 46
      disadvantages of, 47-49
      oral presentations, 46
      proposal meetings and conferences, 45
      proposal team formation, 45
      questions from bidders, 45

questions from outsourcing organization, 46
      release of RFPs, 44
      written proposals, 46
   progressive acquisition model
      advantages of, 54-55
      for medium to large projects, 52-54
      for small projects, 49-52
      weaknesses of, 55
   two-stage procurement processes, implementing
      artifacts for contractors, 256-257
      contract types, 254-255
      cultural changes, 253-254
      second phase bids, 255
Ada Software Development System, 27
adapting processes, 29
advanced users, 210
Agile Manifesto, 40
agility of RUP, 40-41

analysis and design, verifying quality in, 35
analyzing cleansed data, 205-206
architects, 86
architecture
   component-based architectures, 34
   three-tiered architecture, 32-33
artifacts (Inception phase)
   Business Analysis Models, 117
   Business Cases, 114
   development process, 116
   functional prototypes, 117
   Iteration Plans, 116
   project glossaries, 116
   risk lists, 115
   Risk Management Plans, 115
   SDPs (Software Development Plans), 115-116
   software development environment, 115

279

THIS BOOK IS SAFARI ENABLED

INCLUDES FREE 45-DAY ACCESS TO THE ONLINE EDITION

The Safari® Enabled icon on the cover of your favorite technology book means the book is available through Safari Bookshelf. When you buy this book, you get free access to the online edition for 45 days.

Safari Bookshelf is an electronic reference library that lets you easily search thousands of technical books, find code samples, download chapters, and access technical information whenever and wherever you need it.

TO GAIN 45-DAY SAFARI ENABLED ACCESS TO THIS BOOK:

- Go to **http://www.prenhallprofessional.com/safarienabled**
- Complete the brief registration form
- Enter the coupon code found in the front of this book on the "Copyright" page

If you have difficulty registering on Safari Bookshelf or accessing the online edition, please e-mail customer-service@safaribooksonline.com.

PRENTICE HALL

informIT

www.informit.com

YOUR GUIDE TO IT REFERENCE

Articles

Keep your edge with thousands of free articles, in-depth features, interviews, and IT reference recommendations – all written by experts you know and trust.

Online Books

Answers in an instant from **InformIT Online Book's** 600+ fully searchable on line books. For a limited time, you can get your first 14 days **free**.

Safari
TECH BOOKS ONLINE

Catalog

Review online sample chapters, author biographies and customer rankings and choose exactly the right book from a selection of over 5,000 titles.